OUR LADY'S WAY

THE STORY OF OUR LADY OF PEACE CHURCH & SHRINE

Cultivating the Fruit of Peace

OUR LADY'S WAY

THE STORY OF OUR LADY OF PEACE CHURCH & SHRINE

Cultivating the Fruit of Peace

ROSEMARY ALVA

Dedicated to

Our Lady of Peace

and

her devoted sons and daughters, the priests and religious whose love for Christ, his Mother, and humanity brought to life the remarkable story that fills these pages.

Thousands of individuals, families, priests, religious, staff members, groups, and organizations have made a personal mark on the story of Our Lady of Peace Church and Shrine. Though it is impossible to name each, or to tell every story, the testimonies spoken here seek to represent the historical and spiritual background shared by many.

If you are of Our Lady of Peace, this is your story. If you are a newcomer, this is your heritage. And if you are a stranger, this is your invitation.

Contents

Introduction

"Peace I leave with you; my peace I give to you. Not as the world gives do I give it to you. Do not let your hearts be troubled or afraid." (John 14:27)

How do we get to this point? God has shown us the way to this peace, it is along Our Lady's Way: Mary leading us to Jesus and Jesus entrusting us to Mary. Thousands of faith-filled souls have walked and continue to walk this path at Our Lady of Peace.

Our Lady of Peace lives and breathes love of Jesus and love of Mary, which is it's secret—plain and simple. "Always Jesus and Mary; always Mary and Jesus." (*IVE Directory of Spirituality*, no. 325) Here, Mary waits for her children *with a serene and kindly countenance*, with her arms extended and open to receive her children. She then, assuredly, invites her guests to make a prayerful visit with her Son Jesus, who silently and lovingly awaits us in His Eucharistic form.

In a simple and authentic way, one experiences the love of the Blessed Virgin Mary and the love of the Eucharist, which from these spring forth true peace. This peace, then, produces love. Unlike worldly peace, which leads to love of things such as prosperity and comfort, this peace produces love of God and love of brethren. Peace produces love and in turn, love produces peace.

For this reason, at every hour of every day, with faith, hope and love, we offer the simple prayer: "O my God, I believe, I adore, I trust, and I love You! I beg pardon for those who do not believe, do not adore, do not trust, and do not love you." It is Mary's children sincerely responding to their mother's request by praying for those who do not pray, staying awake with her Son while the world sleeps—to love Him, to adore Him, and to trust in Him. And they make this prayer through the Rosary, recited while adoring her Son in the Eucharist. The countless Rosaries prayed here in Eucharistic Adoration in some ways feels like the vessels by which blood is being pumped from the Sacred and Immaculate Hearts all throughout this valley.

This is the simple yet profound story Our Lady of Peace has to tell, which is really just a page taken from the one written with a divine pen—the good news of the Gospel!

Fr. Brian Dinkel, IVE
Pastor, Our Lady of Peace Church & Shrine
May 13, 2019 Our Lady of Fatima

CHAPTER 1
Historical Legacy Through the 1960s

On Holy Ground

Lord, we pray Thee let our doings be prompted by
Thy inspiration and furthered by Thy help so that
every prayer and work of ours may begin from Thee,
and be through Thee accomplished. Through Christ our Lord.

Mary, pray for us to learn the spirit of generosity
and sacrifice. Amen.

*Prayer for the establishment of
Our Lady of Peace Catholic Church, 1963*

The story of Our Lady of Peace Church and Shrine includes a theme, from her earliest days, of setting no limits on reaching souls with an invitation to draw closer to Christ. Souls who yearned for Christ, souls who were distant from Christ, and souls who did not even know Christ have been invited in, welcomed, and nourished. Under the steady guidance of holy priests, this parish community has established fruit-bearing ministries yielding a rich harvest for over half a century.

Unbeknownst to many, such missionary zeal began long before Our Lady of Peace opened for services in 1963: the original parish

1

boundaries encircled holy ground.

A NEW MISSION

Before farmers planted orchard upon orchard, before highways, expressways, and off-ramps, before Silicon Valley, colleges, hotels, amusement parks, and stadiums, a humble expedition trekked through the original parish boundaries of Our Lady of Peace Church in search of a site for Fr. Junipero Serra to establish California's Mission Santa Clara de Asís. Their dream was to bring Christianity to the native people.

On January 12, 1777, traveling by foot or by horseback, the mission scouts stopped at the mouth of the Guadalupe River and gave thanks for the terrain they chose for this inspired endeavor. On the quiet land of the Ohlone and Costanoan Indians, serenaded only by sounds of nature, their thanksgiving was the highest form of gratitude: the Holy Mass. And so this ground, later known as Alviso, was consecrated to God through the first Holy Mass offered in what is today known as Silicon Valley.

The Roman Catholic Church had been established in present-day Santa Clara County during the era of the Provincias Internas of New Spain. Originally a part of the Diocese of Sonora in Mexico, in 1840 Santa Clara and the rest of the Californias became part of the Diocese of Alta and Baja California, headquartered in Santa Barbara. In 1850, two years after the Mexican Cession, the Diocese of Alta and Baja California was split between American and Mexican territories and Santa Clara became a part of the Diocese of Monterey. In 1853, the northern half of Santa Clara county became part of the Archdiocese of San Francisco, while the areas around Gilroy and Morgan Hill remained in the Diocese of Monterey. In 1922, the American Catholic Church decided to use county boundaries for the dioceses, and the southern half of Santa Clara county was transferred to the Archdiocese of San Francisco, which included the City of Santa Clara.

Floods and earthquakes damaged many of the early Mission Santa Clara structures, forcing relocation to higher ground. Four times, the mission was relocated. Six times, the structure was rebuilt. Likewise, the territory has undergone such change that generation to generation recalls a different landscape. As the California population swelled and business enterprises lured prospective home buyers to San Jose, the Archdiocese of San Francisco kept pace and planned ahead for the anticipated housing boom by establishing new parishes to minister to the neighborhoods on-the-way. On June 23, 1961, *The Monitor* announced Archbishop John Mitty's establishment of ten new parishes. Six of these houses of worship were to be constructed in Santa Clara County. In Santa Clara proper, the archdiocese purchased thirteen acres of farmland for $130,000 in a neighborhood developers marketed as "New Bethlehem," and Archbishop Mitty appointed Fr. Joseph G. Sullivan as the founding pastor of the new Our Lady of Peace Church.

A NEW CHURCH

Over ninety years after those first Franciscan missionaries offered Mass in her parish boundaries, Fr. Sullivan established Our Lady of Peace Church to serve the growing Santa Clara community and provide a permanent home, or resettlement, for the faithful who, in 1952, had independently created Our Lady Star of the Sea as their Spanish-speaking Catholic chapel in Alviso. Originally a mission of St. John the Baptist Church in Milpitas, the Archbishop expected Our Lady Star of the Sea to assimilate into the fledgling Our Lady of Peace. The new parish included Alviso, Agnew, and Lakewood Village.

THE MONITOR, JUNE 23, 1961

OFFICIAL

NEW PARISHES

His Excellency, the Most Reverend Archbishop, announces the establishment of the following new parishes:

ALAMEDA COUNTY

Dublin, San Ramon Village, St. Raymond's Parish (formerly a mission of St. Augustine's Parish, Pleasanton).

MARIN COUNTY

San Rafael, St. Sylvester's Parish (formerly a mission of St. Raphael's, San Rafael).

SAN MATEO COUNTY

Menlo Park, St. Denis' Parish.
Redwood City, St. Matthias' Parish.

SANTA CLARA COUNTY

Mountain View, St. Cyprian's Parish.
Palo Alto, St. Albert the Great Parish.
San Jose, Most Holy Trinity Parish (including Guadalupe Mission).
San Jose, St. Maria Goretti's Parish.
San Jose, St. Victor's Parish.
Santa Clara, Our Lady of Peace Parish.

PASTORS

His Excellency, the Most Reverend Archbishop, announces the following appointments:

Rev. John C. Murphy, St. Raymond's Church, San Ramon Village, Dublin (new parish)
Rev. John A. Coghlan, St. Anthony's Church, Hughson
Rev. Thomas I. Kennedy, St. Denis' Church, Menlo Park (new parish)
Rev. Hugh P. McKenna, St. John the Baptist Church, Milpitas
Rev. Thomas C. Rielly, St. Cyprian's Church, Mountain View (new parish)
Rev. J. Garcia Prieto, St. Benedict's Church, Oakland
Rev. Henry A. MacEnery, St. Albert the Great Parish, Palo Alto (new parish)
Rev. Edward R. Allen, St. Thomas Aquinas Church, Palo Alto
Rev. Joseph D. Munier, Ph.D., Our Lady of Mt. Carmel Church, Redwood City
Rev. Thomas E. Lacey, St. Matthias' Church, Redwood City (new parish)
Rev. Thomas J. Bowe, J.C.D., Most Holy Trinity Church, San Jose (new parish)
Rev. Joseph D. Deans, St. Maria Goretti Church, San Jose (new parish)
Rev. James E. Prindeville, St. Victor's Church, San Jose (new parish)
Rev. John P. Tierney, St. Sylvester's Church, San Rafael (new parish)
Rev. Joseph G. Sullivan, Our Lady of Peace Church, Santa Clara (new parish)
Right Rev. Walter J. Tappe, St. Rose's Church, Santa Rosa.

OUR LADY OF PEACE PARISH, SANTA CLARA (SANTA CLARA COUNTY)

EAST: Bayshore and Nimitz Freeway to Coyote Creek to Alviso and Milpitas Road to Zanker to Bay.
NORTH: San Francisco Bay to Zanker.
WEST: Winifred to Mountain View-Alviso Road to Fairoaks, to Bayshore.
SOUTH: Bayshore to Nimitz Freeway.

The Archdiocese of San Francisco publicly announces new parishes and their respective pastors. Published in The Monitor *on June 23, 1961.*

Until the church and rectory were constructed, Fr. Sullivan lived in a temporary rectory on Lakewood Drive in Lakewood Village, Sunnyvale. He offered daily Masses in his garage, confessions weekly, and Sunday Masses at Our Lady Star of the Sea in Alviso. Fr. Sullivan was a warm and personable man who enthusiastically set out to create a God-loving and person-oriented community. He visited parishioner homes daily and established parish organizations such as the Women's Guild/Altar Society (April 1962), the Men's Club/Holy Name Society (May 1962), and the St. Vincent de Paul Society (November 1962). He founded Bible studies and Cursillo groups. He invited the Holy Name Sisters to come from Mission San Jose in Fremont to oversee catechism classes and support the volunteer instructors. Encouraged by their pastor, the faithful involved in these programs met in parishioner living rooms and kitchens until the church and hall were built.

The property for Our Lady of Peace, on the corner of Coffin and Agnew Roads, was "out in the boondocks," as Fr. Sullivan fondly explained. Parishioners came from Agnew Village on one side and the neighborhood of Lakewood Village (at the west end of Agnew Road) on the other. Between these two communities was a landscape typical of vast stretches of the Santa Clara Valley in the early 1960s: acres and acres of orchards and fields. Our Lady of Peace was surrounded by pear orchards and situated on a one hundred year flood plain. Before construction could begin, truckloads of landfill were brought in to bring the property up to grade level.

Spring of 1962 brought new signs of the church becoming a reality. Construction began in March. Fr. Sullivan visited the building site daily to oversee the construction of the church, parish hall, and rectory. On one occasion, he watched a huge crane lift each of the great arched beams into place while carpenters scrambled up to secure them with bolts at the top. Beam by beam, bolt by bolt, the spiritual home for Fr. Sullivan's community was coming into view. Person by person, he worked tirelessly to draw in and warmly welcome the Body of Christ.

The founding 650 parishioners of Our Lady of Peace met hardships and discomforts with a remarkable flexibility during the period of foundation, not withstanding one Sunday in 1962 when plans for a festive first Mass in the new church structure were suddenly pushed forward by natural disaster: flooding in Alviso.

CHRISTENING BY CANDLELIGHT

A town below sea level, Alviso was prone to flooding during the rainy season. From September of 1961 to October of 1962, Fr. Sullivan offered Sunday Masses at Our Lady Star of the Sea. Usually, adverse weather and muddy driving conditions didn't deter him, but on October 21, 1962, three feet of water flooded the town and kept Fr. Sullivan out. Unable to offer Mass in Alviso, Fr. Sullivan officially opened the church of Our Lady of Peace—still in its final stages of construction—with a candlelight Mass. The candles were not for ambiance: there was no electricity! The next day, Fr. Sullivan hastily mailed letters to notify his congregation that Sunday Masses would now be held at Our Lady of Peace.

The church building contractors, the Reardon Company, provided a temporary lighting solution via a generator to provide feeble light until the Santa Clara power company installed electric lines in the area. Gas lines were also on the waiting list, so heat was provided through liquid petroleum gas furnaces. At that first Sunday Mass, the furnaces were fired up and Mass began. Ten minutes into the service, a loud crashing sound startled the congregation. Looking at the furnaces, a parishioner with construction experience noticed the bases had blown out and quickly turned them off. The church had been supplied with *natural gas* furnaces and been told to use *liquid petroleum gas!* The winter months dragged on before the proper type of burner was installed. Fr. Sullivan would later recall, "That first winter, it was overcoats and mittens for Mass."

Finally, on January 27, 1963, His Excellency Joseph Thomas McGucken (appointed new Archbishop of San Francisco in 1961) formally dedicated the new church to the worship of God. At that same Mass, the Archbishop conferred the Sacrament of Confirmation on the first class of young people to receive this sacrament in the new parish. It was a triumphant day for Fr. Sullivan and his community: just two years after the land was purchased, they were finally home.

Meanwhile, movement in the City of Santa Clara planning division was about to rattle this foundation.

A FLOCK WITH FEW SHEEP

The 1961 property purchase for Our Lady of Peace was based on a zoning plan that planted the church in the center of a farming community, set to evolve into a thriving housing development whose families the parish would serve. But in early 1963, the City of Santa Clara voted to re-zone most of the land within the parish boundaries for industrial development. This new plan meant no growth for an already too-small parish. Land owners in an unincorporated area near Our Lady of Peace sought other ways to introduce housing by trying to persuade the County Supervisors to zone the unincorporated land in the parish for homes. Fr. Sullivan, concerned, waited to know "what the fate of the parish" would be.

For the most part, city planners maintained their zoning jurisdiction. Instead of homes hugging the church property, the parish could expect to see businesses. This seemed to mean Our Lady of Peace was fated to close her doors. Even Fr. Sullivan acknowledged

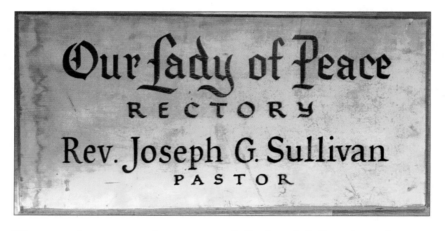

The original rectory sign hanging outside Fr. Joseph Sullivan's residence on Lakewood Avenue, where he resided while the permanent rectory was under construction.

Fr. Joseph Sullivan, first pastor of Our Lady of Peace Church, offers daily Mass in the temporary rectory's converted garage on Lakewood Avenue in 1961. All Masses were in Latin until 1964.

Fr. Sullivan gathers with the parish youth for a picnic in the Our Lady of Peace pear orchards. Circa 1962.

Construction of the church, hall, and rectory began in March of 1962.

Always at the heart of his community, Fr. Sullivan visits with a parishioner in June of 1965.

Our Lady of Peace Church, 1962.

Fr. Joseph Sullivan, founding pastor, at the entrance of his new Catholic church in 1962.

that with no community growth, he now had no plan to either financially support the current church or pay off the monstrous $500,000 debt he was assigned. His parish was small, and a large portion were very poor immigrant boat builders, fishermen, and laborers. Yet he continued to lead with his hallmark dedication and good nature and awaited a decision from the archdiocese.

Undaunted by (and mostly unaware of) the dismal forecast, the Hawaiian parishioners hosted the parish's first luau on September 14, 1963. Because some of the men in the parish were pilots at Moffett Field, contributions such as poi, flowers, and even the roasting rocks were flown in on the daily flights from the Islands, adding authenticity to the event. Hawaiian chefs prepared the food and the celebration concluded with an evening of Hawaiian entertainment.

Also in 1963, Fr. Robert S. Gorman was appointed assistant pastor of the church. His particular gift was in establishing youth activities, and his Catholic Youth Organization (CYO) Teen Club brought in trophy after trophy from athletic wins. He also instituted the tradition of an annual Passion Play performed by teens. When Fr. Gorman was assigned to another parish in 1966, Fr. John Coleman arrived to minister in his place. Another blessing for the parish came through a year of assistance from Spanish-speaking Fr. Crescencio Rodriguez, whose bilingual abilities mostly supported the grateful Alviso Catholics.

CHANGES IN THE CATHOLIC CHURCH

While the roof was being raised at Our Lady of Peace, Pope John XXIII was gathering Church leaders to address the Roman Catholic Church in relation to the modern world. He opened the Second Vatican Council at St. Peter's Basilica on October 11, 1962. Three years later, Pope Paul VI closed the Council on the Feast of the Immaculate Conception, December 8, 1965.

The Council, among various recommendations, encouraged the renewal of consecrated life with a revised charism, ecumenical dialogue with other religions, and the call to holiness for everyone including the laity, which, according to Pope Paul VI, was "the most characteristic and ultimate purpose of the teachings of the Council." Other changes that followed the council included the widespread use of vernacular (local) languages in the Mass instead of Latin, the subtle disuse of ornate clerical regalia, the revision of Eucharistic prayers, the abbreviation of the liturgical calendar, and the ability to celebrate the Mass versus populum (the priest facing the congregation) as well as ad orientem (facing the East and the Crucifix).

As pastor of Our Lady of Peace, Fr. Sullivan was responsible to unveil the recommendations of Vatican II. On November 29, 1964, the "New Mass" was introduced into United States parishes. Though this Mass included a combination of Latin and the vernacular, by 1969 all Latin was phased out. Fr. Sullivan hired parishioner Leonard Quieto to build a second altar at the center of the sanctuary (the original was set against the back wall) so the priests could offer Mass facing the congregation, and the altar stone containing relics of St. Helen, St. Francis of Assisi, St. Thérèse of Lisieux, and St. John Bosco was placed within. Masses were offered in English and Spanish, new Eucharistic prayers were introduced, and most women dropped the tradition of wearing veils in church. Though many pastors followed a trend of removing altar rails, Fr. Sullivan left them intact. While interpretations of Vatican II varied from parish to parish, Fr. Sullivan's careful review and reading of the Vatican II documents before making changes became a hallmark practice of each pastor to come.

THE END OF AN ERA

Fr. Sullivan served as the pastor of Our Lady of Peace for eight years. On December 18, 1968, he celebrated the twenty-fifth anniversary of his ordination to the priesthood and in June of 1969 was transferred to pastor the parish of St. Martin of Tours in San Jose. Fr. John Sweeny arrived to assume the leadership, uncertainty, and debt of Our Lady of Peace Church.

Fr. Sullivan celebrates a wedding Mass in 1965.

The altar in 1968. The original altar, covered in a red cloth, is set against the sanctuary's back wall. In the foreground, covered in white, stands the new altar built post-Vatican II.

*Fr. Sullivan celebrates Mass for a group of First Holy Communicants
in May of 1968.*

A blessing witnessed by Fr. John Coleman (far left), altar boys, and Fr. Sullivan in 1968.

Fr. Coleman leads a procession, followed by altar servers, Fr. Sullivan, and the congregation. Little did they know that prayerful processions, a tradition widely dropped by most parishes after Vatican II, would become a hallmark form of prayer at Our Lady of Peace in years to come.

Fr. Lawrence Goode
Assistant Pastor 1971 - 1978

"In the early 1900s, they were trying to get people to buy property in the area. They had a train line that came down by Agnews and they called the land where Our Lady of Peace is, 'New Bethlehem.' Alviso was called, 'New Chicago,' and they named the streets after the streets in Chicago. It was a real estate scheme to get people to come down and take a look. I don't know why they called this area 'New Bethlehem,' but now we have a statue of the Virgin with Child in the heart of it!"

Fr. Joseph Sullivan, Founding Pastor [†]
as quoted in *The Valley Catholic*, December 14, 1993 and
Our Lady of Peace: A People United Through Prayer

" 'I wanted to be a parish priest,' said Fr. Sullivan. In 1961 [after eight years in prison ministry], he returned to his first love—parish work—as the first pastor of a new parish: Our Lady of Peace in Santa Clara. 'Starting a parish was quite a thrill,' Fr. Sullivan said. 'It's not something every priest gets to do.'

" 'I just loved it. It was rural, with all kinds of birds and little animals around the place. I knew seventy-five percent of the people by their first names, and visited every single family in the parish in their homes. I just tried to provide the best service that I could for the people.'

"Fr. Sullivan feels the best part of the priesthood is 'the privilege of offering Mass. Every day, I'm astounded by the wonder of it. The older I get, the stronger the wonder becomes.' "

Fr. William Stout, S.J. [†]
Serving at Our Lady of Peace 1967 - 2018

"The Archdiocese of San Francisco went out to Alviso and saw the church and decided they had a small congregation, but they wanted to build a good church. The ground was no good in Alviso, so the archdiocese bought a pear orchard over in Santa Clara, built the church, gave the key to Fr. Joseph Sullivan, and said, 'Now it's yours. Here's the bill.' I don't remember the full amount of debt; it was a lot of money. Fr. Sullivan was a good problem solver, but there was very little hope of paying it off because all they had in the parish was Alviso and Agnews. Everyone in Alviso was poor. Agnews was a little town at that time; it's grown a lot since then but back in the 1960s it was small. There was another small neighborhood in the parish, just off Lafayette where the post office is today. About one hundred people came to Mass and the collection was about thirty dollars. They just didn't have the means, so Our Lady of Peace had almost no financial support.

"I started helping at Our Lady of Peace with Fr. Sullivan. When I was a Jesuit seminarian studying at Alma College, Thursday was our day off. They worked out a deal for me to assist in Alviso. Fr. McDonnell was my mentor and was one of those great priests like Fr. Sweeny. (Coincidentally, he was also a mentor to Cesar Chavez.) He had a program for the Spanish-speaking. We helped him and taught catechism. When he moved on, the Franciscans took over. I was looking for another place to volunteer, so I went to Fr. Sullivan and asked if I could give him a hand. He told me, 'I don't have any

*Fr. Joseph G. Sullivan in his early days as founding pastor
of Our Lady of Peace Church.*

money,' and I replied, 'That's okay.'

"When Our Lady of Peace was built and Fr. Sullivan told the people he was going to close the little church in Alviso, they said, 'You can't do that. We were here first.' So he told them, 'If you can get yourselves a priest for Sundays, I'll come during the week.' That's why originally daily Mass was at 8 a.m. at Our Lady of Peace. Fr. Sullivan would then drive out to Star of the Sea in Alviso for a 9:15 a.m. Mass. On Sundays, one of our Jesuit priests from Bellarmine, Fr. Wally Want, would ride his bicycle out to Alviso to say Mass. The people called him, 'Padre Quiero,' which is a direct translation for 'Father Want.' When Fr. Want couldn't do it anymore, I was teaching at Bellarmine so I'd go out when I had the chance and take care of that for him on Sundays. So I started with Fr. Sullivan and then Fr. Sweeny came along and I hung on.

"Fr. Sullivan was a good priest and willing to take on parishes that needed help. Because of this willingness, when he was transferred to another new parish in 1969, it was to St. Martin of Tours in San Jose."

Fr. John Coleman
Assistant Pastor to Fr. Sullivan 1966 - 1968

"Star of the Sea was a place where they had Mass for the migrant workers and such. That little mission was put there by Fr. McDonald in 1951. He bought the church structure for one dollar and moved it from Redwood City over to Alviso. Then Fr. Burke and Fr. George Hague each added a wing of carpentry work, so now it is a cruciform church."

Time for fun! Fr. John Coleman greets Santa.

Jimmy Estrada
Past Parishioner

"When I was an infant, my parents moved from Texas to Sunnyvale, California. When my father and mother heard of the big prospect in Santa Clara in the early 1960s—new homes—they took advantage of it. We moved from our house in Sunnyvale and lived in a trailer in Santa Clara while our home was being built. My folks were building a two-story home and it cost them $17,000. Now that home is worth over a million dollars. It's in the heart of Santa Clara, off Lafayette Street in the Agnew area.

"Our Lady of Peace was our church. Fr. Sullivan was here, he was a good-hearted man. He had a very low voice and spoke straight to the point. When he'd see me, he'd grab me by the nose in a friendly gesture and say, 'How are you doing, young fella?' "

Irene Barrera
Parishioner 1962 - Present

"When I moved from Texas to California, Fr. Sullivan came over to our home to pay us a visit. Fr. Sullivan would invite us to daily Mass in his garage on Lakewood Avenue. On Sundays, we'd all go to Star of the Sea in Alviso.

"In 1964, I began teaching catechism to the third and fourth graders from Our Lady of Peace in my home. The nuns would come from Mission San Jose and visit classes to see how we were doing. At that time, many parents did not know English and wanted their children to continue speaking Spanish. But the children were going to school in English, so I taught the prayers in both Spanish and English and they received a bilingual catechesis. Fr. Pintacura was a very young volunteer here, and he tested them for me. It was a difficult class to teach because each child was at a different level of catechesis.

"For adult catechesis, we had Bible classes at Jim and Sarah Martin's home. Fr. Sullivan would always come and have coffee with us. He was outgoing and approachable. We had Cursillo meetings with him as well; we met in different homes for those gatherings.

"When the church was built, the area was all pear orchards and some walnut. Our drive to Our Lady of Peace was on dirt roads! It was so peaceful there. The only landmark was the big tree. It was all fields until Lakewood Village was built.

"Fr. Sullivan was excited about the construction of the church. He had a young priest, Fr. Gorman, helping him. Fr. Sullivan mobilized the people into a community and started a lot of parish organizations, such as the Men's Club, Cursillo, Bingo nights, catechesis, New Year's dances, and more. He was very friendly and established a friendly parish.

"When the church was built, it was meant to be an official parish for the people of Alviso. For a while, the people from Alviso came. It didn't work well. They liked having their own space. For example, for the feast of Our Lady of Guadalupe they liked to make a big celebration, dress up the children in Mexican traditional clothes, and have the children present flowers to Our Lady all month long. They had a lot of specific traditions and to bring them into Our Lady of Peace was a challenge.

"At first, the combining of parishes between Alviso and Our Lady of Peace was very cold. One day, Fr. Sullivan asked me, 'What do you think about Our Lady of Peace?' I said, 'Well, it's a new church, it's too cold. People don't talk to you.' He replied, 'Well, why don't you start talking to them?' I had to laugh: that was an idea!

"Fr. Stout was helping, too. (His heart is in Alviso and the people there really love him.) Fr. Stout said Mass in two languages, but many people at Our Lady of Peace weren't comfortable with that. When Alviso was incorporated into San Jose, they started sending a Spanish-speaking priest, Fr. Want, to Star of the Sea."

Michelle Barrera
Parishioner 1972 - Present

"Alviso was considered a little chapel, but not a parish. The church there hasn't changed over the years, it is still the same. It's right in a neighborhood, between two homes. When I was a young child, the marshes in Alviso weren't marshes; there was actually water with boats. Many homes had boats parked in front."

Jerry Richards
Parishioner 1963 - 1975

"In 1962, I immigrated from England with my wife, Frances, and our first child. We bought a house in Lakewood Village in 1963, for the high price of $14,000. We asked about the church and were pointed in the direction of Our Lady of Peace. It didn't look like there was a church there, only pear orchards as far as we could see. As we got closer, we could see the steeple. We entered the parish hall and there was a party there for the first anniversary of the church. A

29

woman named Sis Quieto approached us with a big smile and said, 'Hello. You must be strangers around here.' That's how we came to the church. It was surprising to us how many people jumped up to say hello when they saw a new face come into the parish.

"Fr. Sullivan was an older guy, easygoing, and didn't want to upset anybody but he was strictly a man of the Church. If you went to confession and didn't like what he had to say, he'd tell you, 'Go to Fr. Gorman then. He thinks a lot more freely than I do.' But he was a very nice guy.

"Everybody loved Fr. Sullivan. When Fr. Sullivan was assigned to another parish and Fr. Sweeny came, people thought, 'Who is *he*? Who do they think they are, taking our pastor away?' Apparently the Church ruling was that if a priest was a founding pastor and the bishop asked him to move, he could decline. I asked Fr. Sullivan about that. He said, 'I do what my bishop wants me to do. Whether I like it or not is beside the point.'

"When we came to Our Lady of Peace, I joined the Holy Name Society and at the monthly meeting I asked where to go to purchase religious articles. A couple of places were named that were far away from Our Lady of Peace, in Saratoga and San Jose. I asked, 'Why don't you have anything here?' They replied, 'Nobody has even thought about that.' A couple of meetings went by and I began making some inquiries as to where we could purchase some of these articles to sell. The Holy Name Society loaned me two hundred dollars to purchase some items and see if they would sell. That was the beginning of the Our Lady of Peace Gift Shop, in 1964.

"I contacted a Jewish fellow in San Francisco who sold Catholic religious items. The store was near Golden Gate Park. I told him my limit was two hundred dollars and it didn't purchase much for our inventory. His wife suggested he give us more and I walked out with much more inventory than two hundred dollars would have purchased. We set up tables in the parish hall on the first Sunday of the month and asked the priests to announce after Mass that the store was open. On the first Sunday, people just about cleared out our inventory! We returned to the Jewish fellow for more articles, and eventually learned we could purchase inventory at the seminary in Mountain View, which was much closer for me than San Francisco.

"For years, we never missed a Sunday. As time went on, we moved the inventory into the baptistery and sold from there. My family grew and we were looking for a larger home and moved to San Jose so we left the parish. The gift shop has been moved a couple of times and grown significantly, but when we stop in today, we see they're still selling the flagship items we started with."

Fr. Anthony Hernandez
Religious Education Director and Instructor 1980 - Present and
Religious Vocation from Our Lady of Peace

"My first contact with Our Lady of Peace was when I was a little child. My aunt and grandmother lived in the area and were parishioners. In the earliest recollection I have of Our Lady of Peace, I was about four or five years old. I got lost on the property because everything was orchards, but the cross on top of the church guided me back."

Deacon Daniel Hernandez
Religious Education Instructor 1986 - Present and
Religious Vocation from Our Lady of Peace

"They were starting to construct Our Lady of Peace around the time I was entering elementary school, and my first memory of the church was driving by on Highway 101. We were driving from the north down to San Jose, and the church was under construction. I remember the skeleton: it was not a traditional shape and looked, to me, like Noah's ark.

"Our family attended Our Lady of Peace from time to time with our grandmother. Fr. Sweeny came in 1969; it was the same year man landed on the moon. People liked him. The women would say he looked like Dean Martin and sang like Bing Crosby."

Identified with a sign announcing, "Future Home of Our Lady of Peace Catholic Church," the structure resembled Noah's ark in the eyes of a child.

Start by doing what is necessary;
then do what is possible;
and suddenly you are doing the impossible.

St. Francis of Assisi

CHAPTER 2

To Know Fr. Sweeny

What child hasn't responded to the open arms of a
mother? Even the adult, if we take time to think back a
little bit to our first experiences—experiences of trust,
the open arms of a mother—I guess there's nothing
more endearing, and it is next to God.

Fr. John Sweeny

On Monday, June 30, 1969, parishioners held a reception bidding
farewell to Fr. Sullivan and welcoming Fr. John Joseph Sweeny as
their new pastor. The following Sunday, July 6, Fr. Sweeny was
officially installed as the pastor of Our Lady of Peace Church.

This began Fr. Sweeny's 32-year tenure at Our Lady of Peace. His
quiet, likeable, and deeply spiritual persona would become known
beyond parish boundaries into ecumenical and civil sectors. To fully
understand Our Lady of Peace Church's ministry from Fr. Sweeny's
1969 arrival even to its impact today, it is important to look closely at
the man behind the mission.

A RICH HERITAGE

Like many children born in the 1920s, Fr. Sweeny was the son and grandson of immigrants. Families like the Sweeny and DiMartini ancestors arriving on American soil in the 1800s brought with them great hope, little wealth, and a commitment to hard work. Yet for these families, their most precious legacy was devotedly living their Catholic faith.

From his earliest memories, Fr. Sweeny was formed as a child through three primary experiences: prayer, poverty, and the family. These influences, and how he both received and projected them, would be the fruits of his own family tree that would extend—at times worldwide—through his own spiritual fatherhood as a Catholic priest. From his father and mother, he knew the ways of a holy family. They modeled faith, selflessness, sacrifice, and generosity—as did grandparents, aunts, and uncles—establishing a foundation for Fr. Sweeny's life-long desire that all families achieve unity and holiness. His mother's devotion and gentle guidance drew him to revere all mothers and trust in the intercession of the Blessed Mother. His father's character and deep prayer life foreshadowed how Fr. Sweeny would fulfill his vocation as a spiritual father to many.

Fr. Sweeny genuinely acknowledged the dignity of each human person and the family as God's foundation of personal holiness and essential to Christian society. Of his own vocational calling he would say, "I desire to be an instrument of His Peace."

The depth of Fr. Sweeny's family life and trust in Jesus, combined with a commitment to the God-instilled goodness and potential within the human person, explain his steady vision of hope for the individuals and families in his parish, every person who might drive by his church, and for the whole world. Insightful and profound, Fr. Sweeny's story is best told in his own words and by those who knew him best.

Richard Sweeny

Fr. John Sweeny's Youngest Brother

"My father, John Sweeny, was born in Ireland. My mother, Norma DiMartini, was born in 1898 and raised at the family home in Calaveritas, California.

"My mother's father, Louis DiMartini, was a miner. As a young man, he saved enough money from mining to purchase the family property in Calaveras County and build a family home there. Originally there was only a wine cellar, but by the time my mother was born in 1898 the initial rooms were constructed over the cellar.

"My father was a veteran of World War I. When he came home he returned to the trade he had started before going to war, which was plastering. His uncle was a plastering contractor and cinched the contract to build a millionaire's mansion out in Calaveras County. This millionaire had found some property about seven miles east of where my mother's family lived and my father traveled there to work. In the town of Calaveritas there was a dance hall, and in the dance hall he met my mother. The rest is history. My parents were married in 1923.

"My parents lived in San Francisco. Fr. John ('Jack') was born on April 3, 1924, at St. Francis Hospital and baptized at St. Brigid Church. When he was seven years old, the family lost their home due to the Depression. My father was a plasterer and could not find work. We moved to Calaveras County and lived with our mother's family: her parents, siblings, and a great uncle. It was a very full house. I don't know how they did it!

"Without the input and discipline of my father—and alongside him my mother—to say the family rosary, I don't know whether it would have been possible for my brother, John, to say 'Yes' to leaving as an eighth grader to go to the seminary. With his going my second brother, Louis, followed him at the same time. (Louis had skipped a grade. He was in the same grade as Fr. John. When our mother was the local school teacher in a one-room schoolhouse, she taught all grades and Louis moved ahead to John's grade.)

"People often think of priests as not being super-rated in terms of manly strength or characteristics. That wasn't quite true of my brothers because they were raised on a ranch. There were cows to be fed and milked. There were rabbits and chickens to be fed. And it wasn't work to be shunned. Taking care of the cows was an important job Fr. John took on and I did later.

"My mother would tell a story about Fr. John going out to look for the cows. The cows would go munching wildflowers in the springtime and wander within the many acres of land. A milk cow with a full udder usually meandered back to the barn area because she didn't want to carry it around. That day, Fr. John did not find the cow, but he *did* find an armload of wildflowers for his mother!

"There was a lot that stuck in our makeup from life on the ranch. Even today, I don't know how many trips I've made from the Bay Area to Calaveras County. It ended up being Fr. John and Fr. Louis' favorite place for thirty-some consecutive years. On their day off, my brothers met at the ranch. Once a week, they traveled out there to plant and sow a harvest. Automatic watering systems took care of the plants when my brothers were back at their parishes. They yielded beautiful gardens.

"In 1936, our family moved back to the Bay Area because my Dad heard about some work picking up in the Presidio. Treasure Island was built for the 1938 World's Fair; they pumped it right up from the Bay. On it they built a 400-foot tower called the Tower of the Sun. My Dad plastered that. He would commute from our home in Fairfax to San Francisco and then by boat to Treasure Island.

"In the fall of 1936, we started school in Calaveritas but after a month we moved to Fairfax and attended public school for the rest of that year. Next, we attended St. Anselm Catholic School. My brothers, John and Louis, were recruited to the priesthood from there and entered St. Joseph College in 1938. In October of 1938 our family moved to San Francisco and I finished up my elementary education at St. Brigid School, right back where our family started when Fr. John was baptized."

Fr. John Sweeny [†]
Pastor of Our Lady of Peace Church & Shrine 1969 - 2002

"When I was about six years old, we were living in San Francisco and it was during the Depression. There were a lot of gangs, so the only way the little children would be safe was to go with the older boys. They'd have some choice expressions, you know. Well, I picked up one of these and had never heard it before. So I came home. My brother and I were playing on the kitchen floor and Mother and Dad were getting supper ready, and something came to me, [and I thought], 'I have to find out about this.' So I said it out loud. Suddenly, everything was still in that kitchen. And my father says, 'Jackie, where did you get that?' I said, 'Down the block.' He said, 'Son, you're going to hear a lot of things on the outside, but don't bring them into this house.' So that was a teaching moment: what can I bring to my Dad's house? From that time on, what does my father think is right and wrong, what is worthwhile? And that stayed with me. And that's with all families, that's what we do to one another. In the family, children make up their minds by the choice of their parents, normally. I think that's their first response when

John (right) and Louis Sweeny, San Francisco, circa 1929.

Young Sweeny brothers at the ranch in Calaveritas, California.
Left to right: John, Richard, and Louis. Circa 1934.

they're younger, especially. One of the saddest things in society today is the heartlessness youth have for their parents. They forget the trauma for the parent, what the parent has to go through just to earn a living and so forth to bring the family together. I hope to train [people] to bring families together.

"Another experience I had was in the third grade and I was in school in this one room schoolhouse. Some of the older children were telling me about their older brothers and sisters, and it was rather shocking...something immodest. I was riding home with my mother who was the teacher. I was seated way over at the other side and I said, 'Mother, when I grow up, I'm going to take my sleeping bag, my rifle, my fishing bag, my dog, and I'm going off in the hills.' And she looked at me, looked back at the road. And she looked at me again, and looked back at the road. Then she said this: she said, 'Jackie, when you were a little baby and I held you in my arms, I wondered what great person you would be someday.' And I heard that, I let that sink in. Then she looked at me again and said, 'You wouldn't be that selfish, would you?' Now did you understand what I'm saying here? The effect of what parents say really penetrates. And here I am, at 74, telling what happened to me when I was seven or eight. That's what it means when parents train their children and give them values. It doesn't mean shove it down and force it upon them, but show they care.

"Another [time] was when my father was apparently dying. Through a stormy day came two doctors and a priest. They examined my father and the priest anointed him and they went on their way. I was choking up and said, 'What's going to happen to my father?' I thought maybe I shouldn't go in, but I decided I would go in to see him. And I said to him, 'Dad', I said, 'After all the prayers we have said, God is going to let this happen to us?' And my father, who had a 105 temperature, heard me perfectly. He said, 'Oh Jackie,' he said, 'Don't worry. God will take care of us.' And so that sticks with me.

How right he was. He died when he was 89.

"We said our prayers every night as a family. The deep faith of our parents had a big influence on [us]. We were a very loving family. There was never a drought of caring in our family, and we also had some tremendous priests as examples."

Sal Caruso
Parishioner 1990 - Present

"Fr. Sweeny told his own stories of his Mom and Dad going through the Great Depression. He often said, 'My Mom taught us to pray the rosary very devoutly, and my Father taught us to have confidence in Divine Providence.'

"Fr. Sweeny's family was poor. He told that whenever his father wanted to donate money to a cause, such as orphans or any worthy need, he would go to the jar where they kept their money and take out a large sum. His mother would ask, 'Is this prudent? Is this a good choice?' His father would say, 'Don't worry. God will provide.' Fr. Sweeny said he learned that real trust in Divine Providence from his dad. And that's what he instilled in us when he talked to us or spoke of the Gospel."

The Sweeny boys visit the ranch as teens.
Left to right: Louis, Richard, and John. Circa 1943.

The West Side INDEX
February 17, 2000

"Both brothers eventually entered a parochial school, where one day word went out that the priest was seeking applications to the seminary. Those interested had to ask the priest permission to apply. They separately reached the same decision. 'I was going up the steps to see the priest,' John Sweeny explained, 'and I met [Louis] coming down.' "

Fr. John Coleman
Long-Time Friend to Fr. Sweeny
Assistant Pastor to Fr. Sullivan

"John was the product of a great mother and father. They were devout people. His father was Irish and his mother was Italian. Often in San Francisco that was the combination: we'd say, 'the Mission District (Irish) married North Beach (Italian).' They were devout and said prayers every night with the kids.

"Fr. Sweeny and I go back to 1939, that's 79 years. I started at St. Joseph's College Seminary and he had already been there for a year with his brother, Louis. They were a year apart, but they kept the same grade. Louis and John were about thirteen and fourteen years when they went into the seminary together in 1938. I came a year after they entered.

"They were model seminarians. They were really good guys and everybody liked them. And they were athletic. John was quite a

45

Louis and Norma Sweeny visit their young seminarian sons, John (far left) and Louis (far right).

swimmer and diver. As a seminarian at recreation, John participated in and coached sports. He was our baseball coach. He was also very attentive to his studies and, of course, very devout, with a special devotion to the Blessed Mother. After completing studies at St. Joseph College, he entered St. Patrick's Seminary.

"When we were at St. Joseph College in Mountain View, a fellow student, John Mape, slipped and his arm went through a window in a basement door. John Mape's arm was severely damaged. (Later, it would require a great number of stitches.) He was bleeding profusely from the inner arm and was in extreme danger. John (Sweeny), then about eighteen years, immediately acted! He got what appeared to be a t-shirt or a white sweater and made a tourniquet and wrapped it on John Mape's upper arm. I can't remember if someone called for an ambulance or drove him, but they rushed John Mape to the hospital. John (Sweeny) momentarily released the tourniquet pressure from time to time, as required by first aid.

"John Sweeny was such an ideal seminarian and something happened that, if he hadn't been, he might have been discharged. His brother got sick, and John knew it was bad. But the president was really strict at that time. He'd say, 'Stay up and fight it', as if it was a bad cold. 'You don't have to go to the sick bed every time you get a little ailment, you know.' So he resisted letting John take Louis home. And after a week or so, John knew that it was a serious illness and he told the president, 'I've got to take him home.' The president still was adamant. John took him home anyway. That would be a cardinal offense in those days! You don't do that. One hardly left campus when we were there, except on a hike or a Thursday off. But he just got a car and took his brother out of the seminary and everybody thought, 'Whoah! The ideal seminarian!' He could be expelled for disobeying orders. But it was a matter of life and death. It turned out that Louis had rheumatic heart very bad. John got him to the hospital and got his parents, and they saved his life.

"John and Louis were ordained to the priesthood in December of 1948, a year ahead of time. During the World War II there were accelerated courses to get more chaplains, so we were thus ahead in our studies and ordained one year ahead of our ordinary schedule.

"Years later, we got together one day to go golfing. John said, 'Before we go, we have to say a prayer to the Blessed Mother because I'm going to put something in her hands.' I asked, 'What's that?' He replied, 'A job training center. I'm going to start a job training center. I want to say a prayer that Mary will bless it.' He was living at St. Francis of Assisi parish in Palo Alto and drugs, crime, and unemployment were a grave problem in that area. John went on to explain, 'I'm going to start a job training center to get some of our African American people here jobs.' (There were Latino people, too, but mostly they were African American.) He went back to Pennsylvania to the Opportunities Industrialization Center East (OICE) and studied for just a week or so, and then he brought that out here and made it the Opportunities Industrialization Center West (OICW). That group was praised by Martin Luther King's widow. She visited once. By the time she came out here, some politicians had kind of stolen credit for starting it. Fr. Sweeny said, 'That's okay, as long as it is started.' He didn't care. They hosted a big dinner and he was seated at the back of the big room. Coretta Scott King said, 'Fr. Sweeny, you'd better come up here. I found out that you started this.' After a few years, that group became the Center for Employment Training (CET), which is now booming as a big complex on Vine Street in San Jose. So that was founded by Fr. Sweeny, really, and later brought to San Jose by other dedicated people.

"One of the qualities I remember about him most: Fr. Sweeny would never turn down a poor person. They knew it, you know. They would come from all over and he would give them his last dollar. People would come to the door and he couldn't say no. Of course that created a floodgate of people looking for a few dollars. He would drain himself to give to them. He had the biggest heart for the poor. He would not turn down a poor person, I don't think he ever did. That was his weakness: He was too generous! They took advantage of him because he was generous. If it was a person who was coming constantly or he thought was conning him, he would say, 'Okay, you go into church for an hour and pray and then I'll help you.' They'd go out and pray or sit there looking around in the church.

"Fr. Sweeny's keeping of the older devotions—like the Stations of the Cross and the rosary and adoration of the Blessed Sacrament—this brought a lot of people to Our Lady of Peace. Some of those devotions have diminished in the past thirty or forty years. People were trying to have an ecumenical movement by trying to bring the Protestants back to the faith and to the religion that has the Mass, the sacraments, and the Holy Father, but they were pulling away from the fundamentals. Fr. Sweeny was greatly devoted to the Holy Father, the Pope. He offered solid religion. He didn't go for music that was too liberal, but music that was more reverent. According to liturgical reforms, music is supposed to promote community singing: to give the tone and give the melody a little bit. But in many places it has become a performance.

"He also would say the rosary, sometimes fifteen decades. That takes an hour! When most people were eating dinner, he'd grab a quick bite and go out and say fifteen decades of the rosary. That was in his later years, but I think his devotion to Mary was a big deal. He dedicated everything to the Blessed Mother. He had what they call 'true devotion' to the Blessed Mother.

"Fr. Sweeny also started a monthly meeting of priests. Anywhere from five to ten priests still get together once a month for the rosary, Mass, a discussion of our parishes, and lunch. It's a priest support group which has gone on for thirty years. Priests need to have some support, it affirms us. Also, you see what others are doing and you learn from it.

"Fr. Sweeny was very devout. You could say the three virtues of faith, hope, and charity, he had them all. He was a very holy guy. I saw him put work for his parish first, even on his day off, for years. I saw him totally immersed in the work; in Spanish they call it, 'entregado,' *entrega total,* he had that. That rubbed off on the parishioners. I would be hard put to find some fault in Fr. Sweeny. He was a good man, a good person."

Helen Hovland
Parishioner 1976 - Present

"Before he left the house every day when he was a little boy, Fr. Sweeny's father would say to him, 'Did you kiss the Sacred Heart?' They had a small Sacred Heart statue. Everything was devotion. His father was on his knees all the time. Fr. Sweeny would say that sometimes they'd make plans to go somewhere, but his father took so long in prayer they'd miss the event. He was brought up in a very healthy life that very much regarded religion and faith.

"When Fr. Sweeny was fourteen and his brother, Louis, was thirteen, they came to their mother and asked her if they could join the priesthood. She loaded them up in the car, took them to the parish priest, and went in to speak with him. She asked him, 'Father, is it normal for two of the same family to want to become priests?' The priest came out and looked at them in the car and said, 'Well, with some families it is.'

"When Fr. Sweeny was in the seminary, his grandmother had a stroke. So Fr. Sweeny came home from the seminary concerned about his grandmother. As the doctor was leaving, he said, 'I'll be back later tonight'. He thought she wouldn't live more than a few hours. Fr. Sweeny knelt down at her bedside and prayed the rosary. And he

John Sweeny as a young seminarian in the 1940s.

John Sweeny, right, with his basketball teammates at St. Joseph College in Mountain View, California.

John Sweeny, center standing, coached the sophomore baseball team during his junior year of high school. The future Fr. John Coleman kneels at the front left. Circa 1940, St. Joseph College.

Fr. Sweeny's ordination to the priesthood at the Cathedral of St. Mary of the Assumption (locally known as St. Mary's Cathedral) in San Francisco on December 18, 1948. Fr. Sweeny kneels in the front row, closest to the camera. His brother, Louis, kneels in the second row, third from the camera.

prayed another rosary. And he thought he saw his grandmother blink. So he thought to himself, 'Well, I'll say another rosary. If she moves, I'll sit her up.' Well, she moved! So he sat her up. That night when the doctor came back, she was at the dinner table! They said to him, 'What do you think, doctor?' He said, 'Well! I hope when I have a stroke I have someone praying for me!'

"After he was ordained in San Francisco, Fr. Sweeny was assigned to different parishes. Eventually, they assigned him to East Palo Alto where people came to the door every day for food. There was a lot of unemployment and people were hungry. He said, 'I could give money to these people every day,' (which he did, out of his own pocket) 'but there must be a way they can get a job and support themselves.' He had read an article about a minister in Pennsylvania who had started a work program for the poor people there, and he went to see him. The man told him that he contacted business people who could train poor people and give them jobs. Not only did they train them, but they gave them the material they needed to be trained, such as machinery and tools. Fr. Sweeny—just a young priest—decided he would try it. He contacted seventeen business leaders and told them what he wanted to do, that he needed a way to train people who didn't have jobs, the materials necessary to train them, and someone to do the training. Among those he contacted were Hewlett Packard and Joseph Fessio [father to Joseph Fessio, S.J. of Ignatius Press], who worked with a nationwide trucking company. All seventeen business leaders showed up! This work program is still operating, and they have trained over 30,000 people. He was just on top of everything and pursued whatever he could do to help the people.

"How did he handle difficulties? Prayer before the Blessed Sacrament. That was his answer. If he didn't have a chance to get over there during the day, he'd be there at ten or eleven o'clock at night. And if he hadn't had a chance to say Mass, he'd say Mass. So the people who were there adoring went to his Mass! That's how he handled difficulties: he went to the Blessed Sacrament. He once told me he was praying in front of the Blessed Sacrament and was so sad because a married couple he had been working with was breaking up. As he was praying, 'God, take care of this problem!' he said he heard a voice that said, 'I love them more than you do.'

"Fr. Sweeny was very kind. And happy! He was a happy man, he was joyful; you could feel it come from him. He encouraged us to persevere in prayer: he knew that his prayers would be answered and that if people prayed and gave themselves to God, their prayers would be answered, too."

Mark Powers
Parishioner 1986 - Present

"Fr. Sweeny used to share with us stories about growing up with his brothers, Richard and Louis (Fr. Louis), and how they'd say the family rosary every night. That's what Fr. Sweeny taught us. We pray the family rosary because Fr. Sweeny instilled that in us. He was a very instrumental part in a majority of our success as a family.

"He'd also talk about how, after the family prayed, the kids would go to bed and his father would continue saying two or three more rosaries there by himself. Fr. Sweeny would explain that seeing his father pray was such a learning moment for him and an inspiration. The family rosary was really significant.

"Before buildings were built around Our Lady of Peace, it was all undeveloped land and we'd see Father walking out there praying at all times of the day. He loved the open space because he was a country guy.

"Fr. Sweeny was holy, but he was just a regular guy. What made him holy is no secret: consistency in his prayer life, the Mass, the Eucharist, the rosary, and his work for God."

A young Fr. Sweeny offering Mass at the altar on Calvary, where Christ was nailed to the Cross, during a visit to the Holy Land.

THE FORGING OF TWO LINKS

The Opportunities Industrialization Center West represents the embodiment of the OIC "Self-Help" concept in the Menlo Park - East Palo Alto community. Though separated by thousands of miles, our community shares with Philadelphia many of its problems of unemployment and poverty. Father Sweeny in East Palo Alto and Pat Manning at Philco WDL first saw the need for Dr. Sullivan's type of program — one combining the tremendous potential of community and industrial resources to make inroads on these problems. In scarcely a year, under the tireless leadership of Father Sweeny, OICW has become a firm reality, carrying on the "Self-Help" concept in a West Coast setting and forging links of mutual help with Philadelphia's OIC.

PURPOSE

To organize and recruit the Peninsula community to give equal opportunity for economic and social development for those who have never had it or to whom this opportunity has thus far been denied.

Father Sweeny and Pat Manning

A promotional newspaper article featuring the Opportunities Industrialization Center West (OICW), the job training center founded by Fr. Sweeny.

Fr. Sweeny and his brother, Fr. Louis Sweeny, celebrate the 25th anniversary of their ordination in December of 1973. The anniversary cakes were baked and decorated by Our Lady of Peace parishioner Maria Quinata.

I feel that my mission is about to begin:
to make others love God as I love Him.

St. Thérèse of Lisieux

CHAPTER 3
1970s

A Strong Foundation

Prayer works. I didn't have anything but a prayer.

Fr. John Sweeny

Though many parishioners considered Fr. Sweeny young, he was by no means inexperienced. Twenty years into his priestly ministry, Fr. Sweeny was well-equipped as a spiritual and business leader to guide the parish with creativity and vision. These were necessary qualities for a priest inheriting $500,000 of debt and a parish with an uncertain future. Yet Fr. Sweeny had a simple solution to every problem: prayer. Thus, his first initiative as pastor was to establish prayer as the church's strong foundation.

Behind the scenes, Fr. Sweeny advocated on behalf of Our Lady of Peace with the Archdiocese of San Francisco, pressing the Archbishop to recognize the church's heavy-traffic location as an opportunity to minister to more people. He also believed the people of this generation needed a "forthright expression of faith" to draw them to Christ. He achieved both. Hallmarked by prayer and action, the decade of the 1970s was a time of explosive growth at Our Lady of Peace Church...and Shrine.

APOSTOLATES OF PRAYER

Less than a month after his first Mass at Our Lady of Peace, Fr. Sweeny established the Legion of Mary with one presidium and three members: Judy Kennedy, Bernadette Johnson, and Mary Escamilla. This fledgling group would grow over the next fifteen years to eight small groups (one in Alviso), seventy active members, and 600 auxiliary members. In 1973, the bishop appointed Fr. Sweeny as Spiritual Director for the Legion of Mary in metro San Jose. Among the many prayer-oriented outreaches the Legion offered were monthly Days of Recollection and regular visits to patients at HyLond Convalescent Hospital (later renamed Beverly Manor Convalescent Hospital), where the priests from Our Lady of Peace also offered Masses and prayed the rosary with residents. The Days of Recollection were so well attended they became regular events offered every month for fifteen years. As more and more people attended programs offered by Our Lady of Peace Church, Fr. Sweeny identified this as people clearly yearning for prayer, devotion, and spiritual growth, and dedicated his time and energy to making these available.

Next, Fr. Sweeny sponsored first Friday all-night vigils, hosted in conjunction with the Blue Army. Initiated on October 3 of 1969, all-night vigil ceremonies began with Mass at 7:30 p.m., followed by sermons, songs, spiritual reading, and prayers. The Blessed Sacrament was exposed for Eucharistic Adoration until 5 a.m., and the vigil concluded with Mass. Of the approximately five hundred worshipers, about one hundred and fifty would stay all night to pray. The purpose of the vigils was to pray for the conversion of sinners (including themselves), peace in our country, and peace in the world, in response to Our Lady's messages to the three children of Fatima, Portugal, in which she told them, "Many souls go to Hell because there is no one to pray and make sacrifices for them." Prayers for many intentions, including souls, were offered at the vigils. One man from Los Gatos regularly attended to pray for his children's vocations. Years later, his son, Fr. Mark Catalana, was ordained to the priesthood in the Diocese of San Jose. Fr. Mark was unaware these prayers until after he entered the seminary.

By September of 1971, Fr. Sweeny formalized praying the rosary before every Mass and making confession available during every Mass, in an era when the trend across North American parishes was to decrease the availability and significance of these practices. As more Bay Area Catholics realized they could go to Our Lady of Peace for confession, Fr. Sweeny invited retired priests to assist him in hearing confessions for the increasing lines of penitents. Thus began a long tradition of dedicated priests who voluntarily gave their time and guidance to the parish community.

In 1972, Fr. Sweeny visited Fatima, Portugal, the site where three shepherd children saw the Blessed Virgin Mary six times, on the thirteenth day of the month, between May 13 and October 13 of 1917. These appearances and the messages "Our Lady of Fatima" spoke to the children were carefully studied by the Catholic Church and approved in 1930. Fr. Sweeny's personal pilgrimage of faith became a defining moment in his ministry: moved by his experience in Fatima, he returned even more committed to share the importance of praying the rosary and fostering an understanding of Mary's motherly love. On July 13 of 1972, shortly after his return, Fr. Sweeny, with the leadership of (future priest) Michael Pintacura, initiated the first Pilgrimage to Fatima Mass and procession at Our Lady of Peace. Fr. Pintacura was a young man at the parish who knew the exact format for the ceremony and worked tirelessly—with the support of parishioners and his own family members—to orchestrate the event. In a church that seated only 600 people, crowds of 1000 to

2000 overflowed into the parish hall and onto lawns for Mass, the rosary procession, and prayers for healing. This tradition continues to this day.

In 1973, the Men of the Sacred Heart group formed to encourage families to enthrone the Sacred Hearts of Jesus in their homes. They visited hundreds of homes in the area to share this devotion and pray with families. On April 26 of 1975, the Sacred Heart was formally enthroned (dedicated) in the church. Other devotions started in this decade were the traveling statue of Our Lady of Fatima for families to receive into their homes week by week, the Block Rosary families gathering in neighborhoods to pray the rosary, a True Devotion to the Blessed Virgin Mary weekly study group, and rosary-making classes first for children and then opened to all ages. To date, Our Lady of Peace rosary makers have distributed over eight million rosaries.

Further honoring the Mother of God, Fr. Sweeny had a vision to erect a statue and shrine to Our Lady of the Immaculate Heart. In his plan, Eucharistic adoration would be the shrine's "crowning glory" after the statue was completed. Yet after a visit from Jerry Trimble, a full-time promoter of Eucharistic devotion, Fr. Sweeny decided not to wait. Jerry suggested to Fr. Sweeny, "Maybe Our Lord wants you to build a *spiritual shrine* first." Fr. Sweeny told this to staff member Sr. Mary Jean Kula and she volunteered to help. Sr. Mary Jean contacted hundreds of people to ask them to devote one hour of prayer a week before Our Lord, herself signing up for the hours of 4-8 a.m. daily. Parishioners and local faithful responded to the gospel invitation, "Could you not keep watch with me for one hour?" (Matthew 26:40)

Eucharistic adoration, the jewel of all parish apostolates and truly their foundation, was instituted on August 15, 1976. Since that date, the church has remained unlocked day and night for visitors to spend time with Our Lord in the Blessed Sacrament. If an hour was left open or an adorer did not arrive at their assigned time, the priests would come to the church to pray until a replacement arrived. In 1976, there were fewer than twelve churches in the United States offering 24-hour adoration.

APOSTOLATES IN ACTION

The fruit of prayer is faith in action. Side by side with spiritual growth, Our Lady of Peace parishioners implemented program after program, outreach after outreach, inviting people to share their faith and serve in a variety of ministries.

Recognizing the need for an organized Mass procedure, in 1971 George Burnett founded the Lectors Organization while Tony Breslin organized the Ushers Club. These trained men were critical to assisting with Masses and special events.

Simultaneously, faith formation programs at Our Lady of Peace expanded and grew. Volunteers established an adult inquiry program for those interested in joining the Catholic Church and, in 1972, William Burgan formally began an adult catechesis program. Ahead of its time in the American church, years later this program would become known as RCIA (the Rite of Christian Initiation for Adults). In 1976, Sr. Mary Jean Kula established a Montessori Catholic kindergarten, expanding the already-established religious education offered for grades 1 through 12. Sr. Mary Jean's school offered two half-day sessions, five days a week. She also directed a formal First Holy Communion program.

In the community, Fr. Goode, Fr. Stout, and Fr. Sweeny lobbied for civil rights. For the people of Alviso, Fr. Goode was particularly active in addressing city planners and ambitious businesses whose development plans would push the poor out of their homes and thus out of Alviso. For the unborn and their mothers, the priests worked

*Jesuit priest Fr. Tom Byrne assisted with various parish outreaches,
such as offering Mass and Holy Communion to children at
Agnews State Mental Hospital.*

Fr. Sweeny enthrones the Sacred Heart of Jesus in the Lawless family home, 1978.

tirelessly to pray, protest, and encourage initiatives demanding the right to life. They encouraged parishioner pro-life activity and opened the parish meeting spaces for activists to work together. On January 24, 1974, two buses of parishioners traveled from Our Lady of Peace to San Francisco to attend the prolife rally protesting the anniversary of the Supreme Court decision to legalize abortion. Annually, parishioners traveled by the busload to attend rallies in San Francisco and Sacramento, bringing stacks of signed petitions and speaking personally with Congressmen. In 1977, the parish Prolife Committee was formally established. In that same year, two "walks for life" began: the first on Good Friday morning, beginning at St. Martin of Tours parish in San Jose and ending at Our Lady of Peace; the second was a 32-mile walk from Our Lady of Peace to St. Mary of the Assumption Cathedral in San Francisco. These walks were coordinated by parishioners Mary Nora and Mary Emma Jacques, staff member Tony Ryan, and Fr. Goode.

Tony Ryan also coordinated the Youth Mission for the Immaculata (YMI) program. Beginning in 1978, a four-week summer program brought together young Catholic women to learn and share the Catholic faith. Various priests spoke on topics such as Mariology, church history, scripture, and apologetics. Young men from Our Lady of Peace participated in programs for men at other locations.

Due to Fr. Sweeny's reputation for helping the poor, the St. Vincent de Paul chapter grew rapidly. Situated in a small room near the church entrance, volunteers sought to assist the needy with financial and spiritual support, as well as directing them to professional services. Despite the staffed outreach office, many needy continued to line up at the rectory door to see Fr. Sweeny.

Hard-working apostles still made time for fun! Monthly potluck dinners and entertainment brought families together from 1971 through 1981. The parish barbeques and carnivals offered rich social

Sr. Mary Jean Kula with her Montessori Class of 1976.

gatherings and entertainment for all ages. Our Lady of Peace Church bustled with life.

While at one time it seemed the practical decision for the archdiocese to close Our Lady of Peace for lack of parishioners, in time the outlook began to change. As Our Lady of Peace established a foothold as a parish, the archbishop allowed it to stay.

CHANGING LANDSCAPES

Our Lady of Peace's landscape began the 1970s as a church surrounded by orchards. To help pay expenses and weighty debt, Fr. Sweeny decided the parishioners would harvest the fancy comice pears grown on parish property rather than lease the orchards to farmers. Volunteers came together in a tremendous community effort to pick, package, and sell pears. The first year's yield was fifty tons of pears and ten thousand dollars. The parish continued this effort for a few years until a more lucrative solution arose: selling some of the parish property.

Nearby property values rose as businesses competed for land. The Marriott Hotel, Great America Amusement Park, and Mission College built campuses near Our Lady of Peace. More and more farmers sold their orchards and the landscape changed rapidly as trees were felled and buildings raised. In October of 1976, the Archdiocese of San Francisco decided to sell some of the church's most distant acreage to help pay the parish debt. Later, Our Lady of Peace leased seven more acres of nearby surplus land.

On property in front of the rectory, Fr. Sweeny had pear trees cleared away and set up four trailers for much-needed office and classroom space. He also purchased the land in front of the church—for the proposed Shrine—and cleared more trees. For the first time, Our Lady of Peace Church was fully visible from Highway 101.

Fr. Goode good naturedly anticipates his fate in the Our Lady of Peace carnival dunking booth.

Surveying the businesses moving in, Fr. Sweeny told the local newspaper, "It's going to raise the value of real estate, whether that's good or bad. It's of concern to people on a marginal income. I think it should benefit more than it's going to hurt. It gives jobs to people who live close by. You can list the good points and the bad, but you have to think positively. It's a challenge to each one of us to grow. We're going to be host, like it or not, to millions of people." And host they were.

THE SIMPLE APPEAL OF AUTHENTIC CATHOLICISM

In an era when worship styles between parishes varied widely under different interpretations of Vatican II, Our Lady of Peace offered a quiet consistency and ongoing recognition of the popular response to sacraments and devotions. Though critics touted the parish as "traditional," Fr. Sweeny and the priests who worked with him simply studied and implemented guidelines set forth by Vatican II for the Church in the modern era. So appealing was this implementation that parish enrollment, Mass attendance, and involvement not only flourished, it established deep roots that would support ongoing growth as the parish grew into a landmark.

This tremendous growth at Our Lady of Peace was supported by a tireless commitment and vision from Fr. Sweeny, Fr. Goode, Fr. Francis Shichida (who arrived in 1979 from Nagasaki, Japan to assist at the parish and minister to area Japanese Catholics), a core group of retired priests, and backed by generous parishioner volunteer time. Fr. Sweeny, noting more and more people attending parish functions, acknowledged a yearning for God and continued to offer opportunities to draw close to Our Lord. Concerned about the cultural changes of the 1960s and 1970s, his homilies specifically addressed the Christian response to issues affecting modern culture. He believed the culture needed a forthright expression of faith as a reminder of God's love. His vision was a larger-than-life statue of the Mother of God for all passersby to encounter the love of a Mother who would lead them to her Son.

Irene Barrera
Parishioner 1962 - Present

"In 1969 when my fourth child (Maria Teresa) was born, she had Down syndrome. The doctors told me she wasn't going to make it. I wanted to have her baptized, so I called Fr. Sullivan who had been transferred to San Jose. I was not used to Fr. Sweeny yet. It pained me so much that Fr. Sullivan was not at Our Lady of Peace and I was hurting, so I called him and he said, 'Well Irene, I think this would be a very good time for you to know John [Sweeny].' So I called Fr. Sweeny and told him what was happening. He had just received a call from Fr. Sullivan who told him he needed to go to the hospital to baptize my baby. He was wondering why I hadn't called him first, but you know how it is when you are hurting, and the priest they transferred is the one you know well and like so much?

"Fr. Sweeny came to the hospital and baptized Maria Teresa. It was already 9:00 p.m. when I called him and I was almost asleep when he arrived. The nurse told me, 'There's a priest here to see you.' Fr. Sweeny said, 'Yes, I called and they told me the baby might not make it.' My husband had already gone home, so he looked up a nurse from the hospital who could stand in as a Catholic witness and baptized the baby. That's how Fr. Sweeny and I started to get to know each other.

"I was 38 years when I had Maria Teresa, and when she came along the doctors told me I shouldn't have more children. When I

Facing Great America Amusement Park in the distance, Fr. Goode walks his mother through his vegetable garden. Pear trees stand where the rectory and offices are situated today.

was 41, I became pregnant with Michelle and the doctors told me I should have an abortion. They were very unsupportive, but Fr. Sweeny was there for me again and encouraged me all the way. Michelle was born without any complications.

"Fr. Sweeny helped me often. At one point, he wanted to know why I wasn't sending my children to Catholic school. I told him, 'We cannot afford it.' So Fr. Sweeny fixed it up for me. He called the pastor at St. Martin of Tours and they made it possible for us to take our children out of public school and put them in the Catholic school.

"Fr. Sweeny started the Legion of Mary at Our Lady of Peace and in Alviso (at Our Lady Star of the Sea), and he sent me there to help. He also sent me there to teach catechesis. So Fr. Sullivan told me to build community here at Our Lady of Peace, and Fr. Sweeny was sending me back to Alviso!

"Our Lady of Peace parish has changed so much over the years. It grew more. It used to be that people knew each other well because it was a smaller community. Many people come here now who are not parishioners. This church is very traditional and I feel they come here because they can pray."

Mary Jo Corcoran
Parishioner 1973 - 1998

"There was a lot of confusion after Vatican II. It sounded really good, the day of the emerging layman, but there were those who would take it and run down all kinds of different avenues. Fr. Sweeny always offered Mass, Eucharistic adoration, confession, and devotion to our Blessed Mother—basic Catholicism! Thus, Our Lady of Peace

Statue of Mary and votive candles in the church rear.

was a powerhouse to keep our Catholic identity and get us through those turmoil years of the late 1960s, 1970s, and 1980s, till the dust settled a bit from Vatican II. We are great admirers of Fr. Sweeny, very great admirers. We feel he kept us in the faith during that time.

"My husband and I have nine children. We moved to the Bay Area from Virginia in 1965. It was a time of turmoil and 'anything goes.' Yet if you loved the Church it was constant persecution. Our neighborhood Catholic parish became hardly recognizable as Catholic, and we became an irritation to the priest. We'd send the children to confession and the priest would say, 'Did your *mother* send you?' and belittle them. If sick parishioners asked for a priest to come and hear their confession, he would refuse and tell them the extraordinary minister was good enough. It was wrong. We went through some wild times. The leadership there was a new model of Catholics with a grievance against any traditions, and they really found us offensive. We just went through a storm. It was a hard time to go through so we officially made our home at Our Lady of Peace in 1973 and it kept us going. We were almost completely insane until we found Fr. Sweeny. During those times it was really hard to keep your head on! Fr. Sweeny just leveled us out.

"Fr. Sweeny kept the boat steering in the right direction. He taught us a lot and I thought the world of him. He taught a love of the Blessed Sacrament, receiving the sacraments, keeping my kids going to confession, and keeping a rosary handy and using it. He taught us that we are put here to give honor and glory to God, to save our souls and bring as many souls with us as possible. That was basically his motto. We loved him.

"Our Lady of Peace stabilized and strengthened us while we went through all those hard times when there were people unhappy with the church and wanting to change everything. Attending Our Lady of Peace gave our children the opportunity to experience an authentic

This photo of a Fatima Pilgrimage in 1976 features Mary Jo Corcoran (mother at far right with children) with Amy, Deirdre, Paul, Jimmy, and a young Lucy or Agnes (twins) on Amy's arm, praying in the rosary procession.

Catholicism that we couldn't find in our neighborhood. Today, they are all married in the Church and practicing Catholics because Fr. Sweeny offered the same recognizable Catholicism we wanted to offer our family."

Art Sacman
Parishioner 1971 - Present

"We met Fr. Sweeny in 1970 at a Legion of Mary function in San Francisco. When we moved to Sunnyvale in 1971, Our Lady of Peace became our official parish. At that time, we had one child. Our family grew to seven children.

"Involvement in Our Lady of Peace changed our family dramatically. I never wanted to get involved, actually, and when I came here to America (from the Philippines) I distanced myself from people because of discrimination and such. Yet I needed someone I could talk to. The first people I took confidence with were the nuns at Most Holy Trinity Church and, from there, the priests at Our Lady of Peace: Fr. Sweeny and Fr. Goode.

"Fr. Sweeny would phone and ask me to help him out, so we became active in the parish. We started by picking pears and apples in the parish orchards. Mary Buckley was selling the pears, and Dick Jones was the chief of that effort at the time.

"At first, I didn't want to get involved but Fr. Sweeny told me I was part of the parish now. He asked me to go out for the Annual Diocesan Appeal (ADA). I told him, 'I don't want to go on my own.' He told me a lot of people would get involved, 'but this time we'll go house to house.' I told him, 'Father, there are no houses in Our Lady of Peace!' He said we'd go to those we had and to Alviso. I told him,

'Father, to go to Alviso you need to speak Spanish! All I know how to say is: ¿Como estas?' But I got involved.

"I just tried to accompany the priests. Fr. Goode spoke to me about the people in Alviso needing to establish a health center. He said, 'The City of San Jose is not paying attention, they don't want to get involved in Alviso.' I replied, 'You have to get their attention.' So Fr. Goode set up a toll bridge! There was a small bridge that went over a creek near town. Fr. Goode set up a toll and charged twenty-five cents to everyone who passed there. I said, 'Father, you can do that on your own! I'm not getting involved with that!' It wasn't really about the money, but the exposure. After some time, the *Mercury News* came and put an article in the paper about the priest who was getting attention for the needs of Alviso by putting up a toll booth because the City of San Jose would not respond to them.

"Before coming to America, I met my wife in the Legion of Mary in the Philippines and we were married in the Catholic Church, but I wasn't serious about our faith. When we came to Our Lady of Peace, we knew we had a base. Both of us believed in the Church, but I was not as religious as she was. Though I was baptized Catholic, I didn't establish the difference between the Philippine Independent Church and the Catholic Church in the province where I grew up. The Independent Church has broken away from the Catholic Church but seems similar. Also, my family only went to church at Christmas and Easter. After we had been involved at Our Lady of Peace for several years, I said, 'Father, I would like to be full-fledged Catholic.' He asked, 'What do you want to do?' I told him, 'I would like to be confirmed as Catholic.' He said I didn't have to, because my baptism in the Independent Church was recognized, but I told him I wanted to go to classes and be confirmed.

"My time at Our Lady of Peace has changed my life. Because of our involvement in the Church I came closer to God. People here

Fr. Francis Shichida baptizes John Dennis Sacman in February of 1979.

Fr. Sweeny in 1974.

influenced me because I joined the Men of the Sacred Heart. We bring Jesus into the homes. I am encouraged because I can see people praying in their homes. I was not really a prayerful person, but because of Fr. Sweeny inviting me to services and Fr. Goode asking me to help him, I thought about it. I had thought priests were high up—superior, I suppose. Here I realized that if you look at a circle, all of us are within the circle: priests, nuns, and lay people. We're all in that same circle, yet we have different visions. That's when I realized I had a different vision than theirs, but it was still a religious one. My spirituality built upon that due to my relationship with the priests and the people at Our Lady of Peace."

Ellie Powers
Parishioner 1986 - Present

"When I was a young girl, my Mom had friends who were faithful followers of Fatima and the Fatima message. They told her about Fr. Sweeny and the Fatima pilgrimages. It was the first year he began hosting them, and we went on October 13. I remember attending with my Mom and it was very simple, yet due to the simplicity it was an amazing experience. I was in the sixth grade, probably eleven years old. About six years later, my entire family began to attend regularly.

"As an adult, I continued to attend Our Lady of Peace. I felt Fr. Sweeny had a remarkable grace to give spiritual direction on a very large scale. When he spoke at the Tuesday holy hours or at a Mass, he was able to touch a lot of people individually, though speaking to a group. He could make the gospel, devotion to Our Lady, or the Eucharist applicable to entire groups of people and how it addressed what was going on in our individual lives. It was because of this gift I believe people were constantly gravitating toward him: they felt the grace that came from his words. He got into peoples' hearts. He would weigh into the soul of a person and help them with issues they were dealing with, yet it didn't have to be on a one-to-one basis."

Sister Mary Jean Kula [†]
Parish Staff Member 1975 - 2007

"I met this incredibly holy man, Fr. Joseph Devlin, S.J., in 1975 [when I began working for Our Lady of Peace]. He radiated holiness, warmth, and humor, all rolled into one wonderful priest. (Fr. Joe Devlin was a retired Jesuit priest serving at Our Lady of Peace.)

"When dear friends phoned me, needing a priest for their ill ones, I saw Fr. Joe in the church hall and mentioned our desire for anointing of the sick. Before I finished my sentence, he volunteered and said, 'Honey, we have to go right now.' He was dead serious. We left that moment to tend to four families. Whenever we went on sick calls, which were at least ten calls a week, Fr. Joe would say whether the patients would make it or whether they'd live a while longer, and it was true.

"Shortly after the terrible weather storms in 1978, we were called to visit a family on the Loma Prieta fault line. We visited twice, and then the wife phoned that her husband was not doing well. I told Fr. Joe, who became radiant and very serious and said, 'Honey, we have to go right now. He won't live until Friday.' We went on Wednesday and the man passed away early Thursday morning. I had learned, being with Fr. Joe, that God did give him the gift of knowing the outcome and future of certain souls.

"Fr. Joe was a true missionary, zealous and on fire to the last days of his life. He told me I should call him any time, day or night, and he phoned *me* any time, 10:00 p.m. or midnight, 'Honey, is anyone sick or dying now? We can go right now. I am ready.' It would be difficult to find another priest as ready and filled with such love of souls."

Maria Quinata
Parishioner 1969 - Present

"The St. Anthony Novena is every week. This was brought to Our Lady of Peace by my aunt and uncle, Mr. and Mrs. Pedro Ada. They lived in Los Altos during the winter. They are from Guam, and their church there was St. Anthony Church. When they came to Los Altos, they called on my husband to taxi them around, so they were coming to this church. One day, my aunt asked me to ask Fr. Sweeny if they could have the St. Anthony devotion here every Tuesday. They would furnish the statue in the church.

"Fr. Sweeny agreed, so they ordered a statue from Spain. It happened that Fr. Castro was here helping, and he was living with us for a short time because there was no room at Our Lady of Peace. Fr. Castro helped us to put the novena together, then I brought it for Fr. Sweeny to approve, and he created a booklet in the format of a novena to St. Anthony. It has continued for over thirty years.

"Fr. Stout has led this devotion since Fr. Castro left. Fr. Stout had a list of parishioners and religious who have died and he prayed for them at the novena every week. He included Mr. and Mrs. Pedro Ada. No matter where we are or what we are doing, we race over to the church on Tuesdays for the St. Anthony Novena."

Fr. William Stout, S.J.

Sal Caruso
Parishioner 1990 - Present

"Fr. Sweeny told me a story about a Jewish man and woman whose daughter was very sick. She was in a Catholic hospital, and the doctor told her parents she would not live through the night. She was their only child. In despair, the man asked the doctor, 'Is there anything else we can do to help her?' The doctor replied, 'If you are so inclined, you can pray.' So the man went to the hospital chapel and knelt down. He saw an image of Mary and said, 'I do not know you, but will you help my child? I promise that I will do whatever you need of me.' When he returned to his daughter's bedside, he found her completely healed!

"Later, Fr. Sweeny was looking for a way to make large quantities of rosaries for his Rosary Crusade and visited a business owner whose machines made beaded curtains. He asked him, 'Are you able to set up your beading machines to make beaded rosaries?' The business owner remarked, 'I've been waiting twenty years for you!' He was the Jewish man, and told Fr. Sweeny the story of his daughter's healing through the Blessed Mother's intercession. Then he said, 'You can have the machinery for the rosaries.'"

Justino Escalera
Parishioner 1972 - Present

"We moved into the area in 1972 and attended St. Lawrence and St. Martin churches, and even taught catechism classes at St. Justin.

There were new changes coming into all churches from the Second Vatican Council. We weren't quite comfortable with the other churches but we were just going along until we came to this church. Wow. It felt like home and had all the traditions I grew up with. Even though it wasn't the Latin Mass of my childhood, there was more reverence. The people themselves were reverent and we were nourished. In other churches when they'd ask for money, you'd think, 'But you're not giving us a strong faith.' But here, when Fr. Sweeny would ask, you would want to give as much as you could! It was different. Also, after Mass people didn't just leave, they'd stay around and talk a lot. So we just fell in love with it.

"This year we'll celebrate the 40th anniversary of perpetual adoration. It started with Fr. Sweeny, and through the years that he was here he was a very busy man. I had two days that I'd come in: I picked an hour from 2-3 a.m. and another from 1-2 a.m. When I'd arrive, Fr. Sweeny would be there in adoration. Or, I'd just be coming into the church and he'd be going out. Not all the time, but often enough I'd see him and think, 'My God. He's a busy man and he takes time for adoration.' You might say he led by example a lot. You see other priests who are energetic and running around, but he was very quiet, kind of laid back, but what he did...he practiced what he preached. Some say actions speak louder than words; he fit that.

"When Father gave a homily, what he said really got to you. In Spanish we have a saying when priests are not giving enough weight in a sermon: 'Mas canela' which means he needs 'more spice.' But when Fr. Sweeny would speak, he'd make sense. He'd even speak about subjects that were a little hot. He wasn't known as a speaker and homilist, he was known for other qualities. But when he did have something to say, oh boy, you were awake and you were listening. His voice was quiet, slow, and toned down. Yet he was a prime example for everyone.

"Every year they asked volunteers to pick pears and sell them at Christmas. We all worked the orchards. I grew up as a migrant field worker, so I'd bring my boys to come and help pick pears. The parish would serve sandwiches in the hall for lunch, and people would pick pears for as long as they could. My kids didn't know anything about picking crops. They'd get dirt in their eyes and they complained left and right. They didn't like it. I took advantage of the opportunity and told them, 'You don't like it? I used to do it all the time. But if you don't like it, the next time you're sitting in the classroom daydreaming and not paying attention, this is what you're going to do. Pay attention at school!' That influenced them. At lunchtime my wife would bring us tacos, so we'd eat the way we ate when I worked the fields. It was fun. Working in the fields together was great, everyone had a lot of fun. Fr. Sweeny and Fr. Goode were there. I enjoyed it.

"We sold pears at St. Simon Church in Los Altos; it was pretty ritzy compared to Our Lady of Peace. One time the priest from St. Simon was talking to us and said, 'So, you're volunteers?' I said, 'Nope!' He replied, 'Oh, I see. You got railroaded into doing this?' I laughed, 'Right!' We sold quite a number of pears there.

"The greatest impact on my faith life was my parents. They taught me to always try to live the way God wants me to live. Coming here to Our Lady of Peace really reinforced that. It made one want to progress up the ladder of perfection. It taught my children what is right and what is wrong, and that if you really want to live the religious life you're going to suffer. With the world the way it is and so immoral, it did prepare them. A good example of that is my son who is a deacon in Colorado. As a side job he teaches at a high school. They have a dress code, and one time a girl came in dressed out of line with the code. He told her, 'You know, you shouldn't dress like that.' She was very upset, called him names, got bent out of shape,

"Lancey Reyes arrives to give Fr. Sweeny a hand during pear picking at Our Lady of Peace Church in Agnews...."
–The Santa Clara American, August 29, 1973.

C O M I C E   P E A R S

from

O U R   L A D Y   O F   P E A C E   O R C H A R D

2 5 ¢   per   LB.

(Available in 5 lb, 10 lb, and 25 lb quantities)

to

BENEFIT

OUR FUTURE SHRINE

of

THE IMMACULATE HEART OF MARY

"Try a comice and your hunger will cease!" was the catchy slogan for parish comice pear sales in the 1970s.

and her parents came in to complain. But he knew he had to say something to hold her accountable.

"Fr. Sweeny was a quiet man but he accomplished a lot. If he was in a crowd, he wouldn't stand out. You probably wouldn't even notice him. But in dealing with the church, he stood out. To me he lived by example. He talked and taught, but you could see that he was living it. He lived a tremendous faith. No matter what the obstacle, he could get up, dust off, and keep going. Whatever he was aiming for, you could see that he had a strong belief. Yet at the same time, you could talk to him. And the kids could talk to him, that's why they liked Fr. Sweeny and Fr. Goode, too. The kids just really loved them."

Helen Hovland
Parishioner 1976 - Present

"When Mary and Sam Houston took Fr. Sweeny to Fatima in 1972, he was overwhelmed by the processions they held there. When he returned, he spoke of it with his fellow priests. (They would meet every Monday for a holy hour and Mass, and all the priests would concelebrate Mass). He said it was so beautiful it would help to cultivate a love for Our Lady if we could have it here. So they encouraged him to do it, and he did. From the 13th of May through the 13th of October we had the Our Lady of Fatima Pilgrimage. It begins with all the different organizations in the parish processing in with their banners. Next come children dressed as angels and the three shepherd children of Fatima, the Knights of Columbus, the men carrying the statue of Our Lady, the nuns and, finally, the priests. They have reserved seating for the sick and religious. The place is full! People are standing and overflowing to the outside. During Mass, Father would talk about Our Lady of Fatima and the message she gave in that particular month and stressed her message: pray for repentance, pray the rosary for an end to war, and so on.

"Another story, just to give an idea about who this man was: I helped out at the Notre Dame Sisters retirement home in Saratoga. One Saturday a month, a friend and I would go deliver meals to the Sisters in their rooms or help them out to the refectory in their wheelchairs. We'd visit with them or help with whatever they needed. One day, they asked me what parish I attended. I told them I go to Our Lady of Peace. They said, 'Oh! Fr. Sweeny comes here every month to hear our confessions!' That was just one thing he did. He was so involved with everyone, especially anything that had to do with the faith. He didn't have to do that, but he made himself available to so many people.

"He also made himself and the parish available for important causes. When an abortion clinic opened in Sunnyvale, Fr. Sweeny immediately called a meeting of men and they started a pro-life crisis pregnancy center right next to it. He was constantly on top of the pro-life issue. When the Juan Diego Society started (the pro-life crisis pregnancy center in San Jose), he supported it completely and found other people to support it. People from Our Lady of Peace continue to do so.

"There are so many examples of Fr. Sweeny's generosity, they filled his every day. Once, a friend of mine brought a priest from the Ukraine to meet him. The priest told Fr. Sweeny about his work and how poor the people were. They were building a church yet they had no roof. Father took out his personal checkbook and wrote him a check for five hundred dollars. That was what money was for—to give away. That's something about his background and why I think Our Lady of Peace is what it is today: because of Fr. Sweeny.

"I never saw Fr. Sweeny take time to renew himself or recharge except before the Blessed Sacrament. Many times at night he was so exhausted he would sleep in his chair. (I was told this by the housekeepers who found him in the morning.) He was too tired to get up and go to bed! But the Blessed Sacrament sustained him and made him a man of joy."

Fr. Michael Pintacura
Serving at Our Lady of Peace 1970 - Present
Religious Vocation from Our Lady of Peace

"My interest in the priesthood began in grammar school. When I was entering high school, my family moved from Chicago to California. It was at Santa Clara High School where I acknowledged my vocation to the priesthood. At that time, the public schools in this area were attended mostly by Catholics. Most of the teachers were Catholic and we'd see many of them at daily or Sunday Mass. We prayed before and after class.

"Every day, I served the 5:30 a.m. Mass for the Jesuits at the Mission Santa Clara. From there, I'd go to the 7:15 a.m. Mass at the Carmelite nuns' monastery to serve again. Finally, I'd walk over to school. At noon, I'd visit the Blessed Sacrament at a nearby church and bring a group of my classmates with me. Some of them were not Catholic. This was my routine all through high school. Priests were often visitors in my parents' home and I knew Fr. Sweeny as an acquaintance even then.

"When I graduated from high school, the next step was to attend San Jose State for my teaching degree. I was seriously studying to be a teacher, but not necessarily a priest. After San Jose State, I did post-graduate work at Loyola University in Chicago and studied music at DePaul University. From there I taught in a Catholic school for eight years. Along the way, one of my dreams was to work at NASA with

Fr. Sweeny, with Fr. Warren, S.J., raises the monstrance in a prayer of healing for the sick at a Fatima Pilgrimage Mass at Our Lady of Peace Church in 1976. Fr. Michael Pintacura kneels in the background.

Pilgrims of all ages pray at the Fatima Pilgrimages. 1976.

the space program; an opportunity arose and I left my teaching career to work for NASA, not far from Our Lady of Peace. I often attended Mass and Eucharistic adoration at Our Lady of Peace and became good friends with Fr. Sweeny. The thought came to me about being a priest and I spoke with him about it. I also wrote to about 25 different religious orders and gathered information.

"At that time, I helped Fr. Sweeny on the altar at the all-night vigils. The vigils began at 7:30 in the evening and ended at 6:00 the next morning. The church was packed all night long with teenagers, young children, and adults. And there was action all night long. We scheduled priests to speak every hour, on the hour. Throughout the night, people would take breaks: half the church would go to the hall for refreshments, and the other half would stay in prayer. It was so organized. People came from all over the Bay area and lined up for confession throughout the night. Attendance grew and grew.

"One day, Fr. Edward Warren was at Our Lady of Peace (I had known him since serving Mass for the Jesuits in high school). He told me, 'Fr. Melatesta just came in from Rome and he teaches at one of the pontifical seminaries there. I'll have you meet him.' When I met Fr. Melatesta, a Jesuit priest, I was so impressed with his enthusiasm and youthfulness. He said, 'Come to Rome and study for the priesthood. I'm selecting five men from the United States to represent the United States and I'm selecting you.' He spoke with the rector and the Vatican and made arrangements for me to move to Rome. I entered the seminary in 1970, studying at the Beda and Gregorian Pontifical seminaries. I truly enjoyed the time there. It was one of the best seminaries. For my post-graduate work preparing for the deaconate, I went to Kentucky and studied with the Benedictines. During breaks from studies, I returned to Our Lady of Peace.

"When Fr. Sweeny told me, 'The archbishop wants me to sell this parish because it is in the boondocks,' he was very upset. During my seminary vacations, I had been involved in setting up the sanctuary and museum in Fatima, Portugal and knew how to organize the processions. So I told him, 'There is a future for this parish, and we're going to put it together. Let's start with the Fatima procession. I'll get it all organized. We have to bring Our Lady of Fatima here. I'll get her statue and prepare the people. We'll have a procession outside the church.' Father replied, 'Not many people are coming to Mass, who will come?' I met with a parishioner, Mrs. de la Cruz, and we discussed it. Then we told Fr. Sweeny, 'We'll put it in the San Jose *Mercury News*.' We made our own stop signs with wooden posts set in coffee cans and secured with cement, rope guides to control the cars coming in, and our own altar and carrier for the statue. Three hundred people came! That was a big number at that time. Every 13th of the month when we hosted the procession, it became larger and larger.

"We invited priests to give talks related to the theme of the apparition for that month, and they came. We had Fr. Warren, Fr. Stout, the Dominicans, the Maryknolls, and many others. They also made confession available throughout the evening. Eventually the Fatima processions grew so big we had twenty priests here every month. Fr. Sweeny always served a dinner for them.

"There were many miracles at the Fatima pilgrimages. One I remember in particular was a young mother in the 1970s. She had an incurable disease. She was dying. She came to Our Lady of Peace for the Fatima procession and was cured miraculously. When the doctors saw her, they asked, 'How can this be? She is perfectly healthy!' There are records about this cure in Fatima.

"In 1974, the summer and winter Olympians came to Santa Clara. The city had a parade in old Santa Clara on downtown Main Street to welcome them. The parade coordinators asked Fr. Sweeny, 'Can we have your statue of the Virgin in the parade?' The statue was unknown in those days. So we made it big! We dressed in our cassocks, the Dominicans came in their habits, and children carried Our Lady with such precision she never tilted. The ladies of the parish got together and made gigantic rosary beads to carry as we walked in the parade. There was applause for Our Lady all through the event, and the Olympic champions came to have their photos taken with us. Then the city of San Jose wanted us in their parade, so we processed through downtown San Jose! There we were, in the city parades between the drum corps and cheerleaders, and the people were moved. They asked if they could have our rosaries. The cheerleaders were all making the Sign of the Cross, and even the parade queen reached down from her float to request a rosary! Once, however, we were not well-received and a complaint came in about us: we passed down a street in San Jose with adult movie theaters and bars. The business owners all complained they lost money that day because no one came into their establishments after Our Lady passed by!

"People were touched because they had never seen anything like this before. More and more people started coming to daily Mass. Our Lady of Peace became well known and eventually the bishop changed his mind and did not close the church.

"All this time, I was a seminarian not associated with a diocese. I wanted to be a missionary, but needed to be more robust for that life. My spiritual director told me, 'They need missionaries in Amarillo, Texas.' I asked, 'Where's Amarillo, Texas?' But I traveled to Amarillo and the bishop was so welcoming. It was really a missionary diocese! He kept in contact with me while I studied in Rome.

"My seminary class was ordained by Pope Paul VI, but the bishop in Amarillo wanted to ordain me in their new cathedral because the people in Amarillo rarely saw ordinations. I was ordained in 1976 and served as a priest in Amarillo for ten years. I also became a priest for the canonization of saints.

"Next, I served at Our Lady of Peace for two years, and then served in the Diocese of Stockton. After some time, the bishop was receiving so many international calls about my work regarding Blessed Ana Maria Taigi, he released me from parish work to work full-time on her cause and sent me live and work in Santa Clara.

"My background—all the jobs I've held—has enhanced my priesthood. My priesthood has been very, very happy. I've seen miracles happen: people being cured, others finding jobs, people in despair finding peace once again. Fr. Sweeny and Fr. Stout were a great influence and source of encouragement for me, as were the visiting priests who came to assist them at Our Lady of Peace.

"I love everything about the priesthood: To be a priest as a priest should be, an alter Christus. I have a passion for it. Even when others didn't recognize my vocation, I never doubted it. My father always told me, 'Never take no for an answer when you know you're right.' So I didn't! I've been so blessed."

Sister Marie Colette of the Infant Jesus, P.C.C.
Religious Vocation from Our Lady of Peace

"Our Lady of Peace was, for me exactly, what the name signified: an oasis of peace which comes from (and only from!) immersion in God and obedience to His will. This was the life of the Mother of God.

"An awkward teenager who felt herself to be unlovely and unwanted, coming from a family situation that was fractured by divorce, found in this holy place what she was really yearning for: God.

Fr. Michael Pintacura with his traveling statue of Our Lady of Fatima in 1975.

The Our Lady of Fatima procession joins the 1975 Olympian Parade, by invitation, in Santa Clara. Led by children carrying a giant rosary, Fr. Sweeny, Fr. Warren, and adult parishioners accompany the statue.

Fr. Edward Warren, S.J., speaks with Rex Harris, long-time supporter and assistant to the Fatima Pilgrimages. Children dressed as Lucia and Francisco, the Fatima visionaries, are in the foreground. 1975.

"It was at Our Lady of Peace that I heard God's call through the preaching of Fr. John Sweeny. At one of the Pilgrimage to Fatima nights, Father said that Our Lady wanted souls who would dedicate themselves to prayer and sacrifice for the conversion of sinners. This sounded like a bell in my heart—this was what I wanted to do! Father often repeated this message and each time it felt like a personal call to give myself to God through Our Lady for the conversion of sinners.

"Of course, the first miracle that took place was my own conversion! I spent much time praying before the mystical image of Our Lady near the altar of the church where all the vigil candles were burning. Those little candles would be the symbol of my own vocation.

"When Saint Francis was converted from his worldly way of life, he heard God speak to him through the crucifix in the Church of San Damiano. He, too, had heard words which rang true in his own heart: 'Go, Francis, and rebuild my church which you see is falling into ruin.' After that experience, he wanted to keep a vigil light burning always before that crucifix. Years later, when he founded the Order of the Poor Ladies (one day to be known as the Poor Clares), he brought Clare and her Sisters to that Church of San Damiano. There they would testify to God's Presence by their lives of total consecration to Him in the silence and hiddenness of the cloister. The Sisters' lives were the vigil candles burning before the Lord by night and by day.

"It was at Our Lady of Peace where I spent many days and nights! I helped to staple the very first booklets for the first Pilgrimage of Fatima. I was privileged to help put the flowers around her image and set up the church for the Fatima nights. I attended the first all-night vigils there, strengthened both by the Blessed Sacrament and by the witness of a policeman who came when he got off work just to be with Our Lord. It was at Our Lady of Peace that I was confirmed and where

I made the total consecration to Our Lady witnessed by Fr. Sweeny. I taught catechism in the first 'school,' the trailers that had been moved in for that purpose. I was also privileged to help with the first junior Legion of Mary.

"But above all, it was here that an awkward teenager with a lukewarm faith was overwhelmed by the immensity of God's personal and unconditional love. I spent the happiest years of my life helping at this parish. On the morning of my entrance into the monastery, I attended Holy Mass and went to confession to Fr. Sweeny. It launched my little ship out into the ocean of God's love and mercy, into the fulfillment of my dream, and set me on course to give myself totally to the Giver of all good gifts, the Father of Mercies, in His beloved Son, through the blessed Holy Spirit.

"The confirmation name given me at Our Lady of Peace was 'Colette,' which is my religious name. I will be forever indebted to Fr. Sweeny, Fr. Goode, my dear friend Judy Kennedy who was so close to Fr. Sweeny, and to the wonderful oasis of peace found in the church named for Our Lady of Peace."

Fr. Lawrence Goode
Assistant Pastor 1971 - 1978

"Our Lady of Peace was the third parish assignment I received after my ordination to the priesthood. I thought I was heading to a parish in San Francisco, and was then told it was Our Lady of Peace. They told me I could go straight to the assignment or go through the process to talk to my confessor before I decided. So I told them, 'I do NOT want to go there.' The next day, I received a letter in the mail sending me to Our Lady of Peace anyway! So much for democracy!

Sister Marie Colette of the Infant Jesus, at the Convent of the Poor Clares in Los Altos, California.

That was the last time I ever did that; from then on I decided whatever the Bishop wanted me to do would be fine. I was the assistant pastor at Our Lady of Peace from 1971 to 1978.

"In the 1970s, there were few parishes offering confession and even those were cutting back on opportunities for people to go to confession. There were a lot of unusual practices post-Vatican II and people were questioning everything, such as: Should children have to go to confession before they make their First Communion? (Many parishes decided to wait until children were in the fourth grade.) What exactly defines sin? Should confession only be for mortal sins? Do people really need to go to confession before going to communion? These were some of the ideas that were floating out there. Priests were not encouraging people to use the sacraments and thus many people now only consider six sacraments—as if confession doesn't exist. In the meantime, Fr. Sweeny offered the Sacrament of Confession at every Mass.

"I had started learning Spanish and working with the Spanish-speaking community in Gilroy, but that assignment was followed by time in Burlingame and there was no Spanish Mass. I was anxious to get back into that and when I arrived to Our Lady of Peace I discovered that we were taking care of Alviso. Fr. Stout would say Mass there on Sundays, and we would go during the week and say Mass. It didn't take very long before I got caught up in what was going on in Alviso. There was probably a lot more going on in Alviso as far as day-to-day stuff than there was at Our Lady of Peace where the nearest houses were in Sunnyvale and Santa Clara. So we had three communities: Alviso, Sunnyvale, and Santa Clara.

"I became very involved in the Alviso community during my seven years at Our Lady of Peace. We organized marches to City Hall to try to get Alviso back from San Jose (it had been incorporated by a narrow vote). We realized after a while that the struggle was going to be political, which meant trying to get publicity to our situation. There were some big business interests, enterprisers who had other plans all along, though they gave the impression to the local people they were going to make it better for them. They had plans for a Foster City, a marine world, and an airport that would come right up to Alviso. So all these different plans were being talked about under the table and hadn't surfaced yet because they didn't have the peoples' best interest. We found out about all these plans one by one. Our big concern was that people would be relocated because they were being offered money to relocate but they would not have houses if they did so. The people had old houses, made with real nails and real wood, and they worked in construction so they knew they had something better than what was being built in the surrounding areas. We were actually successful in keeping the community. We got streets put in and convinced the city to do a lot of things to improve the community, most important being to not relocate the people.

"I also became involved with the pro-life efforts in 1973 when abortion was made legal. Fr. Sweeny was very good about creating a crisis pregnancy center in Sunnyvale. It was right near Planned Parenthood and created an option for women. People who were picketing outside of Planned Parenthood tried to send people over to the pro-life center. There was a woman who ran it, and she was terrific. She would get a hospital to take in a woman and the doctors would give her free care. I remember one woman who had no insurance. She went into labor around 2:00 a.m., phoned me, and asked, 'What do I do?' I had her call the director of the pregnancy center, who then got on the phone and called the doctor, who called the hospital, and they said, 'Tell her to come right away.' She went to the hospital and they were ready for her.

"We also organized pro-life marches. Our first one was from Mission Santa Clara to Mission Dolores. It took us three days. We'd

108

stay overnight in Menlo Park, then walk up to Daly City and stay overnight in the hall there, and then walk up Mission Street to Mission Dolores. It was kind of fun because, in the story of St. Francis and St. Clare, they got together one time to pray. This was toward the end of his life. When the two saints prayed together, a bright light was created. It looked like there was a fire, and firemen came up with buckets to put it out! I mention this because we began in Mission *Santa Clara* and ended up at Mission *San Francisco*, so I'd say, 'Tell the firemen not to worry!' Our group of walkers met up with a prolife event in San Francisco. We walked from one church to another and there were speakers at each church. This was before the Walk for Life; that's what they did in the early days. By that time there were people from all over who identified with Our Lady of Peace, so the people who joined our group weren't just Our Lady of Peace parishioners, though a number of parishioners came.

"During a drought, we also had marches from St. Martin of Tours parish to Our Lady of Peace to pray for rain. Fr. Sweeny's friend, Fr. McDonald, got a fruit crate, put a statue of Our Lady on it, and set it up in the field, symbolic of the Shrine statue that was to come. We did this every year for three or four years and it rained every time.

"Another important event to me was perpetual adoration. I was there for the start of it and that was really exciting. There was a man who came to promote perpetual adoration at the parish. He came on a Holy Thursday when we had adoration in the church. He stayed all night long. After, he came in and told us, 'Don't say you're *going* to do it, say you're going to do it *on this day*.' Fr. Sweeny was talking about waiting until we had the statue, and the statue would draw people to enter the church with the Blessed Sacrament. The visitor said, 'Do it.' So Fr. Sweeny got on the phone and called Monsignor Burns from the archdiocese asking permission to start perpetual adoration. He said, 'Go right ahead. Just be careful.' He never questioned anything Fr. Sweeny did and he knew he would be careful.

"The interesting story about perpetual adoration was that Sr. Mary Jean got it all organized, confirmed people for every hour, and told everyone we were ready to start. After the first week, she had to get on the phone and start calling people all over again because the American people didn't understand perpetual adoration! They didn't know the meaning of *perpetual* adoration. It was not part of their tradition. She called people and they'd say, 'I already did it last week.' They had no idea of doing it regularly. The Hispanics and Filipinos understood. If it weren't for the Hispanics and Filipinos, we would not have gotten it off the ground.

"We each had our hour for adoration. I had my turn at 2:00 a.m. once a week and I'd get to know some of the people who would come. The middle of the night was the easiest hour to keep because nobody had appointments and, unless they were sick, they would be there. They were very faithful about coming. A lot of them were older people.

"When I was serving at Our Lady of Peace, Fr. Sweeny and I talked a lot. I had been in other parishes where I didn't really know the priest, but his door would be open at the end of the day and we'd sit down and talk. There were a lot of things that we developed a relationship upon. For example, Fr. Sweeny gave me a book about intensive gardening and I started to garden at Our Lady of Peace. It went for about two or three years and I had nearly twenty beds when they placed classroom trailers on top of it. That was the end of my garden! When I came to St. Francis of Assisi, I started another garden. Then they put the food pantry on top of it, so that was the end of that! I waited until they were all finished and now I have my own garden in another area. I had never gardened in my life. The appeal was in learning how to do it and having a hobby.

"Our Lady of Peace was offering opportunities that were not being offered in other parishes, like the perpetual adoration, all-night vigils, the Fatima Pilgrimage, and confessions with every Mass. Fr. Sweeny was good: when we were not able to do it, he asked other priests to come in. He made sure there were priests for confessions at every Mass. One day, however, a lady went into the confessional and began hearing confessions! She was doing fine until she gave someone a rosary to say for his penance. He was upset and she was found out.

"In 1971 when I was assigned to Our Lady of Peace, I didn't want to go there. In 1978, when the bishop concluded my time at the parish and sent me to another, I didn't want to leave and petitioned to stay! Our Lady of Peace was probably my best parish ever. I thoroughly enjoyed myself."

Fr. William Stout[†]
Served at Our Lady of Peace 1967 - 2018

"The parish was surrounded by comice pear orchards, very fancy pears. Down the road there was an old Portuguese gentleman. In the springtime he came to see Fr. Sweeny and said, 'Would you come and bless my orchard?' Fr. Sweeny said, 'Of course I will.' And he went down and blessed the orchard. Later, someone told Fr. Sweeny, 'Don't you know this is the year of pear blight and it is going to wipe out all the pears in this valley?' And it did, almost. The pear blight was in all the orchards surrounding the Portuguese gentleman's property, but *his orchard was just fine.*

"Before Mission College and the Marriott Hotel went in, that property was also pear orchards. Hollywood's Fess Parker came along and was looking for a new location for his Frontier Village

Fr. Lawrence Goode at Our Lady of Peace in 1977.

[amusement park]. He was looking out beyond Fr. Sweeny's church where the Marriott is today. He couldn't put the finances together, and that's when Marriott came in.

"When the Marriott was built, they got the six-lane highway. They must have had a lot of clout [with the city] because how often did you see a six-lane highway go over a freeway? It just didn't happen. Next, Marriott wanted to buy Our Lady of Peace. They offered to move the church. Fr. Sweeny said, 'No way, I'm not moving this church. It is staying right here.' While they were building the Marriott, they had to re-route the road to get into Our Lady of Peace, and if you got in the wrong lane you wound up going back to where you came from. You had to be very careful. Fr. Sweeny helped them with water: he had a well on the parish property for the building of Marriott and the amusement park [Great America].

"At the same time, Fr. Goode was involved with Alviso city development. The city had taken over to consolidate Alviso and was hoping the property values would increase and discourage the poor from living there. But the poor people didn't want to leave. They wanted to stay as the City of Alviso or go to Santa Clara (the City of Santa Clara was taking care of the Alviso school system). San Jose came in and said they were going to fix the streets, but they never did. In one place, they sprayed 'Stop' on the ground and the letters were crooked because they sank into the potholes! So Fr. Goode put up a sign to stop people as they came into Alviso. If they weren't a resident, he'd ask them for twenty-five cents so they could fix the streets. Someone complained and got the police to go out. But the city manager was a Catholic and said, 'No, leave him alone,' because it would really look bad to arrest a priest. Fr. Goode is quiet and easygoing, you don't expect it but he's a real dynamo. Eventually they got some money from the government to gravel the roads in Alviso."

Steve Nguyen
Parishioner 1975 - Present

"Fr. Sweeny and the parish sponsored my family to come to California when we had to flee Vietnam. Coincidentally, Fr. Joe Devlin was also on our journey.

"My family was all born in Vietnam. On the last two days of the conflict in Vietnam, we took refuge in a seminary. My extended family has many relatives who were priests and nuns. We also had distant uncles who were martyred and defenders of the faith. In fact, we have a relic of a great-great uncle who was decapitated for having defended the Church; he was a priest. So we took refuge at a seminary right outside the naval shipyard. We prayed about what to do next, and got on a boat.

"The original idea was to travel down to South Vietnam. We had never intended to leave the country. The intent was to evacuate from Saigon down to South Saigon. There was talk about regrouping the forces. We hoped the Americans would jump in and help, but they pulled out and gave it up. When that happened, we were in the South Asia Sea (now the South China Sea). We were there during the fall. The next plan evolved when the American government acknowledged there were a million refugees and almost half a million floating around on boats. The world told America they were responsible. Some refugees went to Europe or Australia, but the majority went to America.

"We were put on a World War II Navy ship, we spent a few days on the open sea, and were supplied food. The Navy ships convoyed (escorted) us and eventually we made it to Camp Pendleton. I was

Archbishop Quinn (of San Francisco) and Fr. Stout celebrate Mass at Our Lady Star of the Sea Church in Alviso, 1977.

Archbishop Quinn addresses the congregation at Our Lady Star of the Sea Church in Alviso, 1977.

fourteen years old.

"My parents wanted to come to California because of the warm weather. There were three refugee centers: California, Florida, and Arkansas. We missed the opportunity to go to Florida, so we were offered Arkansas or California. My Mom refused to go to Arkansas. She said, 'I prayed about it and we can't go to Arkansas.' There was a slot open in Florida, but she said, 'I prayed and the Lord said for us to go to California.' So we waited.

"I still remember the first time I served Mass for Fr. Joe Devlin. I was a fourteen-year-old rambunctious kid, and in Vietnam I had been an altar server. At Camp Pendleton in California, I found myself serving Mass for Fr. Joe. I knew of him when I was in Vietnam and stories about his heroic deeds, and that a lot of the United States Marines admired Fr. Devlin. Father was a tall man. Kids loved him. They'd hang on him. He was a saint. Everybody flocked to him. What was unique about him was that he said, 'I'm just another guy. I'm not anyone special.' He made every attempt to speak Vietnamese. His Vietnamese was quaint but it was understandable.

"I was very fortunate to serve daily Mass for Fr. Joe when he was at Camp Pendleton. He spoke with a certain amount of grace. When I was a kid and went to him for confession the first time, I couldn't communicate well with him but he knew a bit of Vietnamese. So he said, 'Are you sorry?' I said, 'Yes.' Then he asked, 'Can you say the Our Father?' I said, 'Yes.' So he told me, 'Go say the Our Father.' That was Fr. Joe. But something about him made me want to try harder. He made people want to be more holy. He knew people would make mistakes again, and would just encourage us to keep trying.

"Fr. Joe was at Camp Pendleton from the month of June until late August or early September. Then he said, 'I have to go. There are people who need me more.' A lot of people asked him to stay, but he still said, 'There are people who need me more.' So he went to Thailand because he knew if an American priest was there, the Thai government would think twice about abusing people. He knew nobody spoke on behalf of the refugees. So he went to minister to the Vietnamese refugees in Thailand. From there he went to the Vietnamese refugee camp in the Philippines.

"Meanwhile, we were praying for a place to go and praying to go to California. My Mom and Dad had always wanted to find a quiet, Catholic community. My mother prayed and prayed, and our location felt somewhat predestined: there were, at times, up to 200,000 refugees at Tent City [Camp Pendleton]; we were among the first refugees to come to Camp Pendleton and among the last to leave.

"What was unique was that it was raining the day we arrived to San Francisco. It was October of 1975 and there had been a drought. It was the first rain of the year and it was pouring. San Jose wasn't much of an airport, so we flew into San Francisco. Our group included my parents, four brothers, and two sisters. (One of my older brothers was studying in Europe and came later.) Fr. Sweeny drove his red Dodge Challenger to meet us, and there was another family car. My older brother rode with him, and I went in the other vehicle with Fr. Stout, Fr. Goode, and a gentleman by the name of Bill. Everyone wanted to take my family to the rental house we would live in, but my mother said, 'No, I want to see the church.' So we went to Our Lady of Peace. To this day I still remember it. We were singing, 'Ave, Ave, Ave Maria'. Fr. Sweeny prayed the rosary with us. He would lead the Our Father in English, and we would say the second half in Vietnamese. We prayed the Hail Mary the same way. Talk about the Catholic Church and its universality! Two separate cultures in a church, and praying the same prayers. Up to the end of his life, Fr. Sweeny never forgot that. He remembered that my mother wanted to see the church and give thanks to God. She wasn't worried about anything. My Mom and her faith are incredible. When she prays for what she needs, God seems to listen to her! She endures all kinds of things and never has a moment of doubt in God's providence.

"Right out of the driveway at Our Lady of Peace, there was a street that led to our house. We would walk to church and were happy the church was within walking distance. People would stop their cars to give us a ride. It was funny to us. We were happy to walk! Eventually we got a car.

"The people in the parish looked out for us. Dick Jones and his family took care of us a lot. We were sponsored in part by the parish of Our Lady of Peace, and in part by Fr. Sweeny himself. It was mostly Fr. Sweeny because the parish was poor.

"We were the poorest parish in the Archdiocese of San Francisco. Our collections did not meet what the church required. We were lucky, on Sunday at the 10 a.m. Mass, if the church was sixty-percent full. At the other Masses, such as 7:30 a.m., it may have been thirty-percent full. So we've seen a huge increase in attendance since the 1970s, huge! My family has been at Our Lady of Peace church since we arrived here. We have lived on the same street for the past 40 years.

"On April 30, 1976, one year after the fall of Vietnam, Fr. Joe Devlin and his brother, Fr. Ray Devlin, were here. (Fr. Joe was in Thailand and he fell ill because he didn't eat well. That was typical of him. He also had an infection in his foot, so the Jesuits told him he had to return. He came back and stayed with Fr. Sweeny in the rectory.) I served Mass with Fr. Joe. He brought a Vietnamese flag and said Mass for all the people who died in Vietnam, all the Marines who died in Vietnam, and he declared Communism would lose and fall if the people were devout enough and pray hard enough. He said, 'I will live long enough to see Communism fall.' And he did. I still remember it like it was yesterday. I was just a fifteen-year-old kid.

"I started running track in high school and, as a sophomore, I lettered in the sport. I was so proud. Both Fathers Devlin (Fr. Joe and Fr. Ray) and Fr. Sweeny would pick on me and say, 'You're not old enough to be a letterman!' When Fr. Joe Devlin heard I made the team, he forked out the money and bought me a letterman's jacket. I didn't know it was him. My coach told me, 'Well, someone bought you a letterman's jacket, so wear it.' I said, 'Coach, was it you?' He swore it wasn't him. I told him, 'You better have not bought this. Because if you did, I need to work and earn it.' The coach assured me it wasn't him, and even swore on the Bible! I told him, 'You guys don't always tell the truth about doing good things. I don't want to owe anyone.' So he swore, but he also swore he would never tell me who paid for the jacket. And he didn't. Fifteen years later, the coach was dying of cancer and his son told me Fr. Joe Devlin had paid for the jacket. The priests always showed they were proud of me.

"Fr. Sweeny had a love for the Vietnamese. I think it is because he fell in love with my family because of our shared faith. Our Lady is a love of our family's. And you know how much Father loved Our Lady. He always loved the people who were faithful. He always told me and my brothers that my Dad reminded him of his Dad. It was a mutual admiration, because my Dad admired Fr. Sweeny because of his strength and his faith, and how he saw through all the complications and the politics and simply loved his faith.

"In 1976, there were more Vietnamese coming to Our Lady of Peace on Sundays and the Fatima celebrations brought even more. There were so many Vietnamese coming to the church that Fr. Sweeny started saying two Masses every Sunday for them. People would travel to Our Lady of Peace even if they lived in other areas. They would travel here to pray together. The church was packed, the hall was used for overflow seating, and people were even sitting outside because there was no room in the church. Fr. Sweeny was shocked by the large attendance.

"Not only did people flock to Our Lady of Peace for their spiritual needs, but Fr. Sweeny attracted all kinds of people in material need because they knew he would help them. So many people came that he'd end up giving money out of his own wallet until it was empty. Sometimes I'd be at the parish helping him, and I knew he needed cash so I'd leave some on his desk. Within twenty minutes, someone would come to the door to ask for help. Fr. Sweeny would tell them, 'You're lucky. Someone just left the money.' He didn't keep it.

"I served Mass as often as I could. I was an altar server until I got married, even when I was in the military and came home. I served for Fr. Sweeny, Fr. Warren, Fr. Joe Devlin, Fr. Ray Devlin, and Fr. Stout (at the St. Anthony Novenas). Fr. Pintacura came along in the 1980s. The priests were wonderful with the people. Kids would come up to Fr. Joe Devlin and, even when he had his bad foot, he would try to pick them up. Both Fr. Ray and Fr. Joe were like that into old age. The kids just loved them, they glowed. Those priests had unfiltered joy!"

Willie Lapus
Parishioner 1983 - Present

"Fr. Sweeny told me how Fr. Shichida came to Our Lady of Peace: Bishop Ito came to the United States to present the case of Our Lady of Akita. He brought Fr. Shichida because he spoke English. His English wasn't that great, but it was better than the Bishop's! Bishop Ito asked Fr. Sweeny if he would like to have Fr. Shichida as an associate pastor here. Fr. Sweeny told me, 'I couldn't

Fr. Stout offers Mass in Vietnamese.

refuse!' They became very good friends and worked together as an excellent team.

"Among the many who appreciated Fr. Shichida, there was a small group of Japanese Catholics who would come to Our Lady of Peace to visit him."

Jerry Richards
Parishioner 1963 - 1975

"We were running Bingo every Friday night throughout the year. It was a big deal. I even built a balcony to stand in when calling out the numbers, right over the doors to the restroom area in the parish hall.

"One night, the sheriff came over to my house and said, 'Do you run a Bingo game out of the parish hall?' I said, 'Yes.' He told me, 'We're shutting you down. There's a person who has filed a complaint that you are gambling, and gambling is illegal in Santa Clara.' I went down to Fr. Sweeny and told him the law shut us down. Then I formed an association with all the places that played Bingo, like Archbishop Mitty High School (they had a huge Bingo program and depended on the income for the school). I went down to see the District Attorney, who was a Catholic, and presented all kinds of caveats we could use to start Bingo again. It took me two years to come up with a solution. He told me, 'It takes this to make Bingo illegal: game, chance, contribution, and winnings.' I realized if we took one leg off that stool, Bingo wouldn't be illegal. So I asked him, 'How about if people donate for the cards instead of paying for the cards? If you don't pay for the cards, you aren't losing money.' So we started again! I put up a sign: Players are under no obligation to pay for Bingo cards. But if you'd like to *donate*, these are the suggested *donations....* Any profit was turned straight over to the church. By the end of the year we were giving ten to fifteen thousand dollars to the church.

"I spent two years getting Bingo back into our churches and schools. Bingo was a source of income for these places and they were hurting like crazy. When we could finally start Bingo again, Fr. Sweeny wasn't excited because we tied up the hall all day Thursday and Friday. On Thursday we had to set the hall up with all the tables and chairs, and on Friday the game was on. Then Fr. Sweeny started the all-night vigils on Fridays, and the Bingo game disturbed the prayer service. People were shouting out, 'Bingo!' right in the middle of the rosary!

"When I left the parish, one of the other guys took over the game. At Our Lady of Peace, if our jackpot got to $1,000 it would bankrupt us. Then the city made it legal for a non-profit to run Bingo, so everybody became a non-profit organization, and there were too many games in town. These other outfits were paying blackout for $2,000, $10,000, $25,000, so of course the people went over there. The fairgrounds now have Bingo seven days a week. We just couldn't compete. There were not enough people to keep it going at Our Lady of Peace.

"The end of my story with Fr. Sweeny is that one day, many years later, I was over at our house in Lakewood Village which we rented out after we moved to San Jose. I was mowing the lawn when my wife stopped by with two grandsons. She told me, 'I'm going down to the store at Our Lady of Peace, we need to buy a crucifix for the kitchen.' I told her, 'I'll go down there with you.' So I got in my truck and she drove in her car and we went to the store and purchased this crucifix. I said to her, 'I wonder if it's been blessed?' She said, 'I doubt it. It just came out of the box.' So we went to the rectory door and rang the doorbell. The secretary came out and we asked if a priest was available to bless our crucifix. She said, 'Sure.' She went back and we waited two or three minutes, when who shows up but Fr. Sweeny! We didn't know he was still there. He didn't remember Frances, but he sure remembered me. Because we often hadn't seen eye-to-eye, I had a lot of weight in my heart toward him, a lot of weight. But as he blessed that crucifix, all hostilities and all that weight left my heart. It was *gone*."

Tony Ryan
Staff member 1977 - 1981

"I met Fr. Sweeny through a good friend of mine who worked for him one summer. Fr. Sweeny told him, 'I really need someone like you full-time.' My friend put Fr. Sweeny in touch with me and I came out from the midwest to meet him and interview. Fr. Sweeny told me his plans for the Shrine and vision for the future. Marcia and I decided to take the leap and move out here. We were just married a year and were expecting our first child. I was 27 years old.

"We moved across the country in an old Chevy pickup truck with a trailer. It took us nine days to get here, and everything that could go wrong went wrong! Our infant, Vincent, was in a cardboard box in the middle of our front seat, and we pulled a trailer I bought to move our belongings. We encountered storms, had car parts blow up, axles break, and brakes go out. It was unbelievable. By the time we arrived, we felt like we had fought the forces of hell to drive to California. I think we did. But it was great when we made it. We arrived in late November of 1977.

"I was the Director of Religious Education and also involved

The Our Lady of Peace Bingo leaders at Friday night gaming in the parish hall.

with the youth group, helped with the perpetual adoration program, and promoted the Shrine. Those were my main jobs. On the side, I helped Fr. Sweeny with whatever he wanted to do. With the Shrine, it was giving out rosary checks, talking to people about it, promoting it, and getting the word out. Anything Fr. Sweeny needed help on regarding the Shrine, I did. I was happy to help him.

"Adoration began a year before we arrived. When Fr. Sweeny interviewed me in 1977, he told me, 'We started this perpetual adoration program in the last several months. I need someone to help me run it.' I said, 'Great, I'd love to help.' That was one of my jobs. Sr. [Mary] Jean was there, too. She helped me a bit. She was a holy woman and would take adoration hours herself and encourage people to sign up, and I kept it going. She had a school there and my children attended her school. Sr. Jean and Fr. Sweeny were a spiritual force.

"When I arrived to Our Lady of Peace, there were two great women, Mary Nora and Mary Emma Jacques, who were (biological) sisters in their late 70's. They were very devout and they were go-getters. When Roe vs. Wade passed and legalized abortion, they said, 'We've got to do something.' They had the idea to organize a nine-mile pro-life prayer walk every Good Friday from St. Martin of Tours Church in San Jose to Our Lady of Peace Church. These older women would lead the people in praying the rosary, walking nine miles, and carrying pro-life signs. When I arrived in 1977, they saw me as a young guy all fired up and asked, 'Would you like to take it over?' How could I say 'No' to these ladies, who were now over 80 years?! I agreed and led it every year until 2015. I had microphones and speakers to lead the people. About 100 to 200 people attend the walk every year. We start at 9 a.m. on Good Friday and pray and walk. Planned Parenthood is on our way, so we stop there to pray an entire rosary. Then we keep going until we arrive to Our Lady of Peace where people serve us beans and bread. We call it a 'penitential meal' but it feels like heaven when we get there, we're so hungry.

"We also started the Shield of Roses. The idea was to meet in front of the abortion mill and pray the rosary. We carried signs emphasizing our witness to life. The roses on the 'Shield of Roses' represent the Hail Marys prayed. My wife and I had participated in a similar group in the midwest and so we started it in Sunnyvale with people from Our Lady of Peace. People would come every Saturday, and we had a sizeable group there praying the rosary and handing out literature. Even though it was a poor parish out in the middle of nowhere, Our Lady of Peace became a spiritual and prolife center with all these things going on.

"As a young man out of college, I had taken part in a youth Marian program called the Youth Mission for the Immaculata, started by the Franciscan Friars in Marytown in the midwest. It was based on the teachings of St. Maximilian Kolbe. I had gone to that month-long program and made my consecration to Our Lady, and it really made an impact on me. When I came to Our Lady of Peace, there was a YMI program in Southern California for boys, so I suggested we start one for young women here. Fr. Sweeny liked the idea, and Fr. Goode helped, so I started the YMI program that summer of 1978. About 20 college-age women came and stayed for a month. We had rigorous programs: spirituality, theology, apologetics, and prayer. It was all centered around the teachings of St. Maximilian Kolbe. I had to go out and find speakers who could teach these classes. After a few years we moved it to St. Simon Church in Los Altos because Our Lady of Peace had too much going on. Then we found other places to host it where there were dormitories for the girls to use. In all, the YMI ran for thirteen summers. It couldn't have started without Our Lady of Peace. Fr. Sweeny was totally supportive and Fr. Goode came every year, all those years, using his vacation time to teach. We used the church for Masses and the hall for class.

"Fr. Sweeny was a devout, holy priest. He really believed in the faith and was a teacher of the faith. He was a true, spiritual son of Our Lady with an authentic love for Mary. He was a spiritual leader. He was a very humble man, very kind, and very gentle. And he was holy. He wasn't a theologian or a scholar, which one doesn't have to be to be holy. He was happy, kind, and generous. He was a man who really wanted to help people get to heaven, and people recognized that in him and came to him. That was the essence of Fr. Sweeny. He wasn't a brilliant homilist or a great administrator, but it was his more important qualities that attracted people."

Barbara Wilkinson
Parish staff member 1986 - 2015

"I was coming to Our Lady of Peace when I lived in Burlingame because Fr. Sweeny was reaching my heart. I was so touched by the Fatima Masses and rosary that I decided that we needed more people to come from the Peninsula. Because I owned two travel businesses, I could orchestrate group trips. So I chartered a bus that started in San Francisco and picked up groups of people in various locations and we'd come down. I wanted to make it easy for people to come.

"Fr. Sweeny was an outstanding spiritual leader. That's why I made such an effort to take people to the Fatima Pilgrimages. He would speak directly to our hearts. He opened up my heart to the Lord: I'd been a Catholic since I was in kindergarten and I studied Theology at the University of San Diego, but it was Fr. Sweeny who opened up my heart. One priest, a brilliant Jesuit, explained it very well. He said, 'We have to bring all this knowledge about the Church into our hearts.' That's what Fr. Sweeny did for me. He brought all the knowledge that I'd grown up with and he made sense out of it. It became a lesson for my heart."

The Youth Mission for the Immaculata gathers in July of 1978. Tony Ryan is in the back row, Fr. Goode stands at the far left, and Fr. Sweeny near the far right.

Irene Barrera
Parishioner 1962 - Present

"My husband knew Fr. Sweeny from the Opportunities Industrialization Center West (OICW—the job training and placement program Fr. Sweeny founded). When Fr. Sweeny came to the parish, my husband told me, 'You know the priest who is there? He's the one whose big picture is on the wall when I go to that program at the OICW.' The OICW was training my husband for welding employment. He had to take classes first in math, and then in the afternoon he would take welding classes.

"Years later, I worked for the County of Santa Clara in the alcohol and drug program. I'd send people to the OICW to get trained because I knew Fr. Sweeny had started the program. People who were getting sober could learn skills there. I'd also host classes in Spanish for the people in the alcohol and drug program and invite Fr. Sweeny to come to speak. He'd speak to the class about how the church sees alcohol: that abuse is bad, but use is not bad. He was available to reach out to those people."

Unnamed Pilgrim

"The Fatima Pilgrimage has such a dramatic and real effect on people's lives that it acts as a magnet to draw them to future Pilgrimages.

"There are miracles at every pilgrimage. They may not be the kind of miracle you can see and describe, nor are they confirmed reports of physical cures. There is, however, some kind of miracle occurring in each human soul who comes and participates. Our Lady dispenses great graces during this time, and it appears to me that she gives to us the gift of neighborly love, so evident in the family spirit among the pilgrims."

Fr. John Sweeny [†]
Pastor of Our Lady of Peace Church & Shrine 1969 - 2002

"When I came, [the parish] was greatly in debt. How do you start? Some things I didn't agree with were in vogue, some of the modernism, but I decided the first thing I would do was begin the rosary before every Mass. So we started the rosary before every Mass, and then someone came along—a group from the Blue Army—and asked if they could use our church on October the 7, a first Friday in 1969, for an all-night vigil in thanksgiving for the gift of the rosary and to celebrate the feast [of Our Lady of the Rosary]. I agreed. About 1,100 people came...not all at once, but throughout the night. We started with a Russian Rite Mass, then Bishop Lane of Maryknoll preached, and then several monsignors and so forth. I said, 'That was wonderful! Are we going to stop now? Why should we stop now?' So I decided I'd send another letter and that time about 150 people came. Then I said, 'What about next month?' I made up my mind: as long as two other people would join me we would have an all-night vigil. [Now] three to four hundred people come. The church is filled at the beginning of the night but then throughout the night [it drops to] a couple hundred. Then we have maybe 450 in the morning. And we have the procession of the Blessed Sacrament.

"What I've found most important is the continuity. You can count on us, like a spring that doesn't go dry. The church provides something that is consistent, 'I can go there. The church is open, [and] there are priests in the confessional.' And then what happened next? We started a Pilgrimage to Fatima. I had been to Fatima and I see great value to prayer and penance. A young man [Michael Pintacura] went to Fatima and he came back describing the procession on May the 13 every year; this is quite large and perhaps a million people go to it. And I said to him, 'Why don't we do that here?' So since that time, in July of 1972, we've had the Pilgrimage to Fatima. We try to copy it almost literally. The bearer, the music, the atmosphere, the whole works. People come by the busload.

"In a parish, there should be opportunity to come close to Our Lord in the Blessed Sacrament, the Mass, and the church being open as much as possible. And I put top priority the opportunity to be able to go to confession: for the individual to be able to get peace of soul as Christ intended. In the present day, when there is so much temptation and people are caught unawares, I think the greatest charity we can work is to be out there in that confessional. I have several retired priests [who come to hear confessions]. We take turns. We have three to four Masses a [week] day and we always make sure there's someone out there hearing confession before Mass. The church is also open 24-hours a day. We have Exposition [of the Blessed Sacrament] every day except Good Friday and Holy Saturday.

"[When I arrived,] the parish was over a half a million dollars in debt. We had to be able to make some progress so, rather than lease the orchard, parishioners worked the orchard and picked the pears. I blessed it and I said to Almighty God, 'Bless not only our orchard. Bless all the land that touches it.' And so we harvested fifty tons of comice pears that year and put ten thousand dollars in the bank. So that was a positive thing."

This aerial photo from 1973 shows Our Lady of Peace Church at the center, surrounded by hundreds of acres of pear orchards. Note this photo pre-dates Great America Parkway, the Marriott Hotel, and the building of a highway overpass.

By 1977, the landscape had undergone significant changes by way of the
removal of farmland and a boom in industrial construction. As Mission
College and the Marriott Hotel moved in as close neighbors, they hemmed in
Our Lady of Peace's property between two new thoroughfares: Great
America Parkway and Mission College Boulevard. A highway exit and
overpass also offered more direct access to the church.

Make frequent visits to Jesus in the Blessed Sacrament
and the devil will be powerless against you.

St. John Bosco

CHAPTER 4

Mary:
A Forthright Expression of Faith

Everyone should have a genuine devotion to
[Mary] and entrust his life to her motherly care.

Second Vatican Council

After the city of Santa Clara re-zoned the neighborhoods bordering
Our Lady of Peace for business and industry, many archdiocesan
leaders saw little future for the church. Yet Fr. Sweeny offered a
unique perspective on the so-called crisis: a parish placed at a highway
exit, in the heart of businesses, hotels, and an amusement park, was
an *opportunity*. The parish property was a prime location to minister
to many. The timing, as well, was perfect. At this pivotal, post-Vatican
II moment in Church history, the world needed a "forthright
expression of faith." In a mid-1970s newspaper interview, Fr. Sweeny
anticipated, "We're going to be host...to millions of people." Thus,
his vision for a statue dedicated to the Immaculate Heart of Mary
began to take shape.

GUIDING A DREAM TO REALITY

Fr. Sweeny lobbied passionately for Our Lady of Peace to not only stay open, but to be dedicated as a Shrine visible and open to people of all faiths. "The world cannot benefit from a hidden faith, love, or hope," he explained. Years later, a retired Archbishop McGucken would say, "That was a brilliant solution for that piece of property."

The Shrine development was many years in the making. The priests had work to do, people to serve, pears to pick, and a parish to run. Also, for a church already laden with over $500,000 of debt and a limited payment plan, it was a bold idea to develop a shrine with a statue the size Fr. Sweeny envisioned: 90-feet high, set on 30-foot pillars, and visible from a 3-mile radius. He passionately promoted his vision, explaining, "We want to make her a statue of such splendid height that no one can ignore it, of a beauty that will attract and inspire all who see it, in the hope that many will respond to Our Lady's invitation to love her Son."

Fr. Sweeny met with Archbishop McGucken to request permission to initiate the statue and Shrine to Our Lady of the Immaculate Heart. The Archbishop agreed, but did not permit him to raise funds. (Unbeknownst to Fr. Sweeny, plans were in motion to divide the Archdiocese of San Francisco and create a new Diocese of San Jose; the Archbishop did not want to commit a new bishop to a fundraising project.) Fr. Sweeny asked, "Can I ask people to donate prayers?" The Archbishop replied, "Of course." And so a campaign began: Fr. Sweeny presented his vision to the people of Our Lady of Peace and asked for one million rosaries as the foundation for the Shrine. When that foundation was established, he would initiate plans for the physical statue. Faith, he said, not dollars, would build the Shrine.

To record the rosary count, Fr. Sweeny sent out rosary checks—

made payable to Our Lady—on which people could write their number of rosaries prayed. As rosary checks poured in at Our Lady of Peace, monetary donations arrived with them. Many donations were not from the parish or local area, but from people across the country and even in Ireland. Whenever someone asked Fr. Sweeny how much money he would need for the statue, his reply was the same: "All I need are rosaries." He never asked for a penny, yet the statue—still just an idea—began to pay for itself. Finances falling into place, Fr. Sweeny began to look for a sculptor who could bring his vision to life. The artist would need to create a piece so personally moving to the visitor or passer-by it would fulfill Fr. Sweeny's desire that, "The Shrine must be of such excellence that whoever comes must leave a better person."

SEARCHING FOR A SCULPTOR

Commissioning a sculptor for the project proved to be a challenge. One sculptor was contacted, but died a few months later. A second sculptor was found, and he also passed away. Then, in 1976, Charles Parks of Wilmington, Delaware, came to San Francisco to present his work at an art show. Mary and Sam Houston, members of the Our Lady of Peace Shrine Committee, attended Mr. Parks' exhibit and were so moved by his work they brought Fr. Sweeny to meet him. The trio explained their mission to Mr. Parks and asked him to consider working with them. Of that first encounter, Charles Parks later recalled, "They drove me down to the site, and I almost told them I couldn't do it. It was Dullsville. The church property is a triangle that extends to the highways. A quarter of a mile away is the Great America Park of Marriott with a Ferris wheel within sight of the spot they've picked for the statue." Mr. Parks objected to the site, yet said that Fr. Sweeny, "won me over. He's a devotionalist and we don't see eye to eye on many things. But he's as close to a saint as a man can be, and I couldn't turn him down."

BRINGING A VISION TO LIFE

Specifics for the statue were not determined until Mr. Parks learned more about Fr. Sweeny's vision and purpose. Because Mr. Parks was not a Catholic, Fr. Sweeny sought to first educate him about Our Lady. They began with a trip to Fatima, Portugal. On October 13, 1977, the two men attended the 60th anniversary of the Miracle of Fatima celebration, honoring the final apparition of the Virgin Mary seen by the shepherd children Lucia, Jacinta, and Francisco, and witnessed by the entire village of Fatima. On that visit, they met with an artist cousin of Lucia's to inquire how she personally described Our Lady's appearance. The cousin told them, "She was full of light, very beautiful, and young." Fr. Sweeny and Mr. Parks viewed existing statues of Our Lady of Fatima, finding them surprisingly scarce and not matching their concept of what the children saw. Mr. Parks later explained, "It was first proposed that I copy one of the existing statues. They were Portuguese concepts out of a different culture from ours. Some were of such saccharine sweetness—they would be ludicrous in the American scene. My Madonna is not historic," Mr. Parks explained. "For one thing, if you look you'll see that her hair is not drawn severely back as the old madonnas wear it." He chose to adhere closely to the peasant children's description, yet striving to convey "sweetness and strength at the same time." This effort was particularly apparent in the outstretched hands—strong and capable with long, tapering fingers—poised in a gesture that bespeaks love, gentleness, and compassion.

Back home in Wilmington, Delaware, Mr. Parks began to sketch his ideas for the statue. He mailed Fr. Sweeny several designs to critique. Though not intended to appear to be with Child, in the final rendering Our Lady's robes reveal her as a mother-with-child which

This early model for the Shrine to the Immaculate Heart of Mary features a 90-foot statue set on 30-foot pillars, visible from a 3-mile radius.

hotel Olid Melia

PLAZA DE SAN MIGUEL, 10
TELEFS. 22 99 71 - 22 45 01
CABLE: MELIAHOTEL
VALLADOLID

Thursday Oct 7-1976

Dear Mother, Dad + Bud:

Today is the Feast of Our Lady of the Rosary. On our way to Lourdes by train. Will be back in Fatima by Oct 9

Contacted the artist and commissioned him to do the statue

Will remember you all at the Grotto.

I'll try to call you tomorrow

Jack.

Hoteles Melia

Madrid: APARTOTEL MELIA CASTILLA ● Madrid: HOTEL MELIA MADRID ● Marbella: HOTEL MELIA DON PEPE ○ Torremolinos: HOTEL MELIA TORREMOLINOS ● Palma de Mallorca: HOTEL MELIA MALLORCA ● Granada: HOTEL MELIA GRANADA ● Cordoba: HOTEL MELIA CORDOBA ● Valladolid: HOTEL OLID MELIA ● Ibiza: HOTEL S'ARGAMASSA ● Puerto de Santa Maria: HOTEL MELIA EL CABALLO BLANCO ● Valdepeñas: MOTEL MELIA EL HIDALGO ● Mallorca: APARTOTEL MELIA MAGALUF ● Murcia: HOTEL 7 CORONAS MELIA ● Alicante: APARTOTEL MELIA ALICANTE ● Tenerife: HOTEL MELIA PUERTO DE LA CRUZ Torremolinos: APARTOTEL MELIA COSTA DEL SOL.

"Contacted the artist and commissioned him to do the statue," Fr. Sweeny wrote in a letter to his parents and brother dated October 7, 1976. This commission officially initiated Charles Parks' work on Our Lady of the Immaculate Heart.

resonated well with Fr. Sweeny.

Both Mr. Parks and Fr. Sweeny were dissatisfied with the first model of a proposed statue. "I was too intent on sculptural lines, too academic. I was losing track of the idea. Fr. Sweeny's concept of a 'mothering' Madonna didn't mean cooking and getting Johnny off to school." Fr. Sweeny's concept was much more "basic and visceral." To the hundreds of thousands of commuters shuttling back and forth past his parish every day, Fr. Sweeny wanted the statue to say, "Peace in the world, and within yourself, is possible." Fr. Sweeny also wanted a sense of the beauty, lightness, and resplendence the three peasant children saw in the 1917 apparition in Fatima. Thus, after both Fr. Sweeny and the Shrine Committee approved Mr. Parks' second clay model, they also agreed on a medium of welded steel strips which would both reflect and allow sunlight to filter through the statue.

Going forward, Mr. Parks continued to refine the statue design. The sculptured stainless-steel tresses fall as a girl would wear them today, "down her breast." She is a young Madonna, youthful, yet still with the warmth of a mother. "I wanted her to be contemporary enough that people wouldn't be saying to themselves, 'Now, where did I see that before?'" Mr. Parks explained. He wanted the perception to be instant, undistracted, and uncluttered. Mr. Parks worked for months before he was satisfied with his final model of Our Lady of the Immaculate Heart.

Several women posed for the face and figure, most notable being the Madonna's face which strongly resembled Laura Watkins, at the time a local college student. Mr. Parks had seen Miss Watkins' face in a 1978 supplement in the Wilmington News-Journal and contacted her to model for him. "I had a veil on [in those pictures], and I guess it just clicked," she remembered. "We talked for a while about the statue, and he asked me to model for him." Watkins knew she was posing for a religious statue, but she had no idea just how

*Charles Parks' initial idea for Our Lady of the Immaculate Heart.
Neither the sculptor nor Fr. Sweeny were satisfied with this first model.*

OUR LADY OF PEACE CHURCH

2800 Mission College Boulevard
Santa Clara, California 95051

Telephone: 244-7366

Compassionate

1) Liked expression in face — didn't like eyebrows — a little too rustic

2) The hair should be covered a little more, more from — I like the hair down on the sides and parted in middle —

3) I didn't like the bust area — its too high — it a little to accent — perhaps because the heart is too small — it looks more like a medallion — The heart has to be bigger. Bust too much like a girl just developing — Perhaps the was

4) The gown was too clinging

5) I like the stance (contra posta) seems to moving, arms also, she is about to speak —

6) The whole face should be a little more refined

Fr. Sweeny's notes to artist Charles Parks offering his critique on the initial
statue design.

important the Madonna would become. "I was an art history major in college, and I looked at the work as a work of art. I didn't really think about the religious aspects," she said. "I was pleased just to be working with Mr. Parks. Part of me knows that it's my face on that statue, but I realize it's not me that's getting the credit. Mr. Parks did the work. It's my face, but he's the one who made it such a beautiful work of art. He's the one who put the spirit into the Madonna."

The Madonna's eyes were the most difficult to deliver. He sought expression, the sense that her eyes met each onlooker with reassurance and compassion, which was the most difficult part yet the heart of the piece. The face also needed an identity, leaving one feeling there is not another face like it in all the world, and yet the same face appealing to everyone who sees it. As for how the public received his piece of art, Mr. Parks sought for each person to receive it as it was personally intended to speak to them. No two people should derive the exact same impression. If they could, if everybody saw the same thing, Mr. Parks explained, his work would be a "failure." He explained, "If I could put into words what the statue says, if I could verbalize it, then I've wasted a lot of time and a lot of stainless steel."

For the hands, Mr. Parks mostly used his own, primarily because "they were right there." He modified and feminized them so they definitely are the hands of a woman, although not those of a hard-working peasant.

Intent on fully articulating Fr. Sweeny's vision through his art, Mr. Parks explained, "I really try to be his hands. I hope the piece says what he wants it to say. Hopefully, there is none of me in it." Due to the technicalities of reproducing art and working with steel, Mr. Parks would need to create multiple versions of the statue, each one increasing in size. His first statue was a 10-foot model that was installed with due ceremony on March 13, 1979, in the churchyard

"Model Laura Watkins, the face of Our Lady of Peace Madonna, stands in front of the statue in Rodney Square [Wilmington, Delaware]."
–News-Journal, *September 1982. Photo by Leo Matkins.*

at Our Lady of Peace, symbolizing greater things to come.

The next would be a 30-foot Madonna, and finally the 90-foot Madonna. He explained, "Visually, I could go from 10 to 30 feet but I didn't feel up to going directly to 90. I don't want to create a monster. Even doing it by scale you're bound to lose something in symmetry."

In 1980, Fr. Sweeny commissioned the 32-foot statue. The clay head, hands, one exposed foot, and heart were completed in the sculptor's Bancroft Mills studio, cast in fiberglass, and then sent to a Peekskill, New York foundry where they were cast in steel. Mr. Parks himself cut the strips of stainless steel and worked from a bridge crane or scaffolding around the statue, cutting the strips of varying widths, then bending and twisting the steel into shapes to give the appearance of a flowing, undulating robe. Using strips of steel enabled light to filter through, giving a different aspect to the statue as the light changed throughout the day, creating a sense of movement. The different treatment also provides a different texture from the other parts of the body, intentionally creating a jarring impression. Once the strips were ready, trained welder Dick Berger connected them with small steel plates.

When Mr. Parks was well into fabricating the statue, an onlooker took up station outside his studio and just stared. "I watched him; he stared for fifteen minutes. I was succeeding; he had found the statue meaningful, and that was enough for me."

In January of 1981 when the Diocese of San Jose was created, new Bishop Pierre DuMaine had several concerns about the statue, including the cost. He determined the 32-foot statue would be the final size and Fr. Sweeny would not commission a 90-foot statue. This was a tremendous disappointment to Fr. Sweeny, who told the *Peninsula Times Tribune*, "I knew there might be a lot of possibilities for problems. There always are disappointments in life—you have to

Sculptor Charles Parks prepares for a crane to lift Our Lady's head onto the stainless steel body at his studio in Delaware. Photo by Jamie Winder.

leave something for heaven."

As the completed pieces came together, the Madonna outgrew Mr. Parks' studio. He sent the clay mold for the statue's head to Our Lady of Peace, where it was unveiled in the parish hall on July 28, 1981. Then Mr. Parks pieced the statue together outside his studio and, to his surprise, created a traffic problem for the city of Wilmington! So many people began to arrive, park, and marvel at Our Lady, the city raised traffic and safety concerns. Wilmington Mayor William McLaughlin made arrangements for Mr. Parks to move the statue into Rodney Square, where thousands of visitors were drawn to her daily. As described by the *Wilmington News-Journal*, "The Madonna—30 feet of cast stainless steel—created by Charles C. Parks [is] touching the lives of thousands of people who go daily to Wilmington's Rodney Square to see the massive work of art, to feel its power, and to pray. 'Our Lady of Peace' will find its home in Santa Clara, California in October, but meanwhile Delawareans have opened their hearts to her." So many people phoned the *Wilmington News-Journal* to praise the statue and ask for reprints of stories and photos, the paper published a special edition titled, "The Madonna in Rodney Square." The 10,000 copies they printed sold out in one day.

Facing legal pressure from the American Civil Liberties Union to remove a religious symbol from a public square, Our Lady of the Immaculate Heart was warmly welcomed by Philadelphia's Archbishop Krol and moved to the Cathedral Basilica of Saints Peter and Paul. From December 1982 until the following spring, she offered an exciting visual against the cathedral's brownstone bulk and continued to receive crowds of Catholic and non-Catholic visitors day and night.

Finally, it was time for Our Lady of Peace to travel West to California. Secured on a flatbed truck in May of 1983, she still had

*Thousands flock to visit the "Madonna of Rodney Square" in
Wilmington, Delaware, 1982.*

"Early risers watch the sculpture being placed on the platform."
–News-Journal, *1982. Photo by Leo Matkins.*

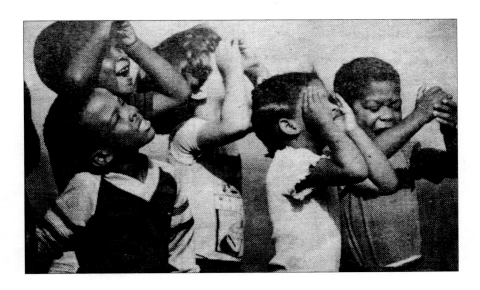

"Children stare up at the 30-foot, six-ton Madonna in downtown Wilmington." –News-Journal, *1982. Photo by Fred Comegys.*

"A woman weeps at the sight of the Our Lady of Peace Madonna."
–News-Journal, *1982. Photo by Fred Comegys.*

"Sculptor Charles Cropper Parks studies the nearly completed statue."
–News-Journal, *1982. Photo by Leo Matkins.*

one more visit to pay: Mundelein Seminary in Chicago. Her timing was such to welcome the U.S. bishops meeting there. In an impressive ceremony held before the statue on May 8, Mother's Day, Cardinal Joseph Bernardin re-dedicated the Archdiocese of Chicago to the Immaculate Heart of Mary. In September of 1983, the statue was finally transported to Our Lady of Peace Church in Santa Clara, California. Volunteers cheered as she rolled into the driveway on a flatbed truck on September 23. They cleaned off the grime from the cross-country journey and stood in awe as she was erected.

On October 7, the Feast of Our Lady of the Rosary, Bishop DuMaine and several other priests concelebrated Mass with Fr. Sweeny, initiating three days of festivities dedicating the statue and Shrine of Our Lady of the Immaculate Heart. Fr. Patrick Peyton, the "Rosary Priest," traveled to Santa Clara to assist with the dedication.

From Fr. Sweeny's first ideas to the formal dedication of the Shrine, the statue was eleven years in the making. For Charles Parks, first-encounters to completion spanned six years. The 32-foot statue alone took two years and 12,000 hours for Mr. Parks and his assistants. About $100,000 was spent in casting and materials (the head alone cost $45,000), shop overhead, excessive rental space, and transporting the 7,500-pound statue to California. Profit was limited, but Mr. Parks was pleased with the outcome. Our Lady of the Immaculate Heart, often referred to as Our Lady of Peace, was fully paid for in $340,000 of unsolicited donations and a foundation of not one million rosaries, as Fr. Sweeny had requested, but three million.

For a world under so many "persuasive forces," Fr. Sweeny desired to give the people "a chance to experience what [the children of Fatima's] experience was all about. Why not put up a figure that nobody can turn down? Who can turn down the purest form of love that exists, the love of a mother for her children? How many times

Dedication of the Shrine to the Immaculate Heart of Mary on October 7, 1983.

Fr. Sweeny speaks at the dedication of the Shrine to the Immaculate Heart of Mary on October 7, 1983.

did we as children, before we were conscious of it, respond to the open arms of our mothers?" In Our Lady of the Immaculate Heart, every passerby receives her invitation to encounter the love of a mother and to step into the love of her Son, in a church that is always open to receive them.

MARY IN MULTIPLES: AN UNEXPECTED OUTCOME

Meanwhile, Fr. Sweeny's forthright expression of faith had made an impression as she traveled across the country. As a result, new, towering, steel statues of Our Lady began to rise up. One of these fulfilled a life-long dream that started with a young boy in Chicago.

One afternoon in 1941, a nine-year-old boy named Carl Demma thought he saw a magnificent statue of Mary, the Mother of God, towering over downtown Chicago. Entranced, he was deeply disappointed when told the statue was Ceres, the Roman goddess of agriculture. Though only a child, Carl decided if a statue of Mary didn't exist for Chicago, he would see to it that one was erected.

Carl grew up, married, opened a successful business, and cherished his wife and two daughters. And though life was busy, he held to his dream. Unexpectedly, in May of 1983, Carl came across the embodiment of his childhood vision: a 32-foot stainless steel statue of Mary stopped at Quigley Preparatory Seminary South for ten days while being transported from the artist's studio in Delaware to Our Lady of Peace Church in Santa Clara, California. At that time, Our Lady of the Immaculate Heart's guaranteed arrival to Santa Clara was still unsure. Carl brought his daughter, Judi, to see the statue and told her, "This is what God wants from me."

In many ways, Carl's journey from first inspiration to physical statue was much like Fr. Sweeny's: many years in the making, difficult to finance, and lacking diocesan support. Cardinal Joseph Bernardin, who had blessed Our Lady of the Immaculate Heart and re-dedicated

Chicago to her patronage, was far less interested when it came to financing a project. He told Carl, "Do you know how many hungry people I can feed with that money?" Yet, like Fr. Sweeny, Carl knew souls were hungry for Our Lady's motherly love and believed the bigger the rendering of Mary, the better the impact. He had seen 5,000 people flock to Quigley Seminary to see Our Lady of the Immaculate Heart and to pray. He felt this was a direct consequence of her size and believed the best way to reach people raised in a visual culture would be through a powerful image.

Most people doubted Carl, but he pursued his dream with purpose. As his health began to fail, he would say, "For every day I'm on this earth, I haven't finished what God wants me to do." Over several years, Carl sent personal funds and even sold his business to pay for the statue. When it was finished, Mr. Parks would later recall, "He had tears in his eyes and just said, 'Thanks'."

The statue, named Our Lady of the New Millenium, was blessed by Pope John Paul II in 1999 and is now permanently established at the Shrine of Christ's Passion at St. John the Evangelist Church in St. John, Indiana.

The story continues. In Delaware, Fr. Sweeny's statue had also left her mark and the faithful didn't want to see her go! The people of Holy Spirit Church in New Castle, Delaware, followed Fr. Sweeny's formula to establish a foundation of prayer and, after praying 500,000 rosaries, commissioned Charles Parks to design Our Lady Queen of Peace. She was dedicated by Bishop Michael Saltarelli on May 26, 2007.

Next is the story of Fr. Harold Cooper of Sioux City, Iowa, who, for many years, dreamed of a statue of Our Lady for the people of his diocese. After visiting Our Lady of Peace Church and Shrine during a trip to California in 1985, he returned to Sioux City to establish a shrine named Trinity Heights, set on a quiet rise just minutes from downtown Sioux City. Fr. Cooper hired a local artist, Dale Claude Lamphere, to sculpt Mary Queen of Peace and later the Sacred Heart of Jesus. Both statues are made of steel and weigh approximately five tons each.

In 1982, when Bishop DuMaine set a cap on the statue size for Our Lady of the Immaculate Heart, it meant Fr. Sweeny's dream of a 90-foot statue would not be realized. Of additional concern to Fr. Sweeny was the sculptor, Charles Parks, because canceling these plans put Mr. Parks out of work (he had not accepted other contracts due to his commitment to Fr. Sweeny). Unbeknownst to either men, Our Lady of the Immaculate Heart would fill that gap as requests for additional statues rolled in. Not only did this provide ongoing employment for the artist, but Our Lady of the Immaculate Heart— in multiples—became a forthright expression of faith across the United States.

Sister Marie Colette of the Infant Jesus, P.C.C.
Religious Vocation from Our Lady of Peace

"When I was attending Our Lady of Peace, there was no large outdoor statue of Our Lady, but the tall tree on the edge of the property looked very much like the Mother of God holding her Child in her arms. It was symbolic of the spirituality of the parish.

"Years later, after I had entered the monastery, Fr. Sweeny one day brought the plans up for the large statue of Our Lady presently on the parish grounds. He asked our superior if the plans could be put near the altar. Mother Veronica, who was abbess at the time, placed the plans behind the statue of St. Joseph which stood next to our adoration altar. Fr. Sweeny's dream was eventually realized and what had always been present in spirit became a reality: the Holy

"Our Lady of the New Millenium" in St. John, Indiana.

"Our Lady Queen of Peace" at Holy Spirit Church in New Castle, Delaware. Our Lady is on a hill overlooking Interstate 295 and greets 40,000 people a day coming to Delaware from New Jersey. Her face is fashioned after Our Lady of Medjugorje.

"Immaculate Heart of Mary Queen of Peace" at Trinity Heights Shrine in Sioux City, Iowa.

164

Mother of God, with her arms extended, welcoming all to her Immaculate Heart."

Art Sacman
Parishioner 1971 - Present

"I tried to accompany the priests when I could, and Fr. Sweeny asked me if I could help him with funerals. One time in 1971, we went to have a funeral service. I drove and Fr. Sweeny smoked and talked. He was telling me about all kinds of visions he had about the parish and what it could become. He said, 'My vision is to have a big statue.' I was thinking it would be a statue like the St. Anthony or St. Joseph statues we had in the church, and didn't understand why he was thinking through the funding so much. I said, 'Sure, Father. You can do it anytime.' He replied, 'Yes, it will take some time.' The picture in my mind didn't match the picture in his mind. So he explained, 'This will be a place where people will see a big statue as they commute to work.' Then I understood, and asked him to tell me more. He said, 'We'll have to fix the church first.' He mentioned first a statue, rebuilding the hall and facilities, and rebuilding the church. He wanted to build the hall first, so it could be used for Masses while the church was rebuilt.

"A few months later, he asked me, 'Have you thought about what I talked to you about in the car?' I said, 'No!' I was about 26 years old, I had other things on my mind. Our relationship was good, we talked about our families to each other and things that were important to us. Yet his vision for Our Lady of Peace Church and Shrine was beyond my comprehension at first. I could not visualize what he was talking about. Eventually, he showed me a drawing.

"Fr. Sweeny wanted the land in front of the church for the

Fr. Sweeny presents a vision for the Shrine to the Immaculate Heart of Mary in 1978.

Shrine. He told me, 'We need to ask the Blessed Mother to help us to get this land.' Then the property was to be sold and Fr. Sweeny wanted to bid on it. It went up for sale at an auction hosted by the City of Santa Clara. When people realized Fr. Sweeny was bidding on the land, everyone backed off. No one else bid on the property.

"Fr. Sweeny would talk to me about a lot of big projects; I was like a sounding board for him. I was concerned about them because we didn't have money and had to think of a way to pay for the land and the statue. Fr. Sweeny wasn't really concerned about that. He told me, 'We'll have rosary checks.' I was incredulous. 'Rosary checks?' He told me, 'We're not supposed to ask people for money. So we will ask them for rosaries. The Blessed Mother will help us.' So the rosary checks went out requesting prayers, and people started sending in their rosary prayers...along with monetary checks. He just asked for prayers, and money came in that paid for the project.

"Fr. Sweeny's thinking was a statue as big as the tree and underneath would be a presentation hall. If you've been to Disneyland, below each large exhibit there's a hall that explains it. The Bishop of San Jose limited the project, reasoning we didn't have enough money in the diocese. He had us stop at the second phase of the statue, the 32-foot statue."

Steve Nguyen
Parishioner 1975 - Present

"Fr. Sweeny proposed the idea to the Vietnamese about having a devotion to Our Lady. The Vietnamese wanted to contribute money to the statue project, but Fr. Sweeny told them, 'I don't want your money. I want your prayers.' We filled out those rosary checks. From that I learned to give people prayers instead of money when I wanted to thank them: prayers are genuine and intentional, and mean more than a million dollars. Fr. Sweeny would also say, 'You can't just write a check without the money in the bank. You have to say the prayers first. Then you can write the check.' The rosary checks were for the establishment of the Shrine and the money that happened to come in with them went toward the statue of Our Lady."

Fr. Lawrence Goode
Assistant Pastor 1971 - 1978
Collaborator on Shrine Vision and Planning

"Fr. Sweeny wanted a Shrine to Our Lady because he felt like the times we were living in required a 'forthright expression of faith,' as he would say. He saw the Church becoming wishy-washy and not sure of itself and thought the Church needed a forthright expression of faith. That seems to have been the inspiration for the Shrine.

"He was invited to go back to Philadelphia and work with this job training program that he started in East Palo Alto (OICW). The minister [director] wanted him to specialize in bringing this to Hispanic neighborhoods. At that time he was up to his neck in the Shrine and he told them he could not direct the training center. He loved his work in East Palo Alto and talked about it all the time. But he also realized the Church needed him to do what he was doing.

"I took the flyer that Fr. Sweeny used to promote the rosaries with me to Ireland and they caught on right away. Of course they saw the name, 'Sweeny,' and that was the part of Ireland where Sweenys were from, so it got on the radio, in the news, and someone even sent me a newspaper article about the rosary checks that said, 'This is a great idea. For all our projects, we should do this.' Hence, that's how it began: with the rosaries.

"One of the projects we did when I was at Our Lady of Peace was to research shrines. I wanted to see what other shrines were doing. I visited the National Sanctuary of Our Sorrowful Mother (The Grotto) in Portland, Oregon, the California missions, the Basilica of Our Lady of Guadalupe in Mexico City, the Knock Shrine in Ireland, and the Shrine of Fatima in Portugal. But Fr. Sweeny had this idea: he wanted to provide people with piety (devotion to Our Lord in the Blessed Sacrament) and theology (knowledge). He had the idea they'd come to pray, then they'd go out into the vestibule or the hall and find machines where they'd push a button and could learn about anything they wanted to know about the faith. He wanted to teach religion so people would know their religion or be able to find out what the Church teaches, why it teaches what it does, and so on. It would be prayer, knowledge, and action. Visitors could even find out about the organizations in the church so they could get involved.

"It gave us the idea to create the story of the Shrine mission. We knew the first Mass in the Valley may have been said in our parish. I visited the priest who was in charge of the archives, who showed me books that had Junipero Serra's signature on them. He showed me the history that referenced the first Mass being a stone's throw from the Guadalupe River and we figured that could have actually been in the parish boundaries of Our Lady of Peace. It was blessed land before we even got there. The Mass was not said by Fr. Serra [but probably by Fray Tomás de la Peña].

"Fr. Sweeny wanted the land in front of the church next to the highway for the Shrine. The land was being put up for auction and a construction company was bidding on it. The architects who designed the original plan for the Shrine had included a long esplanade where visitors could walk up to it; it was very ornate. (None of this was actually implemented.) The architects knew this construction company and had done some work for them. So they talked to them and told them, 'Fr. Sweeny has only one bid to make.' The construction company wanted the property simply because they wanted work for their men. So we made a gentleman's agreement if there was any work to be done, they would be involved in providing labor. We got the property for the amount it was being sold for before more changes happened in city zoning. When we went to bid, the property was still being sold as farmland so it was a lower value. Within a week of our purchase, all the property around Our Lady of Peace went sky-high in value.

"Later, we leased out another parcel of unused parish land. With the increased property values, the going rate for a lease was impressive. In 1981 when the Diocese of San Jose was created, there was no cash flow. They had a lot of land that was given to them by the Archdiocese of San Francisco, but no cash flow. The only parish that had cash flow was Our Lady of Peace! Our Lady of Peace, what had once been the poorest parish, ended up assisting the Diocese of San Jose!

"There was a man in San Jose who built statues. Fr. Sweeny interviewed him, but in the process the man died. Then there was a priest, a Dominican, who created the statue of Our Lady of Fatima over the entrance of the Basilica of Our Lady of Fatima in Portugal. I was at the interview when Fr. Sweeny met with this priest. He told us he had interviewed Lucia, one of the visionaries in Fatima, and asked her, 'What did you see? What did it look like?' He only got 'yes' and 'no' answers as they went back and forth, but what she told him was, 'It was light on light.' Hard to imagine. That artist never got started on the Shrine project either, because he died. Then Mary Houston, a woman from Orinda who was the head of the Blue Army for Oakland, called one day. She heard about an artist who had come to San Francisco. She went up to see his art and it was realistic. That's what she wanted. She and Fr. Sweeny went up to meet him in San Francisco and he liked the idea. He had never built anything that big but was willing to do it from his studio in Delaware. The man's name was Charles Parks.

"Mr. Parks had no idea what he was doing when creating an image of Our Lady. So Father sent him a book of poems on Our Lady. He went on a pilgrimage to Fatima to experience it, and met the artist there who created the statue of Our Lady of Fatima that is at Our Lady of Peace. Little by little, Mr. Parks got the idea.

"The statue was supposed to be 90 feet tall but, in the end, the bishop approved it to be 32 feet. Fr. Sweeny was a little bit disappointed, and the day he dedicated the statue (I had already been reassigned to a new parish) we walked up to the statue together. I could see he was disappointed and I said to him, 'I suspect Our Lady was very good at bargaining when she went to the marketplace. Just think how small the statue would have been if you had started at 30 feet. But you started at 90 feet and got a 32-foot statue out of it!' It sort of relieved that suffering I knew he was going through, because it bothered him that he didn't have a 90-foot statue. The way things are today, a 90-foot statue would fit in perfectly there with all the buildings around it.

"Later, my Dad and I went to Delaware and met Mr. Parks at the studio where he made the statue. It was right along the Delaware River. To complete the statue, Mr. Parks needed more space and put it out front. People would come to see it. So many people were coming the mayor called Mr. Parks and said it was too dangerous to have so many people stopping there. They loaded it on a truck and put it in the town plaza. It was apparently in a neighborhood with a lot of crime and violence, and all of a sudden it became very peaceful. When we drove into town we stopped at a restaurant and a young waitress served us. We asked her where the statue had been because we wanted to see the plaza. She said, 'You mean Our Lady of Peace?' We said, 'Yes.' She wasn't Catholic, and told us, 'I asked my minister: Why was it so peaceful around there when she was there?' He told

The pear orchard Fr. Sweeny purchased and had converted to the lawn and Shrine to Our Lady of the Immaculate Heart as we know it today.

her, 'Mind your own business!' The statue stayed there until the American Civil Liberties Union (ACLU) got news of it, and they complained and were going to take Mr. Parks to court. Before they could do that, it was moved up to Philadelphia where the Archbishop allowed them to put the statue in front of the cathedral.

"Next, it moved to Chicago. The bishops were meeting in Mundelein, the seminary there, and it was right outside the seminary when the bishops arrived.

"When the statue arrived to Santa Clara and was installed, Mr. Parks came and spoke with the people. I was at Alviso and translated for him into Spanish. He said he wanted the experience of Our Lady, the love of Our Lady, and the heart of Mary to reach out to the people driving by or visiting the Shrine. That was a wonderful time for me to be there at the parish, to experience it and to meet the artist."

Helen Hovland
Parishioner 1976 - Present

"Fr. Sweeny met Mary Houston, the head of the Blue Army for the Oakland diocese. She brought Our Lady of Fatima to Our Lady of Peace Church for the parish to honor her for a week. Fr. Sweeny and Mary Houston became close friends because they both had a great love for the Blessed Mother. Mary heard about Fatima in 1946 and she was inspired to want to flood the world with rosaries, because Our Lady had asked for rosaries. Fr. Sweeny had wanted to build this huge statue. He wanted a 90-foot statue, which would have towered over all the buildings around here. That didn't happen, but we did end up with a beautiful statue.

"This friendship blossomed and, in 1972, Mary and Sam Houston took Fr. Sweeny to Fatima. They were looking at statues and

Fr. Sweeny with the statues of the Immaculate Heart of Mary and the Sacred Heart of Jesus he brought from Fatima in 1972. This photo was taken on Easter of 1982.

wanted something they would use as a model for the statue at Our Lady of Peace. They met the nephew of the sculptor who did the statues for Lucia. He was also a sculptor, and created the statues that are in our church: the Immaculate Heart of Mary and the Sacred Heart. When they saw those statues in Fatima, Fr. Sweeny decided to bring the one of the Blessed Mother. Mary said, 'Father, you can't leave the Sacred Heart here.' So they brought them both.

"When Charles Parks completed Our Lady of the Immaculate Heart and she was moved from Philadelphia to Chicago, a small group of us, including Mary Houston, flew to Chicago to watch the happenings when the statue finally began her journey to Our Lady of Peace. We actually saw them laying her down on a flatbed truck and hauling her across the country. When we returned on the 23rd of September, she was already up, in place, and fastened to the foundation. The Immaculate Heart of Mary Shrine was dedicated on October 7, 1983. Fr. Peyton came for three days to recognize the occasion."

Tony Ryan
Staff Member 1977 - 1981

"When the statue was dedicated in 1983, Fr. Patrick Peyton came. That was a big deal: Fr. Peyton was one of the great church men of the 20th century. He started the Family Rosary Crusade, which became such a huge crusade that, until Pope John Paul II was elected Pope, Fr. Peyton had spoken to more people than anyone in the history of the church. (The Family Rosary Crusade got so big that 500,000 people attended when Fr. Peyton came to San Francisco. In South America, a million people would attend.) When Fr. Peyton came for the dedication of the Shrine, he was elderly yet he was still a great spiritual leader. I just couldn't believe Fr. Sweeny got him to come! I was in awe we had him there. Today, his cause has already been opened for sainthood."

Joanne Schott
Wife of Larry Schott[†], Civil Engineer for the Shrine Establishment

"All the companies involved with preparing the land and constructing the pedestal for the statue provided donated service. My husband, Larry Schott, provided the civil engineering. He and his group, McKay & Somps, drew out the plans for how the land would be set up. He drew the plans for the site, where the statue would go, the pathways around the parking lot, and so on. This included plotting the land, the slope, and soil. He had a number of other partners who were also Catholic and very happy to be participating in the project. They were friends who knew each other from their studies at Santa Clara University.

"Participating in the statue project was an exciting time for our family. The whole idea of Our Lady coming across the country on a flatbed truck was intriguing. The truck driver even got into the experience.

"When the statue arrived we were all there to greet it. It was very exciting to see it pull in. Then dear Mary had to be washed because she was quite dirty from the trip. The kids climbed up on top of the statue and cleaned it with buckets of water, soap, and sponges. One of my sons was excited because he gave Mary a high-five! It took us a number of days to clean her. Our children all have very fond memories of that, it was great fun. Our seven children ranged in age from grammar school to college, so they were at good ages to be involved.

Fr. Patrick Peyton, "The Rosary Priest," speaks at the dedication of the Shrine, October 7, 1983.

"The statue project was a very significant part of our family's faith life. It created a closeness to Our Lady of Peace parish for us that we probably would not have had. We also joined the parish on the Good Friday walk from St. Martin of Tours Church in San Jose to Our Lady of Peace. It is a good distance! Some of our children were at Santa Clara University, so we'd stop there on the way, they'd join us, and we'd continue the walk together. We did that for many years.

"Fr. Sweeny was such a beautiful person. He was such a gentle soul; so sincere. He was certainly the most deeply spiritual person we've ever known. His whole demeanor exuded holiness; you could sense it even just talking to him. Also, his causes were worthy and nothing was impossible to him: he had great confidence in the power of prayer and that things would work out. And somehow, things did work out. Fr. Sweeny was gentle, very serene, and never agitated. He was a man of great faith."

Rooney Blach
Wife of Michael Blach[†], Construction Manager for the Shrine

"The first time I went to Our Lady of Peace was for my husband, Mike Blach. He and his friends, such as Larry Schott, were connected to the parish through the Santa Clara Serra Club. They went there for Mass together and so they knew Fr. Sweeny. Because they were in construction, Fr. Sweeny asked them for help with the Shrine statue project. Michael organized all the donated supplies and work to prepare the land and construct the pedestal.

"For me, the day the statue arrived was one of the most exciting days of my life. It was *so exciting!* It took a long time for the statue to come cross-country. When I saw her I thought she was the most beautiful thing, just gorgeous. Her face is so beautiful, so detailed, so loving.

"There were a lot of us there to meet the statue and work on the project, but none of us were parishioners. Our children and children of the other volunteers were all there on Friday night, trying to clean the statue. It was filthy after it drove cross-country. But her face was still so gorgeous, she's got such a beautiful face and we could see it up close and touch it. Her hands were stunning. Fr. Sweeny smiled and smiled, his face radiated joy. It was a dream come true for him.

"Dennis Ahearn was the civil engineer on the project and a very good friend of Michael's. His wife, Michelle, was blind. The Friday night it arrived, Michelle was able to feel the statue and experience it.

"There's a hook on the top of Our Lady's head. They had to bring a large crane and attach it to her head by putting the hook in her head. The crane lifted her up slowly. I still get goosebumps looking at the photos. She was pulled up and up, and then off the truck and over to her base. Then came the difficult part. There were spikes on the base and the statue had to set right on them. Again, it was very exciting.

"It took Michael about six months to complete this project. It didn't 'just happen.' Everything was donated. Galeazzo did all the dirt work, and I can remember men working at night and on the weekends. When you have donated work, you can't work as you do with employees and say, 'Be here Monday at 8 a.m.' It is whenever they are available to do it. So it took longer because it depended on their availability. Then Cupertino Electric, which is Gene Ravizza, did all the electrical. John Albanese and his cousin, Tom Albanese, donated and finished all the concrete work. I believe Collinshaw did all the landscaping, mostly after the statue was raised. We did all the other work.

"You really can't help but see the statue as you are going down Bowers Avenue or Highway 101 exiting onto Great America Parkway,

Constructing the statue pedestal and walkway to the Shrine in 1982. The Marriott Hotel is at the far right. Rides at Great America amusement park are visible between the large tree and hotel.

The completed pedestal would add ten feet of height to the 32-foot statue.

or heading to the convention center. That was Fr. Sweeny's intention: to bring an awareness of the Blessed Mother to the people. He himself had a great devotion to the Blessed Mother. When I pass her by, I always put in a little prayer. Before the statue went up, the church and the property were not noticeable and there was no direct entrance there. Now, because of the statue, there is always someone there and so many flowers left by visitors. There is also always someone praying inside the church. We see a beauty there.

"Fr. Sweeny was so spiritual and his way of having other people share the devotion to the Blessed Mother was unique. It is a place where people can go to pray. I give him a lot of credit because he took a huge risk to put up a statue outside. To see a huge, religious statue outside for the public to view required a lot of forethought and looking into the future knowing that people needed that encouragement and a reminder to pray. You can't help when you go by it to say some prayer, whatever comes to mind. Fr. Sweeny was so open and exuded love and kindness. He was a gentle, gentle man.

"Michael managed the entire project. It was a six-month job, and for us personally it was something. He worked full-time on the Shrine. In the construction business it takes months between first meeting a new client and then beginning a job, so at the end of six months we had no work because Michael had been busy with the Shrine. He was considering going out of business. I told him, 'Blessed Mother is not going to let you down.' It was stressful to realize there was no work, but our faith pulled us through. Sure enough, that's when our business started to take off.

"Michael always had a devotion to Blessed Mother, long before he assisted with Our Lady of Peace's statue. It came from his family: both his parents were Catholic, they prayed in the home, and were people of great faith who raised twelve children. Michael was diagnosed with lung cancer in January of 1989 and died in May of that same year. Fr. Sweeny was one of the celebrants of his funeral Mass."

Fr. John Sweeny [†]
Pastor of Our Lady of Peace Church & Shrine 1969 - 2002

"The statue is lit night and day. It's really touching to see people come to those open arms of a mother. You see the hurts go away or lessen by coming to Our Lady. What child hasn't responded to the open arms of a mother? Even the adult, if we take time to think back a little bit to our first experiences—experiences of trust, the open arms of a mother—I guess there's nothing more endearing, and it is next to God."

Celebrating Our Lady of the Immaculate Heart's arrival are sculptor Charles Parks (left), Dennis Ahearn, and Michael Blach in 1983. Empty lots and the new Mission College create the backdrop.

Teens scrub the statue after the cross-country trip from Delaware to California.

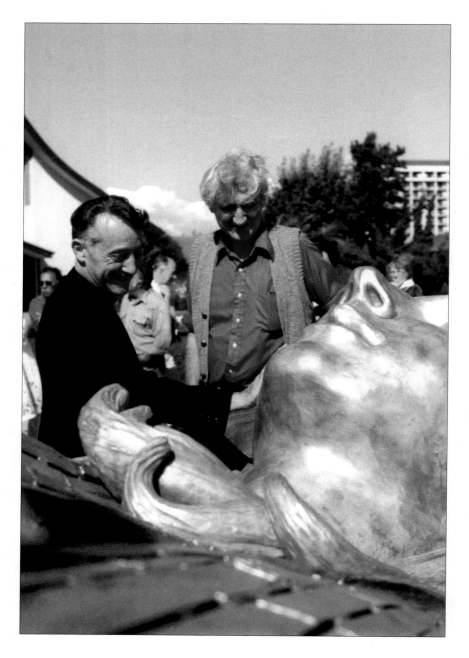

Fr. John Sweeny and sculptor Charles Parks celebrate a great day in the history of Our Lady of Peace Church and Shrine: the 32-foot statue of Our Lady of the Immaculate Heart had finally come home.

186

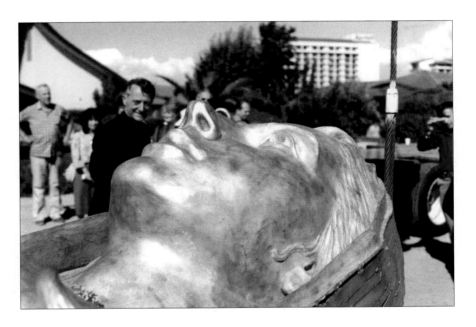

Fr. Sweeny looks on as the crane, fitted into a hook on the statue's head, begins to lift and place Our Lady of the Immaculate Heart on the pedestal.

Onlookers watch as the statue is lifted by a crane. The first crane, in the left background, was proven too small and a larger crane was brought in to install the statue.

A few brave men guide the weighty statue to her permanent location.

Do not be troubled or weighed down with grief.
Do not fear any illness or vexation, anxiety or pain.
Am I not here who am your Mother?
Are you not under my shadow and my protection?
Am I not your fountain of life?
Are you not in the fold of my mantle?
In the crossing of my arms?
Is there anything else you need?

Words of Our Lady of Guadalupe
to St. Juan Diego Cuauhtlatoatzin

CHAPTER 5
1980s

Work and Prayer for Souls

Dear Mother Mary, pour the love of your heart into my heart,
just as you did to Christ, so that I may respond to Him.

Fr. John Sweeny

Mass attendance and activities continued to increase and a thriving Our Lady of Peace Church grew into a hub for worship in Northern California. With a constant vision for forming hearts and saving souls, parish leadership pressed forward with continued zeal. "In Heaven, we shall rest," Fr. Sweeny explained in a Sunday Mass homily. "While we are still here let us consider our work and prayer a privilege. God depends upon our faithfulness, and so do countless human beings who will be saved because of our efforts."

A NEW DIOCESE, A NEW BISHOP

The California population continued to swell and Catholic church attendance with it. To better address the spiritual needs of the faithful, Pope John Paul II created the Diocese of San Jose by annexing the southern portion of the Archdiocese of San Francisco.

A new diocese required a new bishop, and the new bishop brought a new style of leadership. This bishop, Pierre DuMaine, also inherited a stack of real challenges facing the fledgling diocese. In particular, diocesan finances—or lack of—weighed on him heavily. So great were his financial concerns he could not endorse the major expense of the 32-foot statue Fr. Sweeny had contracted, stating that a poor parish in a poor diocese could not take on such tremendous debt. Yet Fr. Sweeny's pray-and-God-will-provide manner gave hope.

MARY COMES HOME

Fr. Sweeny was very disappointed when the Bishop repealed permission for the statue and continued to pray. The people of Our Lady of Peace continued to pray. As their prayers gained momentum, unsolicited donations trickled in. Day by day, money arrived from around the world and paid, in full, for the statue of Our Lady of the Immaculate Heart. Bishop DuMaine gave his consent and she was transported to Our Lady of Peace.

On October 7, 1983, Bishop DuMaine blessed and dedicated the Shrine. That day was also the Feast of the Most Holy Rosary and the fifteenth anniversary of the parish's First Friday all-night vigils. On October 9, the last of the three-day celebration, Fr. Patrick Peyton, CSC, of the Family Rosary Crusade, gave the homily. And to acknowledge this very special occasion, Pope John Paul II sent a special blessing. Our Lady of the Immaculate Heart was finally home, making Our Lady of Peace Church more than just a parish, but also a Marian shrine.

FROM LONELY CHURCH TO LOCAL LANDMARK

Our Lady of Peace Church and Shrine was no longer an

*After the statue was installed and shrine dedicated in 1983, landscaping
efforts continued. This aerial view shows a remarkably transformed
Our Lady of Peace Church and Shrine in 1987.*

unattended parish. On the contrary, as the 1980s became a time of such increased parish activity, Fr. Sweeny leaned heavily on his fellow priests, staff, and volunteers to establish a comprehensive infrastructure to meet the needs of so many people.

Among the many outreaches established or strengthened were catechism classes for children, the Rite of Christian Initiation (RCIA) program for adults interested in joining the Catholic Church, the Knights of Columbus, a Young Adult group, the Family Rosary Confraternity, a formalized marriage preparation program, a home school social group (Regina Pacis), and the Guamanian Catholic annual St. Joseph novena and parish dinner. Fr. Sweeny traveled to Wisconsin to visit the Apostolate of Family Consecration and returned to establish a family prayer ministry that would later lead to building the Family Learning Center.

Education being a constant request and priority, parishioners established Our Lady of Peace lending library. Benefactor Monica Corbitt purchased a satellite so the parish had access to the Eternal Word Television Network (EWTN), and others coordinated an effort to video record Catholic catechesis programs and Shrine Masses to offer for distribution. Classes, talks, and study groups filled the parish calendar. Meeting space became more cramped as classes such as Fr. Pintacura's *Opus Angelorum* overflowed and doubled in size with participants from various local parishes. Active and retired priests including Fr. Edward Warren, Fr. Joe Devlin, Fr. Ray Devlin, Fr. John Coghlan, Fr. Patrick Brannan, Fr. Tom Byrne, Monsignor Edgar McCarren, and Fr. Milan Hlebs dedicated their discretionary time to keeping pace with parishioners' constant yearning for spiritual guidance, confession, and other sacramental needs. The parish was known as a friendly community where families were well-acquainted and enjoyed mutual support for Catholic living. Social time included the establishment of coffee and donuts, and the parish Christmas tree displayed a gold ball for each parish family. Our Lady of Peace was bustling, blossoming, and, in terms of space, bursting at the seams.

On July 1, 1984, the Diocese of San Jose recognized Our Lady Star of the Sea in Alviso as an independent parish. After twenty-three years as a mission church overseen and ministered to by staff at Our Lady of Peace, Bishop DuMaine installed Fr. John Coleman as the first pastor in Alviso. Both Our Lady of Peace and Star of the Sea had overcome the same threat—probable closure—making this celebration all the more joyful. Eager to begin his new assignment, Fr. Coleman slept on a mattress in the lean-to storage shed at Our Lady Star of the Sea until suitable arrangements were made for a rectory.

Two years later, on June 22, 1986, the Our Lady of Peace community celebrated the church's 25th anniversary. Twenty-five years of devotion, sacrifice, hopes, joys, and countless graces were lifted in gratitude at a Mass of Thanksgiving where founding pastor Fr. Sullivan and former assistant pastors Fr. John Coleman and Fr. Lawrence Goode received a warm welcome. Perhaps no parish in the diocese had undergone such a physical and spiritual transformation as Our Lady of Peace. This church, once almost erased from the map, rested on a rock-solid foundation, tirelessly dedicated to the glory of God.

A SOURCE OF STRENGTH

The growth at Our Lady of Peace Church was rooted in a strong spiritual foundation and the zeal to bring as many souls as possible to Christ. As the parish became a center for prayer, peace, and change in the world, growth was visible through physical changes such as the statue, a new rectory and parish offices, expanded parking lots, and outdoor television screens for live broadcasts of Mass for those attending outside in overflow seating. Yet more significant were the individual spiritual and life changes the church's ministry brought forth. In a late 1980s appeal for funds and prayers to support the

Fr. Sweeny, Bishop DuMaine, and Fr. Sullivan prepare to celebrate the 25th anniversary Mass for Our Lady of Peace Church and Shrine.

Fr. Sweeny shares the apostolic blessing sent by Pope John Paul II in honor of the church's 25th anniversary. It reads, "May the Father, and the Son, and the Holy Spirit be glorified in all places through the Immaculate Virgin Mary."

growing parish, the Development Committee shared a few testimonies:

- An East Bay nurse came to Our Lady of Peace Church to take part in the perpetual adoration program. Before long, she made a life-changing decision to join the Missionaries of Charity.

- A sailor from Moffett Field came to a summer pilgrimage. When his tour of duty was over, he entered the seminary.

- Several individuals addicted to drugs or alcohol received enlightenment and strength to radically change their habits. They are now cured of their addictions and leading happy, productive lives.

- One young woman, contemplating suicide, came to pray before Our Lady's statue, imploring God's mother to intercede for her. She now attends church daily and volunteers at a suicide prevention center.

These transformations are among the many encountered in the story of Our Lady of Peace.

As the 1980s drew to a close, the parish pressed on in fervent prayer for the means to continue carrying out God's plan for the hope, healing, and salvation of all souls. Fr. Sweeny told his congregation, "God's gifts and graces that we are using at this present moment are the true foundation of the future. If we are willing, God is certainly willing to give us the help we need to 'grow in nature and grace before God and man.' If we continue the daily rosary, frequent Masses, readily available confession, all-night vigils, perpetual adoration, and other faith-filled efforts, God will provide us not only the persons, organizations, buildings, resources, and skills, but also the spirit to move charitable courageous men, women, and children to do His work. The quality and direction of our future efforts we confidently entrust to the Holy Spirit, in union with Christ Our Lord through the Immaculate Heart of Mary, Our Lady of Peace."

Fr. William Stout[†]
Served at Our Lady of Peace 1967 - 2018

"The Shrine Committee wondered where to put the statue, and Fr. Sweeny wanted to put it in the field where it is now, up against the freeway. The property was up for sale before the city council, so Fr. Sweeny went to the Archbishop of San Francisco and said, 'I'd like to buy this property.' The Archbishop told him, 'You're already in the hole, but I'll lend you $300,000 and that's it. If it is any more, forget it.' With that, Fr. Sweeny went to the city council and bid $300,000. They asked Fr. Sweeny, 'How much is this project going to cost?' He said, 'Many, many rosaries.' They continued, 'When is it going to be done?' He replied, 'When God wants.' He was that way, Fr. Sweeny. He was a man of deep, deep faith."

Ron Hathaway [†]
Chairman, E.A. Hathaway and Co.

"I attended the city council meeting at which [the] property was advertised for sale by the City, with the full intention to bid to secure that property for development. When I went to the Council meeting, I met Fr. Sweeny and other parties interested in securing the property. At that meeting, Fr. Sweeny presented an artist's rendering of a large statue he hoped could be erected on this site. In his presentation that night he indicated his desire to see a shrine of monumental size located on this site.

Catechism students and teachers gather in the parish hall in 1982.

"I was very impressed with his interest and zeal in this matter, and I also felt that the particular site, which is in front of the church property, would lend itself well to that kind of development, which would support his parish and be a fitting monument in these times. As a result of knowing his interest, and not wishing to be a party to seeing his planning destroyed, I announced publicly that I was withdrawing any further interest I had in this property. Had it not been for that type of proposed development concept, I would have continued to attempt to acquire the property for development, for I [felt] it had great potential.

"I was prepared to bid considerably more money to the City for this property than what the City realized from the Diocese. The proposal made for the Shrine caused me to withdraw my interest in this parcel of land. It [will certainly be] a fitting development for the City of Santa Clara and the Church."

Mark Powers
Parishioner 1986 - Present

"I met Fr. Sweeny through my wife, Ellie, but it was within the Legion of Mary that I got to know him and he got to know me.

"Ellie and I were married at Our Lady of Peace in 1986. Before the wedding, we were in the office of the old rectory to see Fr. Sweeny and talk about getting married. A couple pulled up in a brand new truck and the guy came in saying he needed money, that they were homeless. Father gave him a loan. I saw them leave in that brand new truck and said, 'Father, what's going on?' He said, 'Mark, you never know. Only God knows if these people really need the money. You can never turn down any soul.' That was a huge learning experience for Ellie and me. I wanted to punch this guy out for coming in to steal money from Father! That was the saint he was: he could look past the truck and consider that 'only God knows' and it could be God's Providence, that maybe they really did need that money at that point in time.

"However, the most important story we have to tell is about the death of our son, Joseph Patrick, our third child. He was born in 1989. After he was born, I went home to the other children. At three o'clock in the morning, Ellie called me from the hospital and said, 'Joseph stopped breathing.' I returned to the hospital and learned he had stopped breathing for 15 minutes. The doctors weren't sure what it was; they thought it was a metabolic disease. We were told Joseph probably wouldn't make it and was likely brain dead.

"I was frantically trying to get in contact with Fr. Sweeny to have Joseph baptized and for spiritual guidance. I kept calling and calling. We were very close to Fr. Sweeny, so I knew something was going on. We could not get through to him, so we contacted a priest from St. Justin's to come over and baptize Joseph.

"Joseph was transferred to Stanford Hospital and doctors started doing all these tests. His organs were starting to fail and we soon knew we needed to let him go. Through all this, there was still no answer from Fr. Sweeny. We were about ready to pull the plug when *at that moment* Father came through the door, carrying relics and holy books. He was really apologetic: the church had a brand new phone system and messages weren't coming through to him. He was so mad, he was just irate; we saw his Irish and Italian. He was upset because we needed him and he wasn't there to help. But you know, God came through. Fr. Sweeny arrived at the time he was most needed. It was amazing.

"Before and after Joseph died, Fr. Sweeny was there for spiritual guidance. He was there when we took Joseph off life support. Joseph died right there in Ellie's arms, five minutes after Father came. How would it have been if he didn't come? I don't know. It was traumatic as it was. But we received a massive grace, both Ellie and me, and our family, just having Father there. His prayers were powerful, both at that moment and his ongoing prayers over the years. Having him there at that moment was a tremendous grace. It's hard to explain, unless you've ever known someone that holy who has affected you so much at one point in time. After that, I owed him everything. That's why I worked so hard for him.

"About a month before Joseph died in 1989, I started my company, Trinity Technologies. It was a big gamble for us: I didn't really have the money to start it up and had a family and a house. I asked Fr. Sweeny and Fr. Warren for their prayer support, and we consecrated our company to the Blessed Mother. The business was doing okay, but then Joseph died. Next, we lost our big customer. One night at eleven o'clock, I called Fr. Sweeny all distraught and told him what was going on. He said, 'Mark, I'm going to go out to say Mass for you.' I said, 'What do you mean, Father?' He said, 'I'll just go out to the Shrine.' He went out there at eleven o'clock at night and offered Mass for the Powers family and for Trinity Technologies. My company pulled out of that hard time. It's gone back and forth, and I'm sure he's still praying for us now. The company is now 26-years and one of the top in the business.

"The priesthood is a call to holiness, a call to service. That was unquestionable to Fr. Sweeny. With that came his devotion to Our Lady and Our Lord. He loved being a priest and really embraced it. He was notably sincere, humble, and had saintly qualities, such as putting others first and serving God to his fullest extent without complaining. He was a man, a real man, you could call it a 'man's man'. And his work ethic! He worked his tail off completely, entirely, all the time. What made him holy were all these qualities, and his prayer life."

Fr. Sweeny offers Mass before the statue of Our Lady of the Immaculate Heart in June of 1986.

Ellie Powers
Parishioner 1986 - Present

"After our baby, Joseph Patrick, died, I was going to his grave every day. As a mother, I had this deep desire to nurture my baby. I didn't have a baby in my arms yet knew spiritually he was still alive.

"One day, I went to confession and told the priest I was visiting the baby's grave daily. The priest, who was probably Fr. Sweeny, told me, 'He's not in the grave. He's with God, and he's with the God of the Eucharist.' That's when I started Eucharistic adoration with the children. Every morning, I'd pack up activities and snacks, drive from Palo Alto to Our Lady of Peace, and take the children with me to adoration. I spent hours there before the Blessed Sacrament and that's how I healed. It was no longer relevant to go to the grave. What was relevant was to be with my son and Christ in the Eucharist.

"I was drawn to Jesus in adoration in the Blessed Sacrament through the death of my son, and it was Father's being there that led me to heal. He arrived miraculously at the hospital to support us before the baby died, and prayed for us constantly after that. That was Father, and through it all we received the gift of healing and regular Eucharistic adoration to this day."

Art Sacman
Parishioner 1971 - Present

"My wife and I were both shy. Every time Fr. Sweeny approached us to volunteer, we'd say, 'Father, we don't want to talk to people!'

He'd say, 'You're good at it.'

"One day he said, 'We need a marriage preparation program and I'd like you to help with it.' Before we could refuse, Fr. Sweeny had people from the diocese call us. They said, 'You're highly recommended to the diocese by Fr. Sweeny.' We said, 'What?!' How could we refuse? My wife was also hesitant because we had seven young children. We decided to try.

"We went to a course hosted by the diocese, then observed someone host pre-marriage classes, and got started. We started with classes in our home with one couple at a time and began to really love the ministry. Then Barbara Wilkinson, who was working at the parish, told us to try two or three couples at a time. They would come once a week for four weeks. When we started, we were mumbling and trying to find the words to explain everything. But the couples were just young people, and they didn't know what we were going to talk about, and we actually had fun.

"When the parish grew and so many people were coming for marriage preparation, the parish decided to host it as just one class at the church with many couples attending. We taught marriage preparation for about 27 years, until 2002."

Marilyn Egan
Parish Secretary 1987 - 2015

"I was hired right after the parish's 25th year anniversary when Judy Pelter was planning to retire. I saw all the work she did and thought, 'I can't do all that! One person can't do it all!' Well, I found out yes, one can!

"One aspect I liked most about my job was being around all the

Fr. Sweeny leads Eucharistic Adoration in the 1980s.

Art and Mercy Sacman and their seven children celebrate the 50ᵗʰ wedding anniversary of Mercy's parents, Quintin and Maura Lachica, in 1983. The Sacman children are (front row, left to right) Mary, John, Mark and (back row) Michele, Christine, and Jeannette.

priests, getting to know them and seeing how they are when they're relaxed. They're real people.

"The most challenging part of my job was answering the door all day and taking so many phone calls. At that time, Fr. Sweeny used to help a lot of people and it was non-stop. They came to the door all the time wanting money. At the start of my work day, I'd try to find out if Fr. Sweeny was going to be around and if he was available. Many times he was, so I sent them in to him. The St. Vincent de Paul office was set up and Father saw that Barbara Wilkinson had a good way of talking to people, so she took over that office at the church and we'd answer the door and tell them to 'go see Barbara.' She didn't have money, but she had resources and good counsel and that was very helpful. People who wanted cash got turned off completely or would try again to see Fr. Sweeny. The money donated for candles in the church was used to serve the poor, and when he'd run out of that Fr. Sweeny would give them his own money. Not everyone was grateful. On one occasion, Fr. Sweeny gave a man some bills. The man looked at the money and threw it right back at Father! It wasn't enough! He wanted more. And imagine this: Father still helped him after that.

"Once I asked him, 'Father, why do you receive these people every day?' Sometimes the lines were so long it exhausted him. He explained that when he was a boy and his family was very poor, people left groceries at their door. He knew what it meant to be in need and that was why he tried to respond to others in their need.

"Fr. Sweeny was a real person. He was a man. He worked on a farm so he was very capable and would even make repairs around the church. Mostly, he was like a saint. The way he thought of people: he seemed to love everybody and took their side. If I would think to myself, 'This person is bothering me,' he would have the opposite perspective and say, 'They probably have problems they can't solve and need a lot of help.' He was so understanding and that's why people came to see him: because he was there for everyone."

Barbara Wilkinson
Parish Staff Member 1986 - 2015

"Fr. Sweeny felt very strongly about the poor. He told me he would never turn anyone down. He and I were always working for the people. My office was in the church, but they always went to him first. At four o'clock every day, people would start to line up. He'd have lines of people to see him *every day*. Even the poor who knew him in East Palo Alto (before he was pastor of Our Lady of Peace) would come to see him here. Sometimes they would come to me and I'd give them a St. Vincent de Paul (assistance) voucher. But they always went to him first. It has been many years since Fr. Sweeny left, yet I'm still working with some of the people who came to him. He would never turn anyone down. That was beautiful.

"I know I need to depend on the Lord for everything in my life, and I got that from Fr. Sweeny. Everything he did, he depended on the Lord for it. If he ever worried, he didn't show it. I appreciated his honesty with me and I appreciated his faith. When you were around him, you felt the presence of the Lord. Everyone did. For example, he had back problems and would go to the chiropractor; even the chiropractor said he brought her closer to God! He had a quiet strength, but his homilies were so spontaneous and so filled with the Spirit."

Justino Escalera Family
Parishioners 1972 - Present
Religious Vocations from Our Lady of Peace

"My sons were all altar boys, and what they liked about Fr. Sweeny was that if he knew what they were interested in, he would talk to them about that. My sons were in the Santa Clara Vanguard, a renowned drum and bugle corps. He would talk about that. With other altar boys, he would talk to them about sports or their interests. Some priests were hard to approach or were a bit more stern, but all the altar boys liked to talk to Fr. Sweeny.

"My wife and I have six children. Two of my sons are religious. One is a brother, a Capuchin, and the other is a deacon in Colorado. They both said Fr. Sweeny's way of doing things really influenced them. They wanted to be like him. He didn't push religion on them. If he saw it, he'd cultivate it. In fact, my younger son, the one who is a Capuchin, once told me, 'I want to make an appointment with Father to talk to him about these religious feelings I have.' Recently I asked him to tell me about that meeting. He said, 'Dad, the only thing I remember about the meeting was how down to earth Father always was. I remember him telling me about when he was a young kid in grammar school, and he got into a fight with another student. He told me he won, but it wasn't because he was better. He won because he held his fist straight out in front of him and the kid ran into it!' My son who is a deacon also spoke to Father about a vocation. Father gave him some advice about what to do: to nurture it and pray about it. They both singled out that it was Father who drew them to even consider religious life.

"My son, the Capuchin, would listen to Fr. Goode talk about

suffering and carrying our cross. He was ready to enter the Franciscan order when we found out he had cancer. He had waited too long to tell us about the symptoms and when we got to the doctor he was given only twenty-five percent chance of survival. He was really sick, and they hit him with every kind of treatment they could and as hard as they could. He was young so he was able to take radiation and chemotherapy. It burned his hair off and burned his skin, like he was in a fire. Through all that, he persevered. He kept at it, like Father taught us. He was cured, went into the novitiate for five years, and then he entered the order. His attitude was always, 'That's what God wants.' He would say his ability to find God in these experiences was from what my wife and I taught our children and what Fr. Sweeny taught them."

Fr. Ray Devlin, S.J. [†]
Served at Our Lady of Peace 1972 - 2011

"While [Fr.] Joe was overseas in the last days of the Vietnam War, I taught at the Jesuit high school in San Jose and helped at Our Lady of Peace in Santa Clara. I asked Fr. Sweeny to have the people pray for Joe's safe return to the United States, as the Vietcong, who had tried to assassinate Joe, were about to conquer South Vietnam. At that time, the 32-foot statue of the Blessed Mother Mary, now in front of the church, was not yet in place. It was a future hope. In the meantime, a million rosaries were being said by the faithful, who were also participating in all-night adoration, monthly, on the first Fridays. Finally, the statue of the Blessed Mother, Our Lady of Peace, was erected.

"It seemed a happy coincidence that Joe was attracted to assist at the very parish that had prayed for his safe return. He was unaware of the prayers on his behalf and how they had been answered by the Blessed Mother. Joe often walked on the long procession path in front of Mary's statue while saying his daily rosary. Here, in one of the most active U.S. parishes, Joe gave of himself unsparingly in his ministry."

Willie Lapus
Parishioner 1983 - Present

"My wife and I raised three children. My youngest was three years old when we came here. In the 1980s, a lot of weird things were happening in the Catholic church. I've seen all kinds of things at Masses in other parishes: cheerleaders jumping up and down during the consecration, fountains with spouting water, extravaganzas. They were outdoing each other in showmanship at Mass which concerned me a lot because it lost the solemnity and became a circus act. Our Lady of Peace was there to us to give us a solid faith, to root us in reality, and celebrate the Mass as a sacrifice.

"Sr. [Mary] Jean being here was important, too. She provided all the early education for my children. They went to Sr. Jean's school at Our Lady of Peace until they were entering the first grade and learned a lot from her.

"The devotion to the Blessed Sacrament was a special grace. Once I was coming home with my wife from an office party around 1 a.m. We stopped by the church and, as we entered, the person who was praying before the Blessed Sacrament stood up and left. He probably thought we were his replacement. So we stayed there for a while, but we weren't intending to stay so long. We were getting tired, but we couldn't leave the Blessed Sacrament. There was a sign, 'If you have to leave and no one is here, please call this number.' So I picked

213

The Justino and Diana Escalera family in 1986.

Franciscan Brother Alexander Escalera and Deacon Stephen Escalera today.

Fr. Joe Devlin spent many years internationally ministering to and advocating for the Vietnamese, many of them orphaned children. Of this photo he wrote, "It's hard to conceive greater heroines than these. Same boat, twins' mother and 3-year-old sister die of thirst and starvation. Girl in front loses her captain of boat and father swimming to get help in one of three storms. Haunting memories!" Fr. Joe served at Our Lady of Peace, intermittently at first, from 1972 until his death on February 25, 1998.

up the phone and called. Fr. Sweeny answered. He said, 'Give me five minutes.' He came right over, though he was visibly very tired. He didn't speak to us, but just knelt before the Blessed Sacrament. So we stood up and left. That's the kind of priest he was.

"Fr. Joe Devlin was another wonderful priest. Every Saturday after the 8 a.m. Mass, people would gather and go to the Planned Parenthood on the Alameda and pray the rosary there. Fr. Sweeny and Fr. Joe Devlin would always join us. Every week Fr. Sweeny would tell Fr. Joe, 'Don't bring any signs!' And Fr. Joe would say, 'Okay.' And every week, when we arrived to Planned Parenthood, Fr. Joe would open his car trunk and pull out the signs! They had the same dialogue every week!

"Often my wife and I would visit the homes for the sick, and sometimes there would be people who were dying. So we'd go to Fr. Joe and ask, 'Do you have time? We have someone who is dying and wants to go to confession.' Any time someone needed to go to confession or to receive the Extreme Unction (Anointing of the Sick), he would immediately say, 'Let's go.' He never took a vacation. Never. He was a retired Jesuit, but he never really retired."

Mike Aubin
Parishioner 1978 - Present

"I moved to Santa Clara in 1978 and I didn't want to come to Our Lady of Peace because they didn't play rock music here! I liked to go to other churches in the area that had more folk music.

"Growing up, Catholic living was a way of life for my parents and grandparents. When I came to San Jose for a job in high-tech at the age of 23, I had to choose it and make it my own. As I matured, I started to appreciate Our Lady of Peace.

"Living very close to the parish, I started coming here more and more to drop in for perpetual adoration. Then I met Fr. Sweeny, who had a big influence on me that grew over time. Fr. Shichida also influenced me. He was very genuine, a great assistant pastor, and a very humble man. Spending all night in the church before the Blessed Sacrament at the all-night vigils, as well as the Fatima processions, made a big impact on me spiritually. Fr. Sweeny would stay up all night and into the next morning. I don't know how much sleep he got, but he was always tired. He never stopped working. Fr. Shichida was a very calm, humble, peaceful person. He was a good person to work with Fr. Sweeny, because Fr. Sweeny was more excitable and expressive. (He was Italian! He often spoke with his hands.) Fr. Shichida was Japanese and more reserved, but he had a great smile and a warm heart. He was in charge of the altar servers. Later, I joined the Legion of Mary and he was a spiritual director for the Junior Legion (the youth). My wife, Teresita, was in charge of the Junior Legion back then.

"I met my wife in 1983 when we were both catechists attending a workshop at St. Clare Church for catechism (CCD) teachers. The workshop was for catechists from Our Lady of Peace, but our parish had no meeting rooms so we used the school at St. Clare. I was still young, 28 years old. I taught the high schoolers and she taught the grammar school children. She was very good with that age group.

"Teresita, along with Richard Hernandez (now Fr. Anthony), got me to join the Legion of Mary. Richard was a college student. We became friends while we were teaching CCD. He told me about a training program for catechists at Our Lady of Peace Retreat Center in Beaverton, Oregon. I knew I needed more help learning how to teach kids, so we enrolled and spent two weeks in the program there. After attending for three consecutive years, we received certificates from the Pontifical Catechetical Institute.

"It is important to note that, amidst being very involved in the parish, my life had a balance that included riding a motorcycle, playing racquetball, competing in triathlons, and work.

"I had more contact with Fr. Sweeny when I joined the Legion of Mary. I was assisting with evangelization, which means to help the pastor reach people he can't reach due to his time constraints. We had teams of about eight people who would take assignments of about two hours of active work in addition to our weekly prayers and meetings. My assignment was catechesis, and when the catechism classes weren't in session we'd do other forms of outreach, such as door-to-door evangelization. In that role, I was an active member. Others were auxiliary members who prayed for us.

"Fr. Sweeny was the priest who made the greatest impact on my spiritual life. He spoke from the heart. He'd talk to anyone. He spoke with people in a genuine way, and though he could speak with people on any topic, he focused on a religious perspective; it was always on his mind. He always talked about God, in one way or another: Jesus, Mary, the sacraments, and so on. The kids in catechism classes, especially the high school kids, loved him. He could relate to people.

"I left the Legion of Mary in 1986 when I decided to enter St. Joseph College seminary to become a priest. The seminary was a poor fit for me and I left after a semester. Teresita wanted to join the Franciscan Sisters at Our Lady of Peace Retreat in Oregon. She took a two-week vacation from her job at Lockheed to visit. She was miserable and came home. Both of us were discerning our vocations, we took the beginning steps with religious life, and it didn't seem right. We were friends for about three years, then started dating and were engaged a year later. We married in 1988. We have three children and being a father is the greatest thing on earth!

"Where would I be without Our Lady of Peace? I met my wife! Finding a spouse is hard these days. My friends didn't go to church on Sunday, and when I came to Santa Clara I was somewhat by myself in being Catholic. Our Lady of Peace brought me closer to God in many ways, one being teaching catechism and another being the other teachers I spent time with. For about twelve years, from the ages of sixteen to twenty-eight, I didn't do too much with the Church. Then, I followed my parents' example of getting involved and Fr. Sweeny provided the parish which was a genuine Catholic church—there was no revolt here post-Vatican II. In many parishes, dissent was the norm. I was somewhat protected from that by not being as involved (though still going to Mass) during those interim years and then by becoming active at Our Lady of Peace...even if they didn't play rock music."

Fr. Anthony (Richard) Hernandez

Religious Education Director and/or Instructor 1980 - Present
Religious Vocation from Our Lady of Peace

"My grandmother lived with my aunt, Irene Barrera, here in Lakewood for a time. Whenever we visited Grandma, we would come to Our Lady of Peace. In high school, around 1978 to 1979, I started attending the church more regularly. My brother and I would come here because we liked Our Lady of Peace. We got to know some people here and preferred it.

"In the 1980-1981 school year I started volunteering as a catechist; I was 19 years old. I eventually went to catechetical school and earned a Pontifical Catechetical Diploma, and Fr. Sweeny appointed me as the coordinator for the children's religious education program in 1985. Sr. Jean was here to coordinate First Holy Communion, we were developing a high school program, and we started adult Bible study and RCIA (Rite of Christian Initiation

220

Fr. Shichida delivers his well-known rendition of the "Ave Maria" on September 8, 1984, at the birthday celebration for the Blessed Mother.

Mike and Teresita Aubin on their wedding day, joined by (left to right)
Fr. Castro, Fr. Sweeny, and Fr. Shichida.

for Adults). It was a part-time job for me at first, and then I became the full-time Director of Religious Education (DRE) from about 1985 to 1996. In 1989, we started Catholic Faith Fellowship (CFF) as a weekly faith formation group for adults (and it continues today). In 1996, I entered the seminary.

"I offered to help Fr. Sweeny start RCIA at Our Lady of Peace because they had never formed an officially organized program. A man named Mr. Burgan, who had taught for a long time here, would prepare people to enter the Church. He'd have weekly discussions with them; it was more of an inquiry class than a methodical, planned and implemented program. In the 1980s, RCIA was less common.

"I've heard people say they prefer the RCIA program at Our Lady of Peace because in other parishes there was too much emphasis put on the subjective. For example, Jesus may be the topic for just one class of the year, so they'd only spend just one session talking about Jesus. Also, there were a lot of discussions about, 'How do you feel about this?' At the end, how do you receive the dogma or teaching of the Church? At Our Lady of Peace there is an emphasis on what the Church teaches. We also try to introduce people to Church traditions. Many people are drawn to the Marian devotion, and we do introduce them to the devotional life of the Church.

"I don't consider Our Lady of Peace to be 'conservative' or 'traditional'. One can't use those labels. Our Lady of Peace draws all kinds of people. People are drawn to the Eucharist, devotion to the Mother of God, and a more solemn liturgy. On a political spectrum, there is a lot of variety here. It is a spiritual home for many types of people. I do believe, however, there is a consistency in that everyone strives to be 'orthodox', or truly practicing the teachings of the Church.

"People who were involved in the parish knew a different side of Fr. Sweeny than those who did not work closely with parish life.

Organization was not one of his strong qualities. This happens with me as a priest, too, and it's not a criticism: he could organize people in the sense that he could inspire people who would then put teeth to his ideas and make them concrete. The day-to-day administrative details were not always his forte. He empowered a lot of people but the day-to-day carrying out of parish life was not always easy. Very organized people would tend to be frustrated with him. Yet he found the right people to do the job! The RCIA program was my idea, but it was he who put me into action."

Fr. Michael Pintacura

Serving at Our Lady of Peace 1972 - Present
Religious Vocation from Our Lady of Peace

"For many years, the Fatima processions were coordinated by my family. My brother, sister, and her husband and children all helped. I printed up all the books and we put it all together. We trained the altar boys to military precision; there were about 25 faithful altar servers and each had a role to play. The choir sang. The ushers guided the traffic. We gave our volunteers information to answer any questions the pilgrims had. It was a tremendous effort, working day and night, to prepare each month. The Fatima procession grew, word spread, and busloads were coming! It was a neat feeling to see five or six buses pull into the parking lot! It blew Fr. Sweeny's mind and I told him, 'She [Our Lady] does wonders, doesn't she?' Buses came from Monterey, Los Angeles, Nevada, Oregon, Washington, and some pilgrims flew in. It was huge! The people would stay all night long.

"After I was ordained to the priesthood, my second assignment as a priest was here at Our Lady of Peace in the mid-1980s. I was here

Catechism teachers for the 1986-1987 academic year. Richard Hernandez (now Fr. Anthony) is pictured in the back row, fourth from right.

for five years. Fr. Shichida, myself, Fr. Bob Castro, and Fr. Bob Finnegan were all stationed here with Fr. Sweeny. We worked great as a team. In addition, many other orders of priests and diocesan priests came to help us. The priests were always busy. People came from all over. When the Fatima processions grew to be so huge, many people discovered Our Lady of Peace and kept coming.

"As time went on, we began other activities here at Our Lady of Peace. Adoration, the rosary, and the devotion to the Blessed Mother were very popular. Father would always allow me to decorate the sanctuary on feast days of saints. When people began to see how the priests were working as a team, more people came to help us and also offered ideas. This parish became so active and we worked as a team to educate the people. We brought in a television and showed formational videos. Famous people came here to give talks. Many priests loved coming here to help. Confessions were available at every Mass.

"As a child I was always a great dreamer and just made things happen. That's how Fr. Sweeny and I worked together. We did a lot of dreaming and we always did things out of the ordinary. In fact, often we blew Bishop DuMaine's mind, he just couldn't believe it. He was pleasantly surprised. We never worried about money and God worked out the details.

"The sculptor, Charles Parks, was making the statue before Bishop DuMaine came, and he completed it and was ready to send it to Santa Clara. But the bishop said, 'It's too expensive.' Everyone thought he was so mean, but he wasn't. He was concerned because Fr. Sweeny didn't yet have the money to pay.

"Bishop DuMaine was a well-educated man. His diction was very picturesque, he was so well spoken. He was a very faithful man who loved Our Lady. But he knew some realities about what parishes could afford. Some parishes were closing down. He knew Fr. Sweeny was a very humble man, but he wasn't an administrator like some other priests. He didn't have that gift. Paying for the statue just happened to fall into place. That's what blew the bishop's mind! Fr. Sweeny dreamed and the people just put it all together."

Steve Nguyen
Parishioner 1975 - Present

"As an older altar server, I started to organize the younger servers and direct them. I served all through high school and that was one thing that kept me focused as a young man. I didn't need to have a girlfriend or such distractions. I had the faith and was able to serve God. There was a sense of pride for me, and positive attention coming my way. Kids want attention, whether it be negative or positive. This gave me a lot of positive attention. In fact, it felt like I mattered. Typical teenage boys want to be a starting quarterback or the like. My desire was to be in charge of the altar boys, taking care of things at church. It gave me a sense of pride and a way to focus my energy. After varsity sports for a bit, I found I preferred to serve. Though I was a talented and competitive athlete, sports didn't offer the same fulfillment."

Chris Schaper
Parishioner 1972 - 2003

"I grew up in the Bay Area and my family often attended Our Lady of Peace. At college in St. Louis, Missouri, I met my wife, Mary Grace. We were married in St. Louis at her home parish and came back to California to start a family. Our Lady of Peace was our parish.

Pastoring Our Lady of Peace in the 1980s were (left to right):
Fr. Michael Pintacura, Fr. John Sweeny, and Fr. Francis Shichida.

"We didn't have any children for three years, not by our design but the good Lord made us wait. We were very involved with the high school YMI (Youth Militia Immaculata), which was started by Tony Ryan when he worked for the parish. He became the CCD director, and Mary Grace and I were the fifth grade CCD teachers. From there we took over the high school CCD program and the youth group until Kateri, our oldest child, was born.

"Kateri was born with spina bifida. We were told not to have any more children because, according to the doctors, we could have more children with spina bifida. There we were, at a Catholic hospital, being told to not have children. The doctors and staff gave us every excuse in the world to avoid pregnancy. I was pretty upset with this statement, but that's where the medical mindset was at the time. Our offense at being told not to have children strengthened our commitment to do the right thing. Up until then, we were encouraged by our parents to do the right thing. But when you have a personal experience it enhances the commitment and makes it real. We now have nine children, and none of the subsequent children have spina bifida.

"It was confusing to be under the care of a Catholic hospital that didn't uphold Church teaching, so it was good to come back to Our Lady of Peace and have someone like Fr. Sweeny to talk to. Before we could do that, though, we had some decisions about Kateri's care and surgeries to make right after her birth. With all that pending, first we were sent to the nurse who handles social services and she told us it was okay for us to not have any more children and they could do the surgical procedures to sterilize us to eliminate the 'risk.' I told her, 'That's not going to happen.' At this point, our trust in the doctors and the Catholic hospital completely went out the window. We instantly knew we were getting bad information. This was challenging because we had to trust the same people to uphold the life of our child and make good decisions about her care, and we had just a couple of hours to make those decisions. One of the options, by the way, was to not do anything for our daughter and just let her die. Of course, that wasn't an option for us. My Dad was there with us, and his support, all the formation we'd received, and being involved at Our Lady of Peace enhanced our confidence that we could override those peer pressures and not succumb to that incomprehensible mindset. Why were they even suggesting we just let her die? I made the basic statement to the doctors: 'God gave her to me. Now I'm giving her to you doctors, and you need to do whatever you need to do to fix her. Then give her back to me and I'll raise her. It's as simple as that.'

"We had tremendous support from the priests at Our Lady of Peace and the families of the parish. We were faced with a dramatic situation and had a community to tell us we made the right decision. They supported us one-hundred percent. Through all the years we were at Our Lady of Peace, there was never a moment the love from the families and priests wavered. These are the people and priests who loved Kateri from the moment they saw her, and the minute her wheelchair showed up at the church she was welcomed. I became known as, 'the Dad of the girl in the wheelchair.' "

Fr. William Stout[†] (continued)
Served at Our Lady of Peace 1967 - 2018

"Much of my time was at Star of the Sea in Alviso. If I wanted to do anything, Fr. Sweeny would back me up. For example, Alviso would flood from time to time, so the City of San Jose built the Anderson Dam in the 1950s to hold the water back and to keep it for watering. That caused the water in Alviso to sometimes get stagnant. It did cut down the flooding problem, but in 1983 the dam got full by the end of February and they didn't want to let any water out. A huge rainstorm came in and dumped a tremendous amount of water. It went over the spillway and down the Coyote River. The mobile home park there was supposed to have built a wall, but they didn't and it flooded. The water went toward Lamplighter, but Lamplighter had a dike around it and so the water went toward the sewer plant. The city had a dike around Alviso, but they had a choice whether to send the water into the sewer plant and pollute the bay or to punch a hole in the dike. They chose the latter, sending about four feet of water into Alviso and flooding about a thousand people out of their homes.

"Years before, when Fr. Donald McDonnell was in Alviso, he set up a housing cooperative for most of the poor people and allowed the people to buy their own homes. They bought the houses when Highway 880 was being put in and the cooperative brought in the homes and set them down. In Alviso they could buy a lot for fifty dollars, and then the houses were no more than a thousand dollars. For poor people that was a lot of money, but thirty percent of the people in Alviso owned their own homes because of the housing cooperative.

"When the people were flooded out, the church also had about four feet of water inside. At that time, the Jesuits had sent me to Sacramento. On weekends I would take the bus to serve in Alviso. I came down after the flood. The town was flooded but no one had gone into the church. The tabernacle was on the altar, so I asked Fr. Sweeny, 'Can I go in to get the Blessed Sacrament?' He said, 'Sure, you've got my okay.' In Alviso, the police captain stopped me and said, 'Where are you from?' I said, 'I've got authorization from Fr. Sweeny to enter the church.' He replied, 'Fr. John Sweeny?' I said, 'Yes.' He relaxed and said, 'Oh, he said my wedding Mass!' So he gave me a boat with five cops and we went down to the church. We couldn't get in the church door. One of the local residents, Rich

Santos, was a firefighter in San Jose and came with a boat and got in. The cops were then able to enter. It was flooded inside so they walked on the pew backs, got the tabernacle, and carried it out. If it wasn't for Fr. Sweeny, I probably wouldn't have been able to do that. When I mentioned his name, it was like magic.

"A man from the Knights of Colombus, Mr. Phan, wanted to do something for the people who were flooded out. He came to Fr. Sweeny and asked, 'Can we contact the diocese and ask them to take up a second collection for the people of Alviso?' Fr. Sweeny gave his okay, they received permission, and took the collection. With that money, Fr. Sweeny bought drywall. Floods pollute everything. In Alviso, there was oil storage that polluted the water so the homes were just a mess when the water went down. Homeowners had to tear all that sheetrock off their walls. Other organizations brought food and clothes and personal supplies, but Father knew what they needed to fix up their homes and that they probably wouldn't have money to do it, so he bought these great loads of sheetrock and gave it out. I thought that was a smart idea."

Sr. Mary Jean Kula [†]
Parish Staff Member 1975 - 2007

"An elderly, non-Catholic lady was watching the life of Mother Teresa on TV and was deeply edified by her life. Somehow, she found the [telephone] number for Our Lady of Peace. This is what she asked over the phone: 'Was Mother Teresa a Catholic?' Yes, she was. 'Then I'd like to become a Catholic, so when I die I want to be where she is. Please come soon, I am ninety-eight years old.' I told Fr. Joe [Devlin]. Since it was Sunday, we had to wait until he fulfilled all his assigned duties for the day.

"With difficulty we found the home in the Los Gatos hills. The caregiver for this sweet, old lady let us in. Fr. Joe asked her a few questions and gave her a brief spiritual talk. She answered each question and understood what she was asking for: to be received into the Catholic Church.

"She was not certain if she had ever been baptized, so Fr. Joe baptized her in the living room and absolved her of her sins. Fr. Joe gave all the possible sacraments, including Confirmation and the Sacrament of the Sick. He explained the Holy Eucharist and asked if she believed it was the true Body and Blood of Jesus Christ. She said she believed with all her heart. While we sang, 'O Lord, I Am Not Worthy,' Fr. Joe gave her the Body of Christ on her tongue. She received Jesus very reverently, closed her eyes, and was peacefully silent.

"Afterwards, we all enjoyed an ice cream and cookies party upon the elderly woman's request. The great day was made possible because Fr. Joe agreed to do all this. He was very docile to the inspiration of the Holy Spirit."

Zora Ljoljic
Regular Visitor to Our Lady of Peace 1976 - Present

"In 1976, I moved [from Croatia] to California. My office was very close to Our Lady of Peace, so I would go for noon Mass or for quiet prayers. In 1980, I became pregnant with my son. With multiple problems stemming from different directions of that pregnancy, I am convinced that Fr. Sweeny's prayers saved me and saved my unborn son.

"Every morning, I would stop in at Our Lady of Peace before work to pray. Then Fr. Sweeny would pray over me for two, three, or even five minutes, and I would go to work. If he wasn't outside the church, he told me to ring his bell at the rectory. Sometimes I would ring his bell and he would pray over me right in the doorway. There were even days when he was ill, and he would come out in his pajamas and still pray over me! That level of human care is very, very hard to find. I am very grateful to him for finding the time and having that much love for me. That prayer saved me; it literally helped me to get through my difficulties. He prayed over me daily during the entire pregnancy and in *the end, I was a healthy mother and gave birth to a healthy baby boy.*

"A few years later, I had some serious personal issues and went back to Fr. Sweeny. He literally set me off on my feet again, and told me if all I do is believe and pray to Jesus and Holy Mother, everything was going to be okay. Again, I would come in the morning, he would pray over me, and I would go to work. I was going through some difficult, difficult times.

"Fr. Sweeny was genuine. His faith was very, very strong and his devotion to the Holy Mother was very visible. He simply had love, care, and energy for everyone. I would come for months, every morning on a working day morning, and he would see me. How many people can do that? Not many. I really think that's a characteristic of a Catholic saint.

"In 1983, my family moved to Switzerland with a work assignment. When we returned 1987, I'd go to Our Lady of Peace for noon Mass, during my lunch break, and pray. I reached out to Fr. Sweeny and got a little bit involved and attended the noon Mass...again, not because I was a regular parishioner but because I felt totally connected, totally compelled to be there because I felt the closeness of the Holy Spirit and, quite frankly, the power of Fr. Sweeny's faith that was totally unshakable even with some of the issues he was having. Sometimes he was saying the Mass but usually it was being offered by another priest. I would see him after Mass outside the church. He would always follow up with me, asking me how my son and I were doing. Fr. Sweeny was this incredible force of strength and faith and love that when—even if it was for only a moment—he would put his hand on my head and pray, the day would be easier.

"I cannot say enough about this man. First, his faith was totally unshakeable. Second, his absolute love for the Holy Mother. I remember his face when he was describing the statue he was planning to bring in, that the Holy Mother would have her arms open to people going to Great America. Here it is today, not only Great America patrons but the 49ers stadium, a college, businesses, and millions of people driving by on the Highway 101 and seeing those open arms. I've heard many, many people—Catholics, non-Catholics, and non-believers—say they go there to pray and find peace."

Fr. John Sweeny [†]
Pastor of Our Lady of Peace Church & Shrine 1969 - 2002

"Dear friends, you are loved. Way down deep inside, that's what we really want more than anything else in the world, isn't it? Not wealth, fame, power or pleasure, but someone to love us—without reservation, unconditionally, and forever. Someone who really cares, who knows us completely (our ideals and frustrations, our hopes and fears, our strengths and weaknesses, all the good and all the bad) and loves us anyway.

"We want someone who makes us feel complete and whole inside. Someone who makes us feel worthy and special just by loving us. Someone whose love makes us stronger, freer, and more loving.

"Most of us have come to learn that such a love does not exist in the world of nature. Does it exist anywhere?

"Yes, thank God, it does exist to perfection in the Heart of Jesus formed by the Holy Spirit next to the sinless Heart of Our Mother Mary."

Fr. John Sweeny (left) and Fr. Edward Warren (right) celebrate a First Holy Communion in 1980.

We must forget ourselves,
and put aside our tastes and ideas,
and guide souls not by our own way,
but along the path which Our Lord points out.

St. Thérèse of Lisieux

CHAPTER 6
1990s

The Family That Prays Together

I place all my trust in you, My God.
All my hope is in your mercy.

Fr. John Sweeny

Silicon Valley rang in the decade of the 1990s with the rise of more office buildings, expanded parkways, and thriving tech businesses. The planned corporate development hinted at in the 1960s was now the Shrine's backdrop and left hardly a trace of pear orchards from days past. Daily Masses swelled with additional business people dropping in for a moment of grace, weekend Mass counts averaged 4,550 worshipers, and an estimated 200,000 vehicles exited onto Great America Parkway daily witnessing the outstretched arms of Our Lady of the Immaculate Heart.

Day-to-day activity at the parish continued at an active yet focused pace. Priests and volunteers served the Church with tremendous dedication. Retired priests frequented campus to hear confessions for hours at a time. Fr. Sweeny was available 24-hours—or so it seemed—if someone needed good counsel, sacraments, or a sick call. He did not limit his service and often took calls from people outside his parish in need of a priest. As parishioner Ellie Powers recalled, "You could see his fatigue and yet he'd always give that little bit extra. He went the extra mile to be there for us. A natural, sacrificial love was always there."

SEASON OF LOSS

In the latter half of the 1990s, Fr. Sweeny and the people of Our Lady of Peace experienced the loss of several priests. These men of God prompted faith, hope, and change into many lives.

On August 31, 1995, Fr. Shichida entered eternal life during a visit to Lourdes, France, after a struggle with pancreatic cancer. A native of Japan, Fr. Shichida was known as a quiet, prayerful, and always available priest. His composure was characteristically reserved yet when he joined the choir Fr. Shichida surprised the congregation with his beautiful voice and was particularly remembered for his powerful, "Ave Maria."

Fr. Joe Devlin, S.J., passed away on February 25, 1998. His ministry was so committed that when his brother, Fr. Ray Devlin, took over Fr. Joe's role part-time, he estimated Fr. Joe heard 15,000 confessions a year. Prior to assisting at Our Lady of Peace, Fr. Joe left a legacy of heroically serving the Vietnamese people during and after the Vietnam War. Resettled Vietnamese, many who knew him in Vietnam, flocked to see him at Our Lady of Peace.

The most unexpected loss came on October 10, 1999, when Fr. Louis Sweeny slipped on ice outside his parish in Stockton, California and died soon after from a wound to the head. The Sweeny brothers had entered the seminary on the same day in 1938, supported each other in their vocations, and met weekly for a day off at their family home in Calaveritas. Those close to Fr. John Sweeny would note a visible change in him after his brother's death.

THE FAMILY THAT PRAYS TOGETHER

The 1970s and 1980s building of the Marriott Hotel, Great America amusement park, and Mission College in Our Lady of Peace's neighborhood were huge assets to property values. Fr. Sweeny explained, "It brought us to a time when we could get out of debt because the property went from $18,000 an acre up to $205,000 and acre and then to $410,000 an acre. We had seven acres declared surplus land and were able to work a lease. Because of that, we're out of debt and the Shrine is paid for." Freed from paying off past purchases, the church leadership could make necessary investments in accommodating present and future needs.

An ongoing challenge at Our Lady of Peace was sufficient meeting space. The church and facilities were booked with Masses, devotions, and special events like weddings. Even after adding new meeting space, such as classroom trailers and the new parish offices and rectory (built in 1988), the facilities again crammed to overflowing. Catechism classes met wherever they could find space, which might be the corner of a parking lot or under a tree. As the need for additional meeting space pressed in, Fr. Sweeny formed a planning committee and combined this need for space with a desire to bring families together. His priestly ministry made him acutely aware of the strain on families and their need for faith formation, unification, and support. Additionally, he was moved to action by Pope John Paul II's urgings for marriages and families to strive for holiness. Thus prompted the space planning for what would later become the Family Learning Center and Pilgrimage Hall.

Once again envisioning a large-scale project and no diocesan financial support, Fr. Sweeny and his committee proposed the idea

Fr. Louis Sweeny, left, and Fr. John Sweeny, right, celebrate the
50th anniversary of their ordination to the priesthood in December of 1998.

Groundbreaking ceremonies for the Family Learning Center.

of the Family Learning Center to the parishioners. Their characteristic response was immediate support and they generously funded the construction. After much deliberation on the building design, the completed Family Learning Center opened in 1998 and included a kitchen, gym, classroom space, bookstore, library, and state-of-the art video and sound equipment. Built to form families and welcome pilgrims to the Shrine, it's calendar was soon filled to capacity.

Zora Ljoljic
Regular visitor to Our Lady of Peace 1976 - Present

"I'm a professional woman. I've been a business vice president and/or general manager for many, many years. Fr. Sweeny was that solid rock of faith that would help me lighten my day or my burdens. When you're a manager—I've had as many as 900 people in my organization—people bring you problems. Many problems stem from a lack of faith. Many of the people I've worked with were Hindu, Jewish, or non-believers, yet I talk to them about Our Lady of Peace all the time. I tell them to go over to Our Lady of Peace, to the statue, and pray to Our Holy Mother to help them. Many people would tell me they did and found peace of mind.

"The accessibility of the sacraments at Our Lady of Peace, so close to my office, sustained me from making poor choices. When dealing with so many of other peoples' problems it becomes overbearing, yet I had a place to go to and put things into perspective and help me make better decisions. It helped me to be more patient with people who were not easy to get along with, to sort things out, figure out what was important and what really wasn't. Time in prayer sheds light on big issues.

"I went to daily Mass because I'm a fervent believer in the Holy Eucharist. Just as you have to feed your body, I feel you need to feed your soul, and that is the Holy Eucharist. Fr. Sweeny was a big promoter of the Holy Eucharist. You go to Holy Mass to pray but also to receive the nourishment of the Holy Eucharist.

"There's a sense of a very strong faith community in that church and I like the international flavor. Also, you find people from all walks of life there.

"Our Lady of Peace, in that location near my office, was a comfort to me. It is a very special place and it was Fr. Sweeny's faith, energy, perseverance and a pure, sheer love for Our Lady that made it what it is. He poured himself into that Church and Shrine and people felt it. To meet Fr. Sweeny was like meeting a saint. His eyes radiated faith, love, and devotion. I don't know how to describe it; to me it was holiness."

Ellie Powers
Parishioner 1986 – Present

"One week at the Tuesday holy hour, Fr. Sweeny told a story about when he was driving and felt a wave of great suffering, anxiety, and distress come over him. He had the inspiration to put it together like a cross on his shoulder, and all of a sudden the emotions became very light and he was walking and carrying the Cross with Our Lord. That was how he handled the emotions: he physically gathered them like a cross, put his hands around it, set it on his shoulder, and carried it. Such was his simplicity: being like a child, living the faith in the deepest simplicity. His humility and almost demanding things stay simplistic—not in what he said but what he did—was essential. Our Lady manifests that: faith in its simplest form. Fr. Sweeny kept faith

Fr. Shichida, Fr. Sweeny, and Fr. Pintacura celebrate an outdoor Mass at the Shrine.

so tangible and doable for us. To this day, when I am struggling, I put it into a cross on my shoulder and carry it.

"Fr. Sweeny kept himself in that simplicity, talking about the simplicity of the religious and what they were supposed to be. It challenged us, without saying anything, to live the same way. For example, after the new rectory was built, there was no landscaping in front. He was content with that. Another example was one night when we were expecting him for dinner. Fr. Sweeny phoned and said he'd be very late because he was making a sick call. When he arrived, we had already eaten. I only had apples and cheese to serve him, so I sliced them up and put them on a plate. Fr. Sweeny was so grateful for the meal and raved, 'This is perfect! This is exactly what I needed.' In the littlest things he gave such appreciation."

Fr. Miguel Marie Soeherman, MFVA
Religious Vocation from Our Lady of Peace

"My parents were attending Our Lady of Peace quite a bit and brought me on a Divine Mercy Sunday for the first time as a young adult. Fr. Edward Warren was presiding. At some point, I started attending Mass at Our Lady of Peace more frequently. Then, we started attending the Fatima Pilgrimages from May through October on the 13th day of the month. The pilgrimages were one of the big things that got me to be more of a churchgoer. Fr. Sweeny also had the all-night vigil every first Friday and first Saturday, which I started to attend.

"In my life before I went to college, somehow my plans to attend confirmation classes always fell through, so I attended the confirmation class at Our Lady of Peace and was confirmed. Sometime later, I started volunteering to teach catechism classes with a friend. The classes were on Wednesday. I eventually signed up to cover the Eucharistic adoration holy hour from 11 p.m. to 12 a.m. on Wednesdays, so every Wednesday I'd stay after classes until I finished my holy hour and drive home to Hayward at midnight. The more I went to Our Lady of Peace, the more I preferred to go there.

"All this time, I was working in San Francisco near Fisherman's Wharf as a systems engineer for Electronic Data Systems. So I lived in the Diocese of Oakland, worked in the Archdiocese of San Francisco, and went to church in the Diocese of San Jose.

"In October of 1992, my parents went on a Peace Flight Pilgrimage with Our Lady of Peace parishioners. It was a nearly 4-week trip to various pilgrimage sites all over the world. One of the places they went was Fatima to celebrate the 75th anniversary of Our Lady's apparition there. I didn't go on the trip, but got involved spiritually because the spiritual director of the group encouraged them to find some prayer warriors to pray for them while they were gone. My parents asked me and one of my brothers to do this. We had to do three things every day while they were gone: pray the St. Michael's prayer for their protection, pray the Memorare to Our Lady, and make a daily sacrifice. At that time, I was not attending daily Mass, so to fulfill the sacrifice requirement I started going to Mass during my weekday lunch hour.

"St. Francis of Assisi Church was a fifteen-minute walk from my office to the North Beach neighborhood. I walked there for noon Mass and, as I arrived, a sister from the Daughters of Charity approached me and asked, 'Can I talk to you before you return to work?' We spoke after Mass and she asked, 'Have you ever thought of becoming a priest?' She was the first person to ever ask me that question. I'd always wanted to get married and have lots of kids. It was not until that day the idea of the priesthood ever came into my mind. That's when my vocation journey began. It was around

October 7, 1992.

"She spoke for a little while and then said, 'I promise I will pray to the Holy Spirit for you, that you will make the right decision.' When she said that, I got kind of freaked out. I was thinking, 'I didn't even give you permission to pray for me!' I guess I was scared that her prayer would change my life. Obviously, it did. Because what happened after that day was that more strangers started asking me the same question! Some of those people were parishioners from Our Lady of Peace and some were strangers from somewhere else. In response, I kept giving excuses. My number one excuse was that I had school loans to pay. It was true.

"A year after meeting that nun, I went to World Youth Day in Denver. My intention was to go to World Youth Day because I'd never been, but also for discernment. One of the requests I asked of Our Lord was, 'If this is from you, please send someone to ask me the same question.' My cousin and I traveled to Denver with the group from Our Lady of Peace. Arriving, we went to a church staffed by the Franciscan Friars of the Renewal. I decided to go to confession. After confession, as I was about to leave, the priest asked me, 'Have you ever thought about becoming a priest?' The Lord really didn't waste time to answer me! Still, I didn't want to follow because I wanted to get married and have a family. So I tried to run away from it for a couple of years until I realized, 'Unless I am doing God's will, I'm not going to find the true happiness He wants me to have.'

"A priest friend at home knew about the nun speaking to me and challenged me to consider her words. One day he said, 'You have to make the decision first. You never made the decision. You have to decide first and then the Lord will take care of everything.' He was right: I never made the decision whether I was going to follow or not, whatever that may be: married life or priestly life. His words that day hit me, so I started praying about my vocation. The nun had told me to pray about it, but I didn't want to because somehow I knew I was going to get an answer I was not ready to listen to.

"In January of 1996 I visited my community, the Franciscan Missionaries of the Eternal Word (founded by Mother Angelica in 1987). From the first day when I arrived I knew our Lord was calling me there. The different words people said to me would trigger my discernment (as compared to other religious orders I visited). The defining moment was on Wednesday night when I went to Mother Angelica's Live Show. Before the show went on the air, the floor director mentioned to the audience, 'We have a guest from Lincoln Nebraska, Bishop Fabian Bruskewitz, and the topic will be suffering and vocation.' I groaned, 'Oh, great.' Though I was visiting, I still wanted to get married. But as I listened to the show, one of the points the Bishop spoke about was suffering. He said sometimes a member of the same family may be suffering for the one who has a vocation. All week I had been thinking about my parents because that week my mom was scheduled to have brain surgery and my dad was struggling with his job. It was constantly on my mind.

"After the show, I went to the brothers' chapel to pray. It was the first time I told Our Lord, 'Okay, Lord, I believe you are calling me and I will follow you if you want me to.' It was very emotional. At the same time, it was such a relief to tell Him that. I had been so burdened that I couldn't yet say those words. The next morning, I spoke with the Superior about my discernment.

"My biggest excuse for so long had been the school loan, and even when I told Our Lord I would follow Him, my greatest concern was this loan. There was no way I could pay off that loan right away, it was sizeable. About a month later, I was able to pay off my loan completely! Just like the priest had told me, 'You have to decide first and then the Lord will take care of everything,' He did. I never had to seek additional help. I entered our community on March 25, 1996, nearly four years after that sister spoke with me. On June 5, 2004, I was ordained to the priesthood. Throughout my priestly formation, Fr. Sweeny prayed for me.

"The main appeal to me of our religious order is represented in the image of the monstrance on our habits, which indicates we bear witness to the presence of Jesus in the Eucharist. I was attracted to join my community by the fact the community prays together in front of the exposed Blessed Sacrament. Our Lady of Peace and Fr. Sweeny were very instrumental in helping me to grow in my love for Eucharistic adoration and that's what drew me to the Missionaries of the Eternal Word. Additionally, somehow, within my heart, I was drawn to do the work that Mother Angelica started through the media.

"Eucharist adoration being nourished and so well promoted at Our Lady of Peace was instrumental in my vocation and choice of religious orders. In the beginning, I didn't prefer to attend Mass at Our Lady of Peace because the Mass seemed so long. After I became 'converted' to Our Lady of Peace I wanted to go there because I was nourished well through Eucharistic adoration and Father's wonderful work there at the parish, encouraging the people to be devoted to Our Lord and Our Lady."

Anonymous
Convert to Catholicism in 1994

"Located on the front wall at Our Lady of Peace, behind the choir seating, is a painting of the Holy Family with a fascinating history. The original Holy Family painting hangs in the Santa Clara Mission. It is much larger, approximately 10 by 15 feet, and fills the entire wall of the side chapel. The beauty and detail of the original,

Fr. Sweeny, Mother Anglica, PCPA, and Brother (now Father) Miguel Marie Soeherman, MFVA, during his seminary formation.

Mary's vision upon Jesus, and Joseph's focus on the viewers in the Mission—inviting them to also worship Jesus—has inspired people for over a century.

"In 1926, a fire completely destroyed both the old Adobe Santa Clara Mission and the brick student chapel. We are fortunate that this beautiful artwork was rescued from the 1926 fire by students who rushed into the burning chapel to save the painting.

"When the current Mission was built in 1927, it was decided to place the Holy Family painting in the side chapel intended for baptisms. Traditional baptistries are often located near the front door of the church, and the Holy Family is located in the first side chapel, on the right as you enter the Mission.

"[I am a] local man, a former Presbyterian, who worships at Our Lady of Peace. In August of 1993 at a low point in my life, I was at the Santa Clara Mission praying in front of the statue of Jesus in the main courtyard, and it seemed that Jesus' hand and fingers were pointing me towards the Mission church. Not knowing what lay ahead, I walked to the Mission where they were preparing for a wedding and was told I was welcome to sit in the rear of the church. Seated before the Holy Family painting and absorbed in prayer, I became overwhelmed with a desire to be able to receive the Eucharist as a Catholic. I later learned what I felt was the grace of God. My son and I joined the RCIA program in a local church and received our first Eucharist, together, at the Easter vigil of 1994."

Steve Nguyen
Parishioner 1975 - Present

"When I was twenty years old, I started to teach catechism

because my mother made me. I went to Father and said, 'Fr. Sweeny, I really don't want to do this.' He said, 'Just do it. Just try. Keep your mother happy. What is more pleasing to God is not so much the gift that you lay at the altar but that you obey your parents.' So I started teaching catechism and actually enjoyed it.

"At the time, the Vietnamese people were asking for a permanent place to worship and maintain their culture. The diocese said, 'No' and the situation escalated. The diocese's argument was the Vietnamese were Americans now. Some Vietnamese felt we should agree. Others were adamant to have a Vietnamese church and Masses in Vietnamese. So there was a political split.

"The political divide was upsetting the teens and affecting their friendships because their parents were divided. They asked Fr. Sweeny if they could gather at Our Lady of Peace to pray. On a Friday afternoon they pitched tents to spend the weekend there and used the rectory kitchen to cook. The teens prayed all weekend. Fr. Sweeny was so impressed he came out to see them. They attended the 5 p.m. Sunday Mass and sang for Mass. I was one of the youth directors and stayed with them all weekend.

"The kids worked hard to get through it, and they did. That weekend was an experience of a lifetime they will always remember."

Suzanne Spence
Parishioner 1990 - Present

"Fr. Sweeny was a realist. By that I mean he saw the situation of our society as it really was and knew that we needed to do something different than how we had been doing it. He saw that happening in the home schooling families. He was a realist, a practical man, and a visionary. This is seen in some of the other things he did before he

Fr. Sweeny visits with the Vietnamese teens gathered to pray for reconciliation in their community.

Vietnamese teens camp out at Our Lady of Peace for a weekend of prayer and fellowship.

was at Our Lady of Peace, such as being very involved in job training efforts so people could find work. When Fr. Sweeny moved to this parish he brought the same exact outlook: How can he help society be better from the ground up? I can't even tell you what a great impact that was on our family because it said that what we were doing was not only good, but necessary. He gave us the affirmation that what we were doing was necessary to keep the culture from falling into the abyss. Those are dramatic words but he knew the importance of what we were doing.

"Primarily, Fr. Sweeny supported us as a priest. As a pastor, he was our father: he was someone we could go to when we had a concern or a question. He was ready to support us in any situation because he felt what we were doing was essential. He offered the sacraments, wise council, and was very level-headed when people would get excited about differences or miscommunication. Fr. Sweeny had a great way of leveling the playing field and putting it into perspective so that people wouldn't get into factions over small grievances. He was a diplomat in that way. He kept us unified, supported us, and acknowledged us. Fr. Sweeny gave one the sense of being able to stand up straight and say, 'This is tough, but it is worth it. I am doing something that is valuable not only for my own soul and for my family, but for society at large.' "

Deacon Dominick and Mary Ellen Peloso
Church of the Nativity, Menlo Park, California

"When we came back to more actively practicing our faith, we wanted something dynamic. A traveling Fatima statue had come to Nativity and it moved us to go to one of the Fatima Masses we had heard about at Our Lady of Peace. We were very impressed with the

Fatima Mass and with Eucharistic adoration.

"Our pastor, Fr. Davenport (who was ordained with Fr. Sweeny), gave us permission to begin Eucharistic adoration once a month in 1993. In 1994, we talked to him about going perpetual. He was a bit nervous and wasn't ready to take that big leap, so we increased adoration to daily from 8:00 p.m. to midnight. In 1996, Fr. Davenport was in the hospital with leukemia and we went to visit him. We had been planning to approach the subject of going perpetual again, and when we walked into his room he said, "I've just been thinking about you! I've just decided we have to go perpetual!" He had just finished praying the chaplet of Divine Mercy. We didn't even have to ask!

"Fr. Sweeny and Sr. Mary Jean came from Our Lady of Peace to speak at every Mass one weekend. They explained and promoted the devotion, and encouraged people to sign up. We copied the adoration prayer cards used at Our Lady of Peace, making a few alterations to meet our needs. When we began perpetual adoration, we used those cards and prayed aloud every hour on the hour, like at Our Lady of Peace. After some time, we realized so many people were dropping in to pray in silence, so we discontinued the vocal prayer. People still use the cards, they just pray quietly. We also began the Fatima Masses in 1996, and again copied the program from Our Lady of Peace.

"Fr. Sweeny led a parish that was so vibrant and spiritually active. He transformed it into the beacon of the entire San Jose diocese. At Nativity, we started adoration because Our Lady of Peace had adoration. St. Bruno Church in San Bruno started adoration because Nativity had adoration. When one considers Fr. Sweeny's influence, who knows how many other adoration programs or devotions he inspired?"

Joe Moran
Parishioner 1998 - Present

"We have three sons. In 1997, we decided to try home schooling the youngest. For social interaction, we were attending some Christian group activities. In January of 1998, we heard about a Catholic home school group named Regina Pacis at Our Lady of Peace and went to check it out. What really impressed me was the mix of ages interacting together. The highlight of my 5-year-old's day there was that a 14-year-old boy engaged him in a conversation about Star Wars. We started attending regularly, and the older boys were intrigued.

"By the next fall we looked at our family's travel interests and the older boys' academic development and decided we could educate them ourselves. I had taken a leave of absence from work to try home schooling, and as we increased our schooling commitment I left the company.

"Part of my philosophy is the family should go to church where the children go to school. We found we were attending Our Lady of Peace more and more because it offered the same connection between their education and faith community. Within a year, we started attending Our Lady of Peace for all the Sunday Masses. We told our pastor at St. Nicholas we would be transferring to Our Lady of Peace. He said, 'I understand you need to go where you are being fed.' He was right: we were being fed here. Not only in the church itself but from the home school community that was meeting on first Fridays and, later, every Wednesday.

"The support was for the kids: there were other kids who were somewhat like-minded to them. They'd come here and see the same people. They needed the regularity and it came by way of daily Mass and social time afterwards. It became a habit and eventually they wanted to attend daily Mass not only for the social aspect, but for the Mass. I thought it was great! They got that from the other kids in the home schooling group. Here we could talk about our faith and no one argued against us; we could attend daily Mass and didn't have to hide anything. It was critical for the kids to have that kind of peer group. We saw other families regularly and sometimes we'd go out to eat or visit with them after Mass, but the impetus was our faith. As a family, we became more serious about our faith and this church fit.

"The support from the priests was also encouraging. Fr. Warren usually said the noon Mass and he would encourage us, going up to the pulpit for his homily and saying, 'God bless you all for being here on a day you don't have to be,' or, 'I know you have things to do, but you bring your children, you come here, and you make God a priority.' It was delightful to know he would recognize us. He was so happy and enthusiastic."

Sal Caruso
Parishioner 1990 - Present

"Josephine—my fiancée at the time and now my wife—and I were looking for a parish to go to Mass to together around 1989. We really wanted a place where we felt we could raise a family. A place where there was a loving, nurturing environment with a lot of families and activity. A friend suggested, 'You need to go to Our Lady of Peace.' We didn't really ask why, we just came here one Sunday after we were engaged. We loved it.

"We loved the utter simplicity: there wasn't fanfare, there were no smiley-faced greeters at the front door of the church. The welcome came from the Eucharistic Lord, the presence of Christ. That was the welcome for us. We saw the reverence for the Eucharist, and that filled our hearts fill with joy. Fr. Sweeny was saying that same Mass we attended and he was just amazing. His homily was beautiful and spot-on. He had such a quiet courage. He spoke the Gospel in a way that made it relevant and real.

"We were previously at another parish and I had some experiences that were a bit troubling. I would go to confession and confess something I thought needed attention, and indeed it did. The priest, who was the pastor, was somewhat preaching the gospel of relativism along the lines of saying, 'Oh, that's all fine. You're young. That's all fine.' He put my sin in the context of my youth or of being a man, and excused it. I thought, 'Wait a minute. That's not what I was looking for. I was looking for a true conversion of soul, that's what I'm longing for. I'm not longing for someone to just pat me on the back and say, 'It's all okay.' Reassurance is important in the confessional as well. Obviously, no one wants to be condemned, we want to be saved and forgiven, of course. But in that guidance of reconciliation, we look for a bit more and that is the guidance toward what is right, true, and just. I wasn't finding that in the confessional and there didn't seem to be a great reverence for the Eucharist in the church.

"That was a big, big deal for me. I thought, 'I really want a place where I can see Jesus.' Mother Teresa said very clearly, 'The good news is that Jesus is here with us *today*—body, blood, soul and divinity—in the Holy Eucharist. Although Jesus comes to us under the appearance of bread and wine, His presence is as real to us *now* as He was flesh-and-blood-real to His disciples when he walked this earth.' She would reference that if it is in the Gospel, it must be true. There was a flame alive in her, and that is what I want and desire in my heart and in the hearts of every Catholic. This is not a wafer, it is not a symbolic communion of people, a confraternity thing where people go up and say, 'Amen' and receive the Eucharist. *It really is that intimate connection of the person with Christ, receiving Jesus Christ.* We don't consume the Eucharist; we seek that the Eucharist consumes us. That's what I look for: that God takes over my soul. So many times I hear people say, 'Go and consume the Eucharist.' Well, that's the bodily thing that happens, but the spiritual aspect is that God enters us and really permeates our heart and changes our heart for the better; He conforms us to whatever He wants us to be. We shouldn't be looking for what, 'I want, I need;' if that was the case I would have been happy with that confession. Relativism, 'It's all okay,' is most often what we hear in the world and in society: 'Don't be so hard on yourself'; 'Take it easy'; 'Relax.' I wasn't condemning myself, either, but I really desired more.

"We were married at St. Joseph Cathedral in 1991. Fr. Sweeny said our wedding Mass and later baptized six of our seven children. Our youngest was baptized by Fr. Sweeny and Fr. Mark Catalana, another holy priest.

"The Family Learning Center was built in 1998. I was the architect for the building, but Fr. Sweeny was really the architect. Fr. Sweeny's desire for the Family Learning Center was always the hope that there could be a school here someday. He instructed me to build ten classrooms, a library, a kitchen facility to be able to feed everyone, a large gym because physical activity is critical to stay healthy—body and soul trained at the same time—and ample bathroom facilities. He was very specific that he wanted the downstairs rooms to be expandable. He designed the three downstairs classrooms to expand into one large classroom to host families, marriage encounters, sessions for couples preparing to be married, and so on. Fr. Sweeny had a lot of specifics to incorporate into the building which we incorporated to the best of our ability. He wanted state of the art equipment for the movie projection system. Those were all Fr. Sweeny's visions: to use modern technology to the best of its ability to teach the faithful. He certainly was ahead of his time. That building has been used! And not just by our parish. The diocese has come here and had many conferences and meetings."

Mark Powers
Parishioner 1986 - Present

"Fr. Sweeny asked me to be the chairman of the Family Learning Center and Pilgrimage Hall building committee, which was a three- or four-year commitment and quite an honor. We got the parish together to raise awareness and funds by hosting Hawaiian luaus.

"People said we couldn't do it, but we buried two 400-pound pigs! It was a massive success. I'm from Hawaii and we did luaus there, so I knew how to build them. We set up a huge tent and fire on the property that is now the new parking lot near the freeway, and 800 people attended the first luau (the next one brought 1200). At the first luau, we were surprised when three or four fire trucks arrived! The firefighters said even over in Campbell people saw the smoke from San Tomas Expressway and thought the whole place was burning down. It was all safe, though.

"We didn't build the Family Learning Center and Pilgrimage Hall for dances or for parties. It was for spiritual use. The hall was built for families to get together, for pilgrimages to be made to the Shrine, for education in the faith, and for the bookstore to help people grow in holiness. There's the video projector for people to go in and watch movies as a family. Fr. Sweeny was insistent on supporting the family to pray together and play together.

"One of the retired priests at Our Lady of Peace was Fr. Edward Warren. He was Fr. Sweeny's spiritual director and instrumental in helping to put up the Shrine. Fr. Warren worked tirelessly for Our

The Caruso family and Fr. Sweeny celebrate Joseph Caruso's baptism in 2002.

Lady of Peace. He was the holiest man I ever met. Fr. Warren's prayer life, the real dedication to the faith on the daily basis, made him holy. He lived in Los Gatos, so Manny Nino and I would go over there and Fr. Warren would invite us in for dinner. Fr. Warren always wore his Roman collar and was proud and humbled to be a priest. He'd go around serving people, picking up their plates, serving, serving, and serving. Then we'd leave and do the Enthronements of the Sacred Heart and have Mass at peoples' homes. That was an important ministry for all of us.

"Every Sunday morning, Fr. Warren left home at 6 a.m. to drive to Los Altos Hills from his place way off in Los Gatos to say Mass for the Poor Clare nuns. He told us every time he drove by our house (because we lived in Los Altos Hills on his way to the convent) he blessed himself and said a Hail Mary for our family. So to me, knowing we had those prayers of Fr. Sweeny and Fr. Warren, that's what got us through. They gave us the strength first in our marriage, then for the family, and third for the business. With all the different things we've got to go through, in raising the kids and our first and foremost priority is to raise them with faith, and how do we raise them? Do we trust ourselves? No, we trust in God. God gave us the instruments: he gave us Fr. Sweeny and Fr. Warren to teach us. We had them over to the house a lot, they would have Mass, give sermons, teach the kids, talk about the rosary, and just live an example of true holiness."

Fr. Ray Devlin [†]
Served at Our Lady of Peace from 1972 - 2011

"Sr. Mary Jean helped at Our Lady of Peace for twenty-five years as a director for the Shrine. She arranged the schedules for the

The Mark and Ellie Powers family celebrates Christmas with Fr. Sweeny.

perpetual adoration groups who spent an hour a day in adoration (in the church), rotating for the night and day perpetual adoration. Sister made her own hour of adoration at 3:30 a.m. every morning and would attend the 6 a.m. Mass. In the morning hours, she taught children, then visited the sick or performed other charitable works in the afternoon. Sister's many friends informed her of the serious sick and those in need of the sacraments, and she always promptly went to visit them."

Willie Lapus
Parishioner 1983 - Present

"Fr. Sweeny was the inspiration for the Juan Diego Society when it started in 1986. My wife got involved in the early 1990s and I was pulled in because of her. From what I understand, there was a group of parishioners who thought of the idea and I'm sure Fr. Sweeny was the spirit behind it because whenever we had a financial problem we'd go to Fr. Sweeny and he'd ask, 'How much do you need?' Not only that, he signed our charter in June of 1986, just two months after the Juan Diego Society was founded. It shows he was involved right from the very beginning.

"The Juan Diego Society was founded as a crisis pregnancy center to help women keep their babies and prevent abortion. We are not a medical center, but work with Real Options to provide the medical. We do a lot of training, education, and encouraging people to give life. We share the parking lot with Planned Parenthood, so we have people out there volunteering as sidewalk counselors pray and intercept young women to encourage them not to abort their babies. We also offer training in Spanish to help make the Hispanic community aware, because they have been targeted by Planned

Parenthood.

"We are available in any way we can encourage expectant mothers. Recently, we were in contact with a mother from Sacramento by text and were able to help her. Another time we were in touch with a Chinese woman and helped her; now whenever we have a client who needs to speak Chinese, that woman is on call to help her. Many of the mothers we help do return to help others. They also refer friends to us. We are available to talk 24-hours a day, seven days a week, in various languages.

"Our Lady of Peace is like our home. Many times we have a woman who would like to go to confession and we always recommend her to come here and talk to the priest. We have couples who are unmarried and living together, and we recommend they come to have their situation regularized and get married. Yes, Our Lady of Peace has always been our source of spiritual and financial help. And volunteers! I'm a volunteer, I'm a parishioner here. A lot of people who help us are from Our Lady of Peace.

"The pastor allows us to have a Juan Diego Sunday when we speak at Mass and tell the parishioners what we are doing. If we need, they allow us to do a second collection. If not, they allow us a table outside. We do that every one to two years.

"In 2006, I became the director of the Juan Diego Society. Robert, the previous director, got sick in September of 2005. I was a board member and we were trying to keep the doors open, so I started opening the office. After a couple of months of keeping the doors open, I agreed to be the acting Director until we found someone else. I've been there ever since! It is a full time job, so I let my work as a realtor go.

"We have saved about 820 babies over the years and helped over 11,000 families with diapers, baby supplies, housing, and so on. We have counseled about 1,000 abortion-bound women and of those women over 820 have chosen life for their babies. Yet at Juan Diego we are just the messenger. We don't take credit for saving any babies. We try to be the faithful mouthpiece of our Blessed Mother: to be her heart, her arms, and her lips and convey her message. The presence of the Blessed Mother is very important at Juan Diego. Her intercession supports us and has caused mothers to change their mind. Here is a story of three mothers that demonstrates this:

"Five years ago, Anna and her 18-year old daughter, Marie, arrived at the center late on a Thursday afternoon. Both were anxious and troubled. Anna explained that her daughter, Marie, was two months pregnant and wanted an abortion.

"Upon entering our counseling room, all was not well between mother and daughter. Anna sat on the left side of the sofa while Marie sat as far right as possible. Neither would look at each other directly. I told Marie that she was lucky to have a mother who was willing to give her all the support she needed so she could keep her baby, and that the Juan Diego Center would also be there to assist her in any way possible. After talking for about twenty minutes, Marie still remained unmoved and resolute on having an abortion. Since all my arguments were to no avail, I asked Marie if she would be willing to speak with our head counselor, Patsy.

"While Patsy and Marie spoke over the phone, Anna and I went to pray in our little chapel. There, Anna consecrated her unborn grandchild to Our Lady.

"Sensing that the conversation with Patsy was ending, Anna and I returned to the counseling room. I asked Marie, 'Have you changed your mind about aborting your baby?' She answered, 'Not really.' 'Tell me,' I asked, 'Why do you really want to abort your child?' Marie flippantly answered, 'I do not want to get fat.' Stunned by her reply, I was at a loss for words.

"All of a sudden, Anna stood up and looked at her daughter and with a voice choked with emotion, said 'Eighteen years ago, I came here, pregnant, and decided to give *you* life. Can you not find it in your heart to give life to my grandchild?' Marie broke into tears. Anna cried. I cried.

"Who inspired Anna to say those words? I can guess. At the beginning, I mentioned that there were three mothers involved: Anna the grandmother, Marie the new mother and, the third, Our Blessed Mother. It was she who inspired the words that saved Anna's grandchild. She was with us that fateful afternoon. Marie and her little boy still drop in to visit us from time to time."

Sr. Mary Jean Kula [†]
Parish Staff Member 1975 - 2007

"Fr. Joe Devlin is a hero, a missionary on fire for the salvation of souls. Nothing matters but souls.

"A man had been away from God since the age of thirteen (when) his sister died and he became so bitter he declared he was an atheist. His first wife, now divorced, phoned me and said, 'Please get a priest... and go to him.' I told Fr. Joe and he said, 'Let's go to the hospital right now.' I warned him that we might be thrown out.

"[At the hospital], Father asked him if he would like to be a Catholic, and he said, 'Yes, I want that.' His second wife, in the corner of the room, was shocked.

"Father [heard his confession], anointed him, and then asked him if he would like to receive the Body and Blood of Jesus Christ and if he believed it was Christ. He said, 'Yes, I would like that.' However, his wife said, 'No, he can't have anything by mouth.' The man looked at his wife and at us, and he was very disappointed. Then the nurse said he could receive Communion. The man was so happy, he said, 'Now I'm a Catholic,' and smiled so peacefully. I asked him where he wanted the religious articles we gave him. He pointed to his chest, so we placed them on his chest. All this occurred on December 5, 1995, and he passed away on December 7, 1995. Saved on his deathbed. No one would do what Fr. Joe did. He was fearless when it came to saving souls."

Gloria Relloma
Parishioner 1985 - Present

"When I am here at Our Lady of Peace, I can feel the presence of God and that I really am closer to Him. It is the Blessed Sacrament that is exposed on the altar. The statue of Our Lady draws many people here. Fr. Sweeny wanted to have her facing the freeway to welcome everyone, and it is working. Catholics and non-Catholics, young and old, they come. Maybe they don't go inside the church, and maybe eventually they will, but they stay around. It's hard to explain, but I believe they come in response to the invitation of the Blessed Mother in the extension of her arms. There is a warmth in the statue that draws them here. The local newspaper once published a photo of a man kneeling in front of the statue, at the angle showing her hands reaching out to him. According to the newspaper, he was talking to her and she was responding.

"This place is a house of refuge. Once, I was praying and said, 'Lord, I want to help you carry the Cross.' A few months later, I was diagnosed with cancer. I asked God, 'Why?' There was never anyone with cancer in my family. I knelt before the Blessed Sacrament and told Our Lord, 'I'm scared.' When you are told you have cancer, you think, 'Oh, I'm going to die.' Yet I had a place to go and here felt

Fr. Joe Devlin celebrates a baptism in 1997.

both Our Lord and Our Blessed Mother saying, 'I am here.' At the Shrine, I found peace. My prayer time reduced my fear to the point where I could accept my illness and go forward. Eventually I thought, 'Maybe God is inviting me to help carry His Cross.'

"After surgery, I knelt before Our Lord in the Blessed Sacrament and asked him, 'Please help me with my radiation and make it the radiation of your love.' From my experience, adoration is a radiation of Jesus Himself, God Himself, with love for each of us.

"I stop by the parish every evening, but not always for a full hour of adoration. My adoration time is on Saturday morning from 1 a.m. to 6 a.m. Eucharist adoration gives me peace and strength, even physical strength. At seventy years of age, I work full-time and still have energy to help at the parish with activities like the Simbang Gabi devotion. It is nine days long and begins at 5 a.m. We volunteers arrive at 3 a.m. to prepare for the Mass. The Mass is over at 6 or 6:30 a.m., and then we host a reception. That's for nine days, and I still go to work. Sometimes my sisters ask me, 'Are you taking care of yourself, doing all these activities?' Adoration gives me mental, spiritual, and even physical strength. I could not live the life I lead without the strength I receive from the Blessed Sacrament. If I don't come here, for whatever reason, my day is not complete. I do everything I can to come—even for two minutes—to check in with Our Lord. Jesus is waiting.

"Some people travel to Fatima, Portugal or to Lourdes, France to visit the shrines where our Blessed Mother appeared and miracles happened. But Jesus is here! We have that miracle here at Our Lady of Peace. Jesus is here body and soul, and in the Blessed Sacrament He is waiting for all of us, personally.

"There would be times when I would be crying during adoration, yet afterwards felt greatly relieved. I have observed people at adoration who need that same consolation. Once, in the middle of the night, a teenage girl was sobbing in the back of the church. I went to see her and asked, 'How can I help you?' She didn't tell me exactly what was wrong, but she said, 'I'm really, really sad and I don't know what else to do.' So I said, 'Okay, take this rosary.' I showed her how to pray the rosary and said, 'Just keep praying. Even if you don't finish it, that's fine.' Before she left, she stopped crying and gave me a hug and said, 'Thank you.'

"Another time there was a man who said he came because he was going to jail the next day. He said, 'I want to find something, but I don't know what it is.' I gave him some prayer books we had in the church and said, 'When you go to jail, spend your time praying.' He said, 'Okay, thank you. I'm going to be okay.'

Frank Achondoa
Parishioner 1996 - Present

"I was a friend to Fr. Joe Devlin and then became a friend of Fr. Ray Devlin. To Fr. Ray, his brother, Joe, was a saint. Fr. Ray was so loyal to Fr. Joe. He was eight years younger than Fr. Joe and held him in high esteem. When Fr. Joe was in Vietnam, it was Fr. Ray who did the fundraising here in the United States to support his mission.

"When Fr. Joe died, Fr. Ray took over his role at Our Lady of Peace. Fr. Sweeny asked him to stay at the rectory because he was alone; Fr. Shichida had also died. So Fr. Ray lived at Our Lady of Peace and spent weekends with the Jesuits. He said the 6 a.m. Mass daily and spent many hours in the confessional.

"Fr. Ray also took over Fr. Joe's visits to the sick. Sr. Jean would drive him to sick calls, but when she wasn't available she would call me when Fr. Ray needed a ride. When Sr. Jean died, I was his primary driver. He would often treat me to lunch or an afternoon snack at the

Hometown Buffet.

"Fr. Ray was tough in many ways. We used to call him 'Cowboy' because he was like a rugged cowboy. He was a very decent priest and very funny in his sermons. He never needed a microphone because his voice boomed. He was full of humor.

"There was a Vietnam veteran who would come into the church with his dog on Sundays at 9 a.m., just because he liked to hear Fr. Ray speak. He was not Catholic. He'd sell San Jose *Mercury News* papers after Mass. He was not well, and a year before he died he asked to become Catholic. I went to the Veterans Hospital in Palo Alto with Fr. Ray to baptize him. Fr. Ray asked me to be his confirmation sponsor because I was there, and he was baptized, confirmed, and received reconciliation and the Holy Eucharist all in one day. Fr. Ray died on December 12, 2011, and the man died soon after."

Lorna Achondoa
Parishioner 1996 - Present

"Fr. Ray spent hours in the confessional and became a popular confessor. Long lines would form outside his confessional and he would not stop to eat. When we realized he wasn't eating well, we made it a point for someone to take him out to eat regularly. There were times he would hear confession before the noon Mass, so Frank would give him a hamburger in the confessional and he would keep going. That's how we got him to eat. One year, he counted 15,000 confessions. That's a lot! And there were always two priests in the confessionals!"

Fr. Ray Devlin.

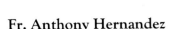

Fr. Anthony Hernandez
Religious Education Director and/or Instructor 1980 - Present
Religious Vocation from Our Lady of Peace

"Our Lady of Peace did play a part in my call to the priesthood. I was raised at St. Cyprian in Sunnyvale and was an altar boy there. In late high school, I came here and helped serve. When my grandmother's funeral was here, I served that Mass. The funny thing about it, however, is that I didn't become a Roman Catholic priest! My vocation, even though I was nourished here, did not flow into a Roman Catholic vocation. Working at Our Lady of Peace, this became the place where I worked and where I prayed. Sometimes I needed to get away, and on a Sunday I might attend Mass at another parish where no one knew me and could approach me to work on Sunday.

"I noticed 'Eastern churches' listed in the phone book. I knew about Eastern churches but had never attended one, so I visited and I fell in love with the liturgy and began attending every Sunday. If I had responsibilities at Our Lady of Peace on Sundays, I started moving those to Saturday so I was free to attend the Eastern church on Sunday. So I was carrying on at Our Lady of Peace but I was also starting to develop a new way of experiencing Catholic tradition.

"The introduction to the Liturgy of the Hours was formative for me. When we started hosting the Catholic Faith Formation classes, a group of us would go to the old cry room and sing vespers together after class.

"I always toyed with the idea of a possible vocation, but for a long time I thought I was just going to become a deacon. One day when I was at the Divine Liturgy, there was a guest there who was a deacon and he was serving with the priest. The priest said, 'The liturgy is more complete when you have a deacon serving.' In the Eastern church, the deacon does a lot. Then he said, 'Maybe God is calling someone here to be a deacon?' The priest's words resonated with me the whole week. The next Sunday the deacon was there visiting again, and I spoke with him. I told him, 'I've been thinking about this all week. It sounds crazy, because I'm a Roman Catholic.' He replied, 'Maybe God's still calling you. Next month Bishop George Kuzma will be visiting. Maybe you can speak with him?' The bishop told me there were no programs for the deaconate. So I said, 'Well, what if I went to the seminary?' And that's how things developed. I started attending the seminary in Pittsburgh, Pennsylvania.

"Our Lady of Peace nourished my liturgical life. I always appreciated liturgy that is expressive and traditional. That's what you get at Our Lady of Peace: a sense of tradition, not just something that belongs to now but something that has been passed on to us. I was already oriented in that way, so when I saw the Eastern Church I saw something that was, to me, even more in that direction.

"In 1999, I returned to work for Our Lady of Peace and was ordained a year and a half later. Once I became a priest, I needed to dedicate myself full-time to St. Basil the Great in Los Gatos yet I still continued teaching adult education at Our Lady of Peace."

Mariano & Maria Quinata
Parishioners 1969 - Present

"When we moved to the area, we'd go to the Catholic Mass at Moffett Field. They told us we had to go to either St. Martin or St. Lawrence. But Our Lady of Peace was closer for us. We chose Our Lady of Peace as our parish home because it offered the comfort of a

Fr. Anthony Hernandez stands between his mother and aunt as they celebrate his ordination to the priesthood in 2000.

place to pray. The people were more down to earth.

"We came here with four children: three sons and one daughter. Our three sons also helped as altar servers through high school. As the years progressed, our children married and moved away. We remained here because we feel this is where God wants us to be.

"One priest who made an impression on us was Fr. Francis Shichida. He was probably a saint. When we needed Mass said in a home for a family member who was sick or dying, he never refused. At that time you couldn't get a priest to offer a home Mass. Fr. Shichida always said, 'Let me check my book,' and he never refused. He also sang in the choir with us.

"At one point, Fr. Shichida became very ill and left active ministry. He sent for us and we started visiting him. We didn't know he suffered from pancreatic cancer. He was a very private person.

"Bishop DuMaine visited Fr. Shichida and asked him, 'Fr. Francis, where do you want to go for your last wish?' Fr. Shichida said, 'I would like to go back to Lourdes one more time.' We were sitting right there listening and Bishop DuMaine said, 'Okay. You pray for us sinners when you get to Lourdes.' Fr. Shichida asked Mariano and I if we would accompany him.

"Fr. Shichida was on oxygen and traveled on a stretcher. I was a hairdresser at the time. When we decided to go take him, I told all my customers that we would be away for at least two weeks. Fr. Shichida wanted to stay in Lourdes for one week. Mariano was already retired from the Air Force and was working part time for Safeway. So we scheduled ourselves to be with him and purchased tickets.

"While we were in Lourdes, it was very quiet. There was no television, just radios and telephones. The first two days, Fr. Shichida was okay. He joined the other priests to say Mass from his gurney, and he was singing! The third day, Fr. Shichida stayed in bed. Then on the fourth day, Fr. Shichida was in very poor condition. The nurse who took care of him, Jeannie, was looking at Fr. Shichida and drew what she saw: the face of the suffering Christ. (She was from England, and took care of him day and night. Priests, doctors, and nurses come from around the world to work there.) The next morning, August 31, 1995, he died. We believe Fr. Shichida knew he would die in Lourdes.

"We had his body transported back to San Francisco and his funeral service was held immediately. He was a very holy man."

Ken Kietzman
Visitor

"Midnight Mass, Christmas 1999, was the beginning of the Jubilee Year for the Church. Our Lady of Peace Church was packed. There were many new faces of people who were not usually churchgoers. The lectors read the scriptures and the choir scrambled to lead the congregation in singing the carols. The entrance hymn, *Adeste Fideles*, began as the priests, acolytes, and altar boys advanced toward the altar. The venerable old hymn concluded and all eyes were fixed at the center where a humble, unassuming man of medium stature began with, 'In the name of the Father, and the Son, and the Holy Spirit.'

"It struck me then how Fr. Sweeny truly believed in his Lord. This assembly wasn't a show time or merely a social gathering, but the Holy Sacrifice of the Mass.

"Through his profound belief and trust in Our Lord and Blessed Mother, Fr. Sweeny has converted thousands of us to understand the deeper meaning of Christmas and to become more ardent followers of Jesus Christ."

Fr. Shichida, far right, smiles at a Mass celebration honoring Mary's birthday in the early 1990s. On August 31, 1995, Fr. Shichida passed away during a pilgrimage trip to Lourdes, France.

Fr. John Sweeny [†]

Pastor of Our Lady of Peace Church & Shrine 1969 - 2002

Excerpt from His 1998 Televised Interview with Mother Angelica
on the Eternal Word Television Network (EWTN)

"My favorite prayer is, 'Dear Lord, make me at this moment just what you intended I should be when you created me. I want to be just what you intended. You had a purpose in creating me. You knew my individuality. Let me be exactly what you intended I should be at this moment.' When I say that, my security is in the efficacy of that prayer. Our Lord says, 'Come to me all you who labor and are heavily burdened and I *will* refresh you.' (Matthew 11:28) It's not 'maybe.'

"[After] completing a Family Learning Center and a Pilgrimage Hall, I hope to develop a program where mother and father and children can come down once a week or more, and together with other mothers, fathers, and children, learn the rights and the wrongs, the do's and the don'ts of living: natural and supernatural. The family unit—the basic unit of society—is the family, not the individual. When this whole unit is working together with the same principles, not in conflict but mother, dad, and children, ... then they can cooperate without attrition, and then we can start building back the whole society. And get people to heaven! I mean, that's the bottom line.

"The family is God-made. God made the family. And so I want to train the whole family... That's what I hope to do in our Center."

"I couldn't recommend anything more efficacious for a happy family than the daily rosary. Give it a priority. Don't make it too long—for the little youngsters they could have a couple of decades—but as they get a little bit older say the whole thing and that's all. It's a bond with Our Lady, [she] promised that. She said to pray the rosary every day for peace. Do we do that? The rosary saved Christian Europe, and we forget that it was on the Feast of Our Lady of the Rosary. We view all the history; history is where you'll find the natural foundation for your faith. You'll see that. And don't be surprised at scandals or weakness of human beings. Weakness was overcome by living the Faith. Read the lives of the saints. But the rosary, yes. It's still no question.

"My judgment is, as much as we talk about prayer, we don't begin to pray enough. Compared to the amount of time we put forth watching television, or listening to the radio, or what it would be. How much time do we actually give to prayer daily? It has to be daily prayer. *Daily.* If you want to live, you have to breathe so many times a minute. If you want to live spiritually, you have to say your prayers every day, because that one day you miss you're all off guard. Prayer works. When I came to Our Lady of Peace Church, I didn't have anything but a prayer."

*Fr. Sweeny places the parish's collective prayers into the
Immaculate Heart of Mary.*

285

Pray with great confidence, with confidence based
upon the goodness and infinite generosity
of God and upon the promises of Jesus Christ.
God is a spring of living water which flows
unceasingly into the hearts of those who pray.

St. Louis de Montfort

CHAPTER 7
2000s

Always Forward

Always forward, never back, for the love of God.

St. Junipero Serra

As the world over anticipated the new millennium, Fr. Sweeny and his staff, retired priests, and volunteers pressed forward with one vision. In a letter addressed to the parish, Father explained, "The most important object of our life upon this earth is to live in the state of grace that we can die ready for heaven, and lead (by our prayers and actions) as many people as possible to do the same."

Pope John Paul II acknowledged Fr. Sweeny's years of exemplary service to the local Church in early 2002 when he formally recognized Fr. Sweeny as a Prelate of Honor. With this recognition came the new title, Monsignor Sweeny. Soon after, his bishop made another announcement that led to a major change in Monsignor Sweeny's priestly ministry: retirement.

Fr. Sweeny, far right, concelebrates Mass with Pope John Paul II in Rome.

TIME OF TRANSITION

In 1999 when Bishop Pierre DuMaine retired as Bishop of San Jose, Bishop Patrick J. McGrath was named his successor. In January of 2002, Bishop McGrath asked Monsignor Sweeny to retire. Though this was to be expected due to Monsignor Sweeny's age, the request stunned and upset much of the parish community. As Bishop McGrath explained to the San Jose *Mercury News* on March 15, 2002, "I'm not out to destroy their world, now or ever. Father Sweeny is the most wonderful priest that has ever lived, he really is. I love John. And people don't want to lose him, and I understand that." Bishop McGrath went on to explain his concern for Monsignor Sweeny's age and health issues prompted his decision.

Some feared a new pastor would alter the style of traditional worship that drew them to Our Lady of Peace Church. For 32 years, they had relied on the steady leadership of one man. In response to their concerns, Monsignor Sweeny simply asked his congregation to "...pray the rosary (5 decades) every day that you may receive a pastor who will help you and your family to keep and grow in holiness until He calls you to Himself." Next, he offered his usual assurance: "Don't worry. God will take care of us."

Bishop McGrath invited the Institute of the Incarnate Word (IVE) religious order of priests to assume leadership and ministry at Our Lady of Peace. They accepted and, in June of 2002, Fr. Walter Mallo, IVE, was established as the new pastor. Shortly after his arrival, the IVE sent additional priests to assist him. In 2004, the IVE's female branch, the Servants of the Lord and the Virgin of Matará (SSVM), brought religious sisters to work at the parish. The IVE priests and the SSVM sisters are a religious family founded to staff parishes and mission outposts worldwide. Their vows of poverty, chastity, obedience, and slavery to Mary so complement the spirituality already established by Monsignor Sweeny, they have

Fr. Walter Mallo, IVE, celebrates his first Mass as new Pastor of Our Lady of Peace Church and Shrine in June of 2002. He is joined by Monsignor John Sweeny and Fr. Gustavo Nieto, IVE, Provincial Superior at the time.

harmoniously upheld and furthered his long-term vision for the Shrine.

FINAL FAREWELLS

When he retired from Our Lady of Peace and active ministry, Monsignor Sweeny served first at St. Frances Cabrini Church in San Jose and later at St. Francis of Assisi Church in East Palo Alto. As his health failed and a terminal lung condition worsened, he spent the last year of his life in the peace of "the ranch," his family home in Calaveritas. Friends, family, and Our Lady of Peace parishioners continued to both visit and care for him. He welcomed them in conversation and prayer, offering Mass in his simple living room where walls of cracking antique wallpaper and photos of generations gave tribute to his spiritually rich family heritage. Diane Murray, Monsignor Sweeny's long-time devoted assistant, voluntarily cared for him until he entered eternal life on March 7, 2006. Monsignor Sweeny's funeral Mass was held at Our Lady of Peace Church and Shrine and his burial at Gate of Heaven Cemetery in Los Altos.

Just one year later, the parish mourned the passing of Fr. Edward V. Warren, S.J. on June 22, 2007. On September 25, 2009, Fr. John Coghlan passed away. Fr. Ray Devlin, S.J., who published his brother Joe's life story in 2001, entered eternal life on December 6, 2011. These holy priests dedicated the decades of their retirement to the people of Our Lady of Peace. The combined confessions they heard numbered in the tens of thousands. Many have testified the prayers, spiritual guidance, and encouragement offered by these men influenced the course of their lives and directed their families toward living more fully in Christ.

SPRING FOLLOWS WINTER

The early 2000s was a time of much change for the parish. After decades of consistent leadership, the transition to a new pastor provided an opportunity for all to exercise patience and flexibility.

The office structure also underwent major changes. Financial aspects of the parish in those early years were very lean and required the most difficult decision to reduce parish staff. The parish office migrated from floppy disks to the "cloud," opened a library, and welcomed more and more major faith-building events at the Family Learning Center. These transitions were hallmarked by creative solutions and much patience!

In 2004, Fr. Mallo designated the old rectory as a convent and planned to make adjustments to the Family Learning Center to house Sr. Mary Jean's educational programs. Ultimately, Sr. Mary Jean moved her classes to an off-campus location but continued to live at Our Lady of Peace. After a battle with cancer, she passed away on July 22, 2007. For thirty years Sr. Mary Jean was an active apostle at Our Lady of Peace, taking middle-of-the-night shifts at adoration, teaching the children, and tirelessly visiting the sick. Two hundred of her previous students were among the 1,200 people who attended her funeral Mass.

In time, the parish began to experience a new springtime. As interest in spiritual and family programs mounted, the IVE Third Order was established in 2003, more IVE priests and Sisters came to assist parish programs, vocations to the religious life continued to spring forth from Our Lady of Peace, the parish benefitted from the ongoing contributions of local priests—still including Fr. Michael Pintacura and Fr. William Stout—and the staff and parishioners faithfully supported the Church's dedication to the greater glory of God and the salvation of souls.

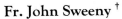

Fr. John Sweeny [†]
Pastor of Our Lady of Peace Church & Shrine 1969 – 2002
Letter Dated January 23, 2002

"Dear Friends and Parishioners of Our Lady of Peace Parish:

"In my 32 years as Pastor of Our Lady of Peace Parish, I have never seen more people at Mass for the New Year than this year of January 1, 2002.

"I was particularly pleased to see the church nearly filled at the 11:00 p.m. prayer vigil and filled to capacity at midnight for the first Mass of the New Year.

"The most important object of our life upon this earth is to live in the state of grace that we can die ready for heaven, and lead (by our prayers and actions) as many people as possible to do the same.

"By church law when a pastor reaches the age of 75 he must submit, at the Bishop's request, his resignation as pastor.

"A little over two years ago at the bishop's request I submitted my resignation; but since he did not accept it I have continued on as pastor to the present time.

"Now Bishop McGrath has requested that I submit another letter of resignation as pastor, which I have done, and he has accepted it.

"Therefore within six months or less you will have a new pastor. Our bishop has kindly allowed me to stay here until June.

"But for the most important part of this letter; and the biggest favor you could do me.

"From the time you receive this letter and until the assignment of the new pastor, pray the rosary (five decades) every day that you may receive a pastor who will help you and your family to keep and grow in holiness until He calls you to Himself.

"When I was about ten years old, my father became critically ill with a strep throat, temperature 105 degrees. We called two doctors and a priest. After they had left I had to get an answer from my father. 'Dad', I said, 'after all the prayers we have said (Dad led us in the family rosary ever night) is God going to let this happen to us?' My father opened his eyes and said with the greatest confidence: 'Don't worry, Jackie, God will take care of us.' Dad lived until he was 89.

"So with the confidence I inherited from my Father, I say to you my parishioners, who are praying the rosary daily for a pastor who will help you and your family keep and grow in holiness until He calls you to Himself, 'Don't worry, God will take care of us.'

"There is one more devotion I recommend to you as a way to remain secure in your faith: The Devotion of the Five First Saturdays (which are exactly the number remaining until June 30th). To quote Sister Lucia in her statement about Our Lady's instruction to her: 'Those who wish to practice this devotion should go to Confession and receive Holy Communion, say five decades of the rosary, and keep Our Lady company for one quarter of an hour on the first Saturday of each month for five consecutive months. While saying the rosary it is necessary to meditate on the mysteries of the rosary. All these acts are to be performed with the intention of making reparation for the offenses committed against Our Heavenly Mother.' When Lucia questioned Our Lady if it was acceptable to go to Confession on another day Our Lady replied in the affirmative, as long as the communicant was in the state of grace.

"Our Lady promised to those who practice this devotion many graces during their lifetime and the gift of final perseverance.

"Let us all pray together for the courage and wisdom to stay faithful and to be at peace."

Sal Caruso
Parishioner 1990 - Present

"Toward the end of the building of the Family Learning Center, Monsignor Sweeny said, 'I want you to meet someone.' It was just weeks before the building was scheduled to open. He wanted me to meet the two Institute of the Incarnate Word (IVE) priests who had come to visit: Fr. Mallo and Fr. Rolando. They were just visiting Monsignor Sweeny, there was no knowledge the IVE would be here, and it was years before Monsignor Sweeny retired. We were standing right outside the Family Learning Center as he introduced me to them. As soon as they walked away, Monsignor Sweeny turned to me and said, 'Sal, when my time comes, those are the types of priests who need to come here. Those are real men.' He said it in such a way that it seemed prophetic, almost like he knew something—or desired something—so deeply. It was very moving to me at the time, yet, at that time Monsignor Sweeny was in his heyday. It was many years before he died.

"Years later when the selection process [for a new pastor] came, the thought had completely vanished from my mind. I didn't know the process, nor did I have any connection to make any influence anyway. Suddenly, at Mass I heard it announced that the IVE was going to come to our parish and take over leadership. I said, 'Of course! That's exactly what Monsignor Sweeny said.' It was only then I remembered they were the ones who should be here. Monsignor Sweeny didn't have any influence on Bishop McGrath's choice for leadership, but the Holy Spirit did. The Holy Spirit worked through him and brought us the priests Monsignor Sweeny originally wanted here. It was beautiful, really, and said to me that as long as whoever is in our church allows the Holy Spirit to influence them, God's will occurs; we are cooperating with God's will.

"What struck me is how God weaves in our lives. When it was announced that Monsignor Sweeny was asked to retire, we were pretty heartbroken. All of us. We just never thought of this parish without him. Obviously we knew that would occur someday, but didn't expect it at that time. Now we see how God took care of the parish at that time with what seemed to be an almost prophetic response by Monsignor Sweeny himself saying, 'When my time comes, men like this need to be here. They love Our Blessed Mother like I do and they will continue on.' The fact that actually came to pass against seemingly all odds was beautiful. I guess maybe because he had that strong trust that was put in him by his Dad, trusting in Divine Providence: Don't worry, it will work out just fine. Don't be afraid.

"Sometimes God wills a different leadership and a different person, and we have to trust that's the will of God and will be for a greater good because He loves us. That was the quiet confidence that Monsignor Sweeny emitted from himself all the time. He allowed people to come, to offer their simple talents, their simple gifts whatever they were, and work alongside him. That spirit of inclusivity that he had in a real way was refreshing, enlightening, and inspiring. He basically brought out the best in everyone, both in physical duty and spiritual gifts. He was a saint of a man.

"Our family feels that going to Our Lady of Peace is really like coming home. The homilies are very direct and honest. They follow the letter and intent of the gospels in a very beautiful way. Having the IVE priests and Sisters here is a continuation of what Monsignor Sweeny started. The Sisters have added a very warm, caring dimension that was here, but they've allowed it to blossom even further and grown it more. They've brought us the Children's Oratory in summertime, the seemingly infinite levels of catechism classes, preparation for First Communion, Confirmation, and so on. All of their discipline and faithfulness has allowed everything to be more.

"It's amazing looking back, though, that Monsignor Sweeny and three or four others basically managed this entire large parish. This is a big parish. Now there's a much larger staff, many nuns, and many priests working hard—these people put a massive effort into what they do and they do it very well—and I just think those previous people did a similar work also, and Monsignor Sweeny always with a smile on his face, always attentive. Any time a parishioner needed him, he was available. He would make time. He was a true pastor. A pastor, leading his sheep, and being there for his flock in a very deep way. He never worried. Some priests need time away from their work, such as living off campus, but here their time belongs to the parish. This has been the hallmark of Our Lady of Peace with Monsignor Sweeny, those who helped him, the IVE...they belong to the flock. They are here: you can knock on the door and they answer. There really is an amazing sense of love and a desire to nurture. I think all of that is part of what we discovered when we first came here over 25 years ago: the availability of grace."

Fr. Walter Mallo, IVE
Pastor of Our Lady of Peace Church & Shrine 2002 - 2010

"As an IVE priest, I was assigned to St. Patrick Church in downtown San Jose from 1995 to 1998. That's when I discovered Our Lady of Peace. I had heard about the 24-hour adoration and was curious. Was it really open 24 hours? One day, I arrived at the airport after midnight so I drove to Our Lady of Peace and saw people

Fr. Joseph LoJacono, IVE, leads a rosary procession. The Monsignor John J.
Sweeny Family Learning Center and Pilgrimage Hall is in the background.
Fr. Joseph's ordination to the deaconate in 2008 was the first IVE
ordination celebrated at Our Lady of Peace.

praying. And I saw, 'It's true. It's open 24-hours.' The adoration drew me to Our Lady of Peace. Among many priests it is known as a good place for prayer because it is always open.

"Later, I was looking for a spiritual director and I met Monsignor Sweeny. I came regularly to meet with him. He was very straightforward. Even his confession was simple and brief. He listened, I'd have the sense that I was heard, and he gave very gentle and good advice. Confession was only three or four minutes, but like many others, I'd leave with the grace, the good advice, and the sense that I was heard. Spiritual direction was longer, maybe 40 minutes, but with the same clarity.

"Monsignor Sweeny insisted on growth, and emphasized to me that as a priest one has to be patient with people. He had a great devotion to our Blessed Mother and would say, 'Whatever you trust to our Blessed Mother, you are going to achieve it.'

"When I heard the IVE was invited to serve at Our Lady of Peace, I told them, 'This is a very special place,' and described it. Because I was familiar with the Shrine, I knew humanly speaking it was impossible to entrust this huge shrine to a religious order. But the IVE has a lot in common with Our Lady of Peace and Monsignor Sweeny. When Fr. Nieto told me I was coming here, I was very happy. I knew it was something big to manage, but I also knew there were wonderful people at Our Lady of Peace.

"The finances were difficult in the beginning. People were very generous but we had to make some adjustments and there were laws and regulations from the diocese. But people were very giving and we never had to worry, in the sense that God provides here in a generous way.

"Monsignor Sweeny was very generous himself. He used to give money to the poor from his personal account. I heard one case about a man asking for money to buy a car. Monsignor Sweeny gave the money. Years later, the man was back on his feet and well off, and he made a sizable donation to the church. He did so because Monsignor Sweeny helped him when he was down. The St. Vincent de Paul Society here at the parish continues this outreach.

"Another tradition Monsignor Sweeny started was to put the parish prayer intentions into Our Lady's Immaculate Heart in the statue. Every year for September 8 (the Nativity of Our Lady), we collect the intentions and then we place them in a box. Then we are lifted in a cherry picker to place them in the statue. Once, I went up to place the intentions in, and when I was done they couldn't bring me down!

"The pillars of this Shrine are the Blessed Mother, the Blessed Sacrament, and confession. In my first parish priest assignment in Brooklyn, the people didn't know what the confessional was for. Coming to Our Lady of Peace is just the opposite! They know about the sacrament and form long lines. This is a special place. It is a joy for the priests because it is the heart of ministry to be that steward of the Mercy of God. We see many conversions in the confessional, and also help people (outside of confession) with counseling and spiritual direction.

"So many people come here because it offers what is needed for people in the 21st century: prayer life, reconciliation, and the opportunity to be part of the Holy Mass every day. Our Lady of Peace is very unique because few parishes are open 24 hours. In daytime and even throughout the night, it's a place of constant prayer, and a place where the non-Catholic community has an opportunity to know the Catholic faith."

Fr. Walter Mallo, IVE, celebrates eighth grade graduation with home-educated student Luke Moran.

"Monsignor John J. Sweeny Pilgrimage Hall and Family Learning Center"
as renamed by Fr. Walter Mallo, IVE.

Fr. Gustavo Nieto, IVE
Pastor of Our Lady of Peace Church & Shrine 2013 - 2016

"I was the Provincial Superior for the IVE, living in New York, when we received the call from the Diocese of San Jose requesting the IVE to staff Our Lady of Peace Church and Shrine. I remember that call so clearly. I called my Superior General and told him about the request. He said, 'You know we don't have any more priests, and we have too many requests.' (Today there are more than 60 bishops with unfilled requests for the IVE to staff parishes; at that time there were fewer but the list was still long.) Regardless, I knew we couldn't say 'No' to Our Lady of Peace and that it was an exception to be considered.

"I told the General Superior what I knew about the Shrine, that we have always had a good relationship with the Bishop in San Jose, and about the very holy priest who was retiring. I believe he knew something about Monsignor Sweeny. We started to see what we could do, and found we could find the priests to go. After much consideration, Fr. Mallo was sent to Our Lady of Peace from his parish in Brooklyn. It is not easy for priests or their congregations when they are reassigned, so there is much to consider.

"Fr. Mallo and I traveled here together when he first came. Monsignor Sweeny met us. We talked for a while in the dining room. The rectory upstairs was practically empty, all ready for the IVE. Monsignor Sweeny had everything ready for us, the staff was established, and this was a great church. After meeting with Monsignor Sweeny, we met some people from the church and then we had Mass. Fr. Mallo told the people his personal story with Monsignor Sweeny and, at the end of his very brief homily, he said,

'I propose to rename the Family Learning Center as the Monsignor John Sweeny Family Learning Center.' Everyone clapped. It was a good beginning. I returned to New York and soon more IVE priests were assigned to Our Lady of Peace to assist Fr. Mallo.

"Everything was very providential about the IVE coming to Our Lady of Peace. I did not have familiarity with the parish, yet I believe we had a spiritual connection because of the blessed Eucharist, devotion to the magisterium of the church, and many such similar devotions. In the IVE, we all take the vows of chastity, poverty, and obedience. We also take a fourth vow of devotion to Our Lady according to St. Louis de Montfort. I didn't know there was a long-time devotion to St. Louis de Montfort at Our Lady of Peace until I arrived at the rectory here. For me, that was such an amazing connection for the IVE to Our Lady of Peace: because we in the IVE are doing the same thing as the people here at this parish.

"When we first came, I recall Fr. Mallo thinking out loud and wondering '...if we really know what we have taken over here.' What he meant was all the Shrine encompasses, it is a big job. We always try to find help but we try to keep three priests here permanently. We still have many others helping us. The people were very good to us: at the beginning there was some skepticism, but we've received good feedback from them and they are positive about the activities we have. We have strong attendance at events like the Walk for Life West Coast and devotions to the Blessed Mother and perpetual adoration of the Blessed Sacrament: those came from Monsignor Sweeny and are very strong here. So you see, on one hand it was a challenge for the IVE to come to Our Lady of Peace, but on the other hand it was easy. We already have so much in common. Today it is the largest parish our order staffs (there are 2200 families registered and many unregistered people who attend the church)."

304

Peter Evans
Parishioner 1999 - 2001

"My wife, Jennifer, and I were members of Our Lady of Peace in 1999 for a little over a year when we lived in the area. I remember Monsignor Sweeny being very authentically devout. He would challenge his congregation and explain the unabridged faith in a logical way. It was remarkable, too, how much the average parishioner revered him.

"We did not know Monsignor Sweeny well, but in 2002—a couple years after we moved away—my brother suffered a stroke and was in rehab for months at Valley Medical. Monsignor Sweeny dropped by to offer Mass in my brother's room with his family, at the request of a parishioner who also knew my brother. We were so amazed and impressed that he would take that much time for a complete stranger."

Suzanne Spence
Parishioner 1990 - Present

"There was one time when Steve and I went to talk to Fr. Warren because we were having probably some very ordinary marital tension. I felt Steve ought to do something in our family situation. Fr. Warren was very kind and he listened to us. He gave us wise council and he even gave us a couple of books to read that were his own books. Fr. Warren's advice to me was, 'There is no reason that you can't do this thing you want your husband to do. There's nothing stopping you from doing it.' I realized he was right! It was an empowering conversation. I had arrived with this well-crafted argument and was ready to say, 'My husband needs to do this.' At the end of the conversation, Fr. Warren looked at me and said, 'There's no reason you can't do it.' So that was really empowering. He closed our meeting by telling us that every evening we should say two prayers: One to St. Joseph and one to the Holy Spirit. From that day until now, we have said a prayer to the Holy Spirit every day. Our children also say the prayer. Recently, Steve found this prayer by St. Augustine, and our family prays:

Breathe in me, O Holy Spirit, that my thoughts may all be holy. Act in me, O Holy Spirit, that my work, too, may be holy. Draw my heart, O Holy Spirit, that I love but what is holy. Strengthen me, O Holy Spirit, to defend all that is holy. Guard me, then, O Holy Spirit, that I always may be holy. Amen.

"Fr. Warren didn't tell us anything earth-shattering or groundbreaking. He just took time for us. He also gave us wise council, was very affirming of me and our marriage, and gave our family a prayer habit we might not have otherwise had."

Sr. María de Los Angeles Garcías, SSVM
Religious Sister Serving at Our Lady of Peace 2003 - Present

"In 2003, I was in Brooklyn, New York, assisting at Saints Peter and Paul Church. We sisters work together with the IVE priests, and Fr. Mallo asked if the group of sisters and seminarians from the East Coast could come to provide a summer program. (We now call this program the Summer Oratory.) We Sisters were not established at Our Lady of Peace at the time; we considered the Oratory as more of a 'mission' because we always lead missions in the summer. I asked Fr. Mallo, 'How many kids do you expect to enroll?' He replied,

'Between 400 and 600.' I said, 'My goodness!' I would later become accustomed to such participation numbers from the people of Our Lady of Peace Church.

"I wasn't used to coordinating activities for so many students, but it was really exciting. About four sisters and five seminarians came in July. The religious education coordinators had taken care of all registrations. We hosted the Summer Oratory for three weeks for children ages 4-16. In my group of children ages 7 through 9, there were 80 students. We taught catechism, played games, and made crafts. It was very interesting for me because this group of children was very different than those I experienced on the East Coast. The children were very engaged. Every day we taught catechism, but one boy raised his hand and said, 'I thought this is supposed to be a Bible study camp!' This was a 7-year-old saying he wanted to study the Bible! I was really surprised because in most situations it was us giving the talk and somewhat 'feeding' the children. He taught me a lesson about the children in my group and the following day we had to change our dynamics to specifically incorporate using the Bible. I would later learn the yearning to grow deeply was a common request at Our Lady of Peace, from both children and adults. Our first Summer Oratory was a wonderful experience: the students had so much fun, but at the same time we learned much from them.

"Our role as Sisters is to work to complement the IVE priests. In the United States, we mostly serve in parishes and especially enjoy working with families and in education. We were soon called to serve full-time at Our Lady of Peace, and the first two Sisters arrived from New York with our Provincial Superior on August 28, 2004 (the feast of St. Augustine). Those first two sisters were Mother Ana and myself. Little by little, more Sisters arrived to help and today (in 2016) we have ten Sisters working at Our Lady of Peace.

"In the beginning, we did whatever we could to assist with the

CCD and RCIA programs. Margaret Sanchagrin coordinated these programs and we taught classes and assisted with the Christmas program. We were able to assist with the Spanish-speaking programs, especially preparing the adults for the sacraments. Mother Ana is a teacher and was very good at instructing and organizing. We taught on Tuesday, Wednesday, Thursday, and Saturday. My classes were Confirmation, First Communion, second grade, and third grade classes. In the beginning, we had about 500 students enrolled in catechism classes. In this current academic year, there are 860 students enrolled. We also started a home school support academy that began with five students and is now nearly 80 students. The parents are very involved, of course.

"I met Monsignor Sweeny briefly when I came here 2003. He was a wonderful, holy man. I also had the grace to meet and talk to his brother, Richard. When Monsignor Sweeny died in 2006, I attended his funeral Mass. It was really something. Before the Mass, however, was the constant line for the viewing. It never stopped! The church is open 24-hours and I believe the viewing may have gone all night. To attend the Mass itself was such a grace and a blessing to me: I thought, 'Here is a holy man and we can take from the fruits of his apostolate and his love for Mary.' There were so many priests concelebrating on the altar: rows and rows! At the end of the Mass it was raining hard but the priests went out in procession; it seems Monsignor Sweeny had asked to be taken to the statue. It was very, very special to witness that. We spent some time there at the statue, returned to the church, and went to the cemetery. At the cemetery people showed a mix of emotions: they were saying how they would miss Monsignor Sweeny, but it was also a joyful moment. One of the parishioners, Mark Powers, started to sing 'Danny Boy', an Irish song. It was a joyful experience, I felt we were saying goodbye to a saint. I think the Sisters and people who were there would agree with me that it was really beautiful.

"When we came, I had never seen parish life like at Our Lady of Peace. We saw it as a true blessing to be here. There are some important qualities that make Our Lady of Peace this way, and they were already in place: love for the Eucharist, the Fatima pilgrimages, and a yearning to grow closer to Christ. As a teacher, it made me go back to studying topics before I taught them, because participants wanted to learn more fully! They also encouraged me in my own formation. Here at Our Lady of Peace, people are asking and ready to learn more and to study more to deepen their faith. We've been able to help so many people because they are open for us to help them with formation. They make us feel so welcome. Even walking from the church to the convent people often approach us, 'Sister! Sister!' They make us feel as if we are part of their family. They know us by name or ask about us; this is a huge parish and you see many people, but at the same time there is a family spirit that is very particular to Our Lady of Peace.

"Lastly, I am also moved to see people kneeling at the foot of the statue of Our Lady. Some of them look like they are going to their Mother but some of them aren't; some of them are Buddhist or non-Christian and still the Mother is opening her arms to them and is there for them. It is beautiful to see."

Fr. Lawrence Goode
Assistant Pastor 1971 - 1978

"I was with Monsignor Sweeny the day he died. Fr. John Direen and I went out to visit him in Calaveritas. We prayed with him, said Mass, and sang. It was getting late so we decided we'd better start driving home because it was a narrow country road. Heading back,

Sister Angeles Garcías, SSVM, sings during an event in the Family Learning Center.

we were praying the rosary. There was a high fog blocking the sun. As we were driving along, all of a sudden the fog lifted and the sun came through, right over us and over the road. I said to Fr. John, 'I think God is telling us something.' I suspect that was when Monsignor Sweeny died.

"Monsignor Sweeny is one of my heroes. We have his picture in the office here at St. Francis of Assisi, and I often mention him to the people—that he was here at St. Francis of Assisi and what he stood for. He was a strong-minded priest. When he'd make up his mind to do something, he would accomplish it. Very few people have that ability as a diocesan priest because we have so many distractions, but he was able to have a vision and follow it through, step by step by step, and accomplish it. I think he did accomplish what he set out to do: to create a forthright expression of faith."

Richard Sweeny
Fr. John Sweeny's Youngest Brother

"The week my brother John died, there were six inches of powder snow at the ranch. That was very, very unusual, perhaps once every fifty years. He passed away in the bedroom there. His secretary from Our Lady of Peace, Diane Murray, took care of him. She ministered to him to his last breath. She had some experience in caring for the sick and went to work at Our Lady of Peace shortly after she lost her husband. She seemed to find it easy within herself to do what she had to do in all aspects of his final care, and served him with a notable grace."

Mark Powers

Parishioner 1986 - Present

"My life was changed by Fr. Sweeny because, first, when he arrived just as our son Joseph was dying and sat with us, that made a huge impact on us. Second, the family rosary: we just can't say how so many times Our Lady has protected us and we had no reason for the protection.

"Father taught us what was right and what was wrong, and he modeled how to teach that to our family. He was an example to our children. What a great model where there's a real man: he was a great guy and an athlete. All these boys want to be athletes, they want to be successful, and they want to be liked. Father had it all: he was a great athlete, he knew how to work with his hands, and he had a strong work ethic. But then as a guy sometimes the world says you're not supposed to be holy, you're not supposed to be praying and talking about God and our Blessed Mother. Father taught me that part of manliness as well. He spoke of loving the Eucharist, understanding it, receiving the sacraments, and going to confession. He gave us spiritual direction and lived the example of faith. I had that growing up from my grandfather and my Dad, actually, but Fr. Sweeny reinforced it. I learned the rosary from my grandmother and I always loved the rosary, but we weren't praying the rosary as a family until Father impressed that upon us. No question about it. That was big.

"Fr. Sweeny had everything that I believe a man stands for: starting with spirituality, then having a good work ethic and knowing how to work and to take care of people, and having that desire to serve God—to know Him, to love Him, and to serve Him—that's what Father did. He knew God. He loved God. And he served God. He was a very holy and faithful priest. His love and devotion to Our Lord and the Holy Eucharist, and to Our Lady with the Holy Rosary, was absolutely amazing. He continues to be completely inspiring to myself, Ellie, and our entire family."

Helen Hovland
Parishioner 1976 - Present

"Because of Our Lady of Peace, my life has been so rich with all of the help from the priests. When I come here in front of the Blessed Sacrament, I feel so much peace I can't stay away. I don't live in the neighborhood, but I come five days a week. It's a little taste of Heaven. That's how it has changed my life.

Paul Duquette
Parishioner 1998 - Present

"Fr. Warren heard my first confession. As I told him my very generic, 7-year-old kid sins, he listened. Then, he took the time to walk me through making a really good confession. As a little kid, confession can seem like a strange and scary thing, but Fr. Warren helped me to see it as something normal that I shouldn't be worried to do; it was not a chore. Because of Fr. Warren, I have never been scared or nervous to go to confession. He was just a really cool guy—I could tell he had been around and knew what was up. I think every young person should have a priest like that to make his first confession. Fr. Warren made me really understand that God still loves me no matter how I have sinned."

Anonymous Parishioner

"I heard that he could 'read souls' and that Fr. Warren was a 'priest's priest.' This was from one of the older parishioners of the *Divine Love Oratory* group which met in the Learning Center kitchen after the noon Mass on Tuesdays, for about ten years.

"About 20 years ago, I had learned what a *general confession* was: that I was to confess all my past sins to the best of my ability, and not only those since my last confession. The main goal is to turn a life of sin into one of devotion. It was Fr. Warren who heard my general confession.

"I approached him coming out of the sacristy, after Mass. I explained I had missed the regular confession time....

"In the sacristy, Fr. Warren was gentle. He stood by me, in front of the vestment drawers. Shoulder-to-shoulder we faced the shuttered window, under the crucifix. He listened to my hushed recital of childhood sins. He listened patiently as I continued through the sins of my youth and my adult life. Something happened as I recalled one serious sin. In that moment, one of Fr. Warren's hands jumped in a spastic jolt. I said nothing more and he said nothing.

"Then, he asked if I had any other sins to confess. He said I had made a good confession, and asked me to say an Act of Contrition. After giving me absolution and penance, Father said: 'You never have to confess these sins again.' I had never heard a priest say that before. I kept repeating in my mind: You never have to confess these sins again. Why did Father say this? He then gave me Holy Communion.

"His words were powerful. They instantly gave me faith and

Paul Duquette celebrates his first Sacrament of Reconciliation.

understanding of the power of confession. They helped me understand why the Catechism of the Catholic Church says that 'there are no limits to the mercy of God (CCC, #1864).'

"Fr. Warren's words have resonated with me to this day. Little-by-little over the years, I have deepened my understanding of the importance of preparing well for confession. That confession confers grace in proportion to how well we examined our conscience and how firm our purpose of amendment is. A well-prepared confession makes the reception of Holy Communion more fruitful. It all began with my general confession with Fr. Warren. I learned that when I forgive I should attempt to show the same mercy and compassion that Fr. Warren taught me."

Sr. Wisdom of the Cross Solomon, SSVM
Religious Vocation from Our Lady of Peace

"I was raised in the Philippines, the youngest of four children in my family. My mother's side of the family was Catholic but not practicing, so I didn't have a good faith example growing up. My older siblings were baptized Catholic but I was baptized into the Philippine Independent Church, or colloquially known as the Aglipayan Church. I grew up knowing my dad attended Jehovah's Witness fellowship. Looking back now, I see that God had been calling me into the religious life as a teen but I didn't understand it.

"When I entered high school, I started searching. I knew God was leading me, and though drawn to visit different churches of different faith traditions, I was always drawn to Eucharistic adoration in the Catholic Church. At this time, God put a lot of good people around me: high school teachers, then college professors, who guided me and instilled good morals that my parents couldn't. He also gave

Fr. Warren celebrates First Holy Communion with Regina Clare Mastroieni on May 24, 1997. Fr. Warren served as a priest at Our Lady of Peace for 37 years between 1970 and 2007.

me a good friend in high school from a strong Catholic family. She went to Mass before school every day, and after school would stop at church for Eucharistic adoration. I'd go with her, but I also had other friends who would invite me to their places of worship: Baptists, Protestants, and Pentecostals. Though I appreciated these experiences, I always returned to St. William's Cathedral in Laoag, in the northern province of Ilocos Norte, with my Catholic friend.

"In my second year of college, a Carmelite nun came to the university for a vocational day and invited the young people to visit the monastery and pray for vocations. She gave a talk to my class, and afterward I asked her how I could be baptized. She referred me to the Daughters of the Divine Zeal. They prepared me and, in my third year of college, I was baptized in the Catholic Church.

"That same year, my mother received notice that her papers were approved to immigrate to the United States. As her only minor child, I was also approved (my father finished some work commitments and followed later). Though I was very happy in the Philippines and wanted to stay and finish college, my family thought I should go with my mother. We came to San Jose and my aunt's family was so kind to host us until we found jobs, became established, and found a place to live. The first church I entered when I came to the United States was Our Lady of Peace. That was in 1993.

"Once anyone starts working, we earn money and acquire more material things. As it is for many women, I wanted to raise a family and have a home. Those were my aspirations. I had just come into the Church and didn't understand a lot of things, and as happens to many people, I fell in my journey of faith. Eventually, however, I came to a point when I felt there must be more to life than getting up in the morning, going to work, and acquiring more material goods.

"The first time I saw the Sisters (Servants of the Lord and the Virgin of Matará) was around 2002. I had just come out of holy Mass and finished my prayers of thanksgiving when I saw a Sister getting out of the car in the parking lot. I was drawn to speak with her and started to walk in her direction. Halfway there, I changed my mind and turned the other way.

"I do believe that God never stops calling us, whether our vocation is for the religious life, or whatever his plans are. He never stops calling because He is the beginning and end of our lives. At that time, I had come to the point of attending daily Mass, but due to my aspirations for a family I was trying to run away from a religious vocation. I didn't want to face it. Whenever I was reminded of a religious vocation, I would always question it or push it off. Why would it be me? Why not someone more deserving? Sometimes I would intentionally go out with friends even when I knew God was calling me to go to church. Yet out with my friends, I didn't have peace because I was going against what God wanted me to do: I realized I wasn't as happy in their company as I once had been, and would end up at Our Lady of Peace to pray—even at late hours of the night. This church was always open for me to come here, pray, and stay as long as I wanted to.

"Finally, when I started to realize there's more to life than work, money, a house, and a car, I started facing my vocational call. I didn't understand it but I knew I had to face and accept it. I knew I couldn't run away from it too long. I started coming to church more and turning again to the sacraments. The more I received Communion, the more I thirsted for it. My supervisor at work allowed me come in early so I could leave early to attend the 5:15 p.m. Mass. Then, one Sunday afternoon I came to Mass and the priest's homily was about vocations to the religious life. After Mass, I approached him and asked if we could talk more about vocations. He pointed me to the Sisters. They gave me a pamphlet about the Spiritual Exercises (a four-day weekend silent retreat according to St. Ignatius of Loyola). I signed up, but a week before the retreat I cancelled. A year later, in

May of 2005, I called and asked again to go. This time, I went. After that, I started spending time with the Sisters and prayed often for the strength to persevere and to understand better what the Lord was asking of me.

"One of my concerns was my financial debt. I needed to pay student loans, a car loan, and to work out financial responsibilities that helped my parents pay for their home. It was God's Providence that not only did everything work out, but even ahead of schedule! I had asked to join the community, the Institute of the Servants of the Lord and the Virgin of Matará, in July of 2007. By God's Divine Providence, I was able to finish paying off my loans by March. There were times when I thought I wouldn't make the next payment, and then everything worked out. When I was debt-free ahead of schedule, I realized my vocation was God's plan because I finished way ahead of time—something that was seemingly impossible for me, yet He had put the pieces together.

"I was drawn to this religious order because I saw the joy the Sisters have in living their religious and community life together. How important it is to have the Eucharist in religious life and love for the Holy Father, who is the Vicar of Christ here on earth, love for the teachings of the Church, centered on the Holy Eucharist, love for the Blessed Virgin Mary, the Mother of God. Being a member of the Religious family of the IVE, we profess vows of poverty, chastity, and obedience, and we have a fourth vow of Marian slavery—it reflects our love and devotion to the Mother of God, consecrating ourselves to Jesus through Mary according to the teachings of St. Louis Marie de Montfort. We give everything to Jesus through the Immaculate Heart of Mary.

"When one truly lives religious life, God is with us and it gives peace, joy, and contentment, for He alone can give us the grace. I was able to answer God's call through Our Lady of Peace parish opening its doors at all times for Perpetual Adoration where I could encounter Christ in prayer. The Legion of Mary group was also God's instrument in my vocation discernment to respond to God's call when I needed to see or hear it. Finally, God led me to the Sisters, drawing me to their joy and love for Jesus and the Eucharist."

Laurel Moran
Parishioner 1998 - Present

"On first Fridays, Fr. Coghlan let the altar boys come into the rectory after Mass to visit. They could ask questions about anything, religious or not. So these young boys from ages eight and up would come to spend an hour with Fr. Coghlan. They saw another side of him. In Mass he was very 'fire and brimstone,' but inside the rectory he had a softer side. He would laugh and joke with the boys and they'd ask him all kinds of questions. My sons couldn't wait to come every first Friday.

"One day, we invited some Carmelite seminarians to play soccer with the home schoolers. When we arrived, the seminarians were already there but the kids asked, 'Where are the seminarians?' They thought the men they saw couldn't be seminarians because they were too young! We realized that, with so many retired priests assisting at Our Lady of Peace, the children thought all priests were old!"

Sister Wisdom of the Cross Solomon, SSVM, with members of her community at the Convent in Hafnarfjörður (Diocese of Reykjavík, Iceland). Sr. Wisdom stands third from the left.

A group of altar servers pose with Fr. Esteban Soler.

Claudia Schussman
Parishioner 1999 - Present

"Fr. Mallo definitely had a sense of humor. The first time I met him was during one of the most stressful times of my life. We were planning our wedding, which was to take place at Our Lady of Peace Church. I had booked the church at least nine months in advance and made all the arrangements needed for a wedding on that specific date. We had ordered and sent out the invitations, booked and paid for a reception space in a nearby winery, selected and paid for my wedding dress, my fiancé had made all the reservations for the honeymoon, our family and friends had booked airline tickets, and everything was finally settled. About a month before the big day, I received a phone call from someone in the rectory letting me know that there had been a booking mistake, because (unbeknownst to us and the rectory staff at the time we made the reservation), the Church does not perform marriages on November 2, All Souls' Day. I was livid. My fiancé and I quickly made an appointment to speak with Fr. Mallo, desperate for a remedy to the situation. Fr. Mallo, with the courage of a lion (have you ever seen an enraged bride?), patiently heard our predicament and assured us that he would see what he could do. He soon let us know our bishop had granted a dispensation and we could be married on that day after all. 'However,' Fr. Mallo added, 'because your wedding will take place on All Souls' Day, you must wear a black dress.' Seeing another storm rising in my being, he wisely said again he would see what he could do. Later, he let us know that my wedding dress would be fine. It wasn't until ten years later, when our friendship was more firm, Fr. Mallo told me the rule about the black wedding dress was a joke!"

Joe Moran
Parishioner 1998 - Present

"The home schoolers were having a weekly park day at another parish with a play yard. When they decided to bring that gathering back to Our Lady of Peace, the big issue was there was no secure area for young children to play, because the parish property is so close to the highway. Suzanne Spence initiated the playground idea and learned that Monsignor Sweeny had left some personal funds to the home schoolers. We voted to use those for a play structure, and she found a fabulous structure on Craigslist. Monsignor Sweeny's funds covered about one-fourth of the total cost to complete the playground. We collected donations for the rest.

"It was quite a project! Dan Devlin, a civil engineer, got all the permits and ended up having to work out a drainage system because of the water issues on the land. It turned out to be a very large project but parents worked overtime on it, Fr. Ray Devlin (Dan's uncle) was out there helping, and at the end we passed inspection! It is a sturdy, safe, and fun place for children to play."

Deacon Daniel Hernandez
Religious Vocation from Our Lady of Peace

"Growing up, my extended family would come to Our Lady of Peace for midnight Mass on Christmas. In 1986, my brother, Fr. Anthony Hernandez, became the religious education director and he didn't have enough teachers. I really had to brush up on what I had learned in Catholic elementary school, but I saw it as a good opportunity because I could teach the classes and they could also help

Fr. Mallo and a group of parish youngsters celebrate the
completed playground.

me to be more social, outside of my independent, single, working life. I remember noticing after Mass the priest would say, 'Go now and serve the Lord by serving one another.' We would reply, 'Thanks be to God,' and leave. I always pondered those words and how to bring them to life. I would leave Mass and realize I was not really reaching out, which made me more egocentric. These words at the end of Mass really helped me. When my brother needed teachers I thought, 'Maybe the Lord is calling me because I have this knowledge that I've really kept to myself and could share that knowledge.' Christianity is about thinking of others.

"I've been teaching catechism classes at Our Lady of Peace for over 30 years. At first I taught high school students to prepare them for confirmation, and then later moved on to teaching sacrament preparation for adult Catholics who haven't been confirmed, and to my surprise many haven't received their First Holy Communion. I also sang in the choir, and for fifteen years served as a lector at Mass.

"Our Lady of Peace had a big part in guiding me to become ordained as a deacon. After teaching here for many years and helping with Bible studies, being in the choir, and lecturing, around 2004 I was at Mass when some visiting priests spoke. They were newly ordained, and one gave the homily. It occurred to me, 'Maybe that's my calling, to take all I've learned and give homilies, too.' I'm from a large family, and that combined with teaching all these years at Our Lady of Peace and going to Catholic school...I saw perhaps I could integrate that into the Gospel. So I went to the pastor, Fr. Mallo, and told him I was discerning the diaconate (becoming a deacon). He recommended me to the diocese as a candidate. It was because of my experiences at Our Lady of Peace I could see how my talents and skills could contribute to the life of the Church, and it was in this church that I felt God calling me to serve through the diaconate. I was accepted into a 6-year program and ordained a deacon in May of 2010.

"The bishop appointed me to serve at St. Thomas Aquinas parish in Palo Alto. The deacon's service role goes all the way back to St. Peter! In Greek, 'deacon' literally means, 'servant.' I do service, preaching, and liturgy. The liturgy would be, for example, baptisms (I do hundreds of baptisms), witness marriages, and participate during the Mass by reading the Gospel, distributing communion, and preaching homilies at Sunday Masses. If there's no priest for a daily Mass, I lead communion services. I also visit people in their homes. My work as a deacon is not full-time; my career is in biochemistry.

"Two scenarios happened at Our Lady of Peace that drew me into the life of the church: the liturgy offered a place I was drawn to pray, and my brother asked me to teach (and thus contribute to the life of the Church). This opened up what had become a boring, humdrum world of work, where everything becomes cliché, to using my skills and talents for my faith. It helped me to overcome individualism and transcend the worldly world. My years of teaching later showed me how I could preach the Gospel to the people and serve as a deacon. If it was not for my brother's personal invitation to teach catechism, I probably wouldn't be a deacon today. It was through the process of attending Our Lady of Peace that expanded service into a vocation."

Charlie Fitzgearl
Parishioner 2006 - Present

"When I was growing up, my family viewed religion as a crutch for people to lean on: it was for people who couldn't make it through life on their own. They did not hold religion in high esteem. In my late teens and early 20s, I became interested in seeing what this was all about, so I read the King James version of the Bible several

At Our Lady of Peace's 50th Anniversary Jubilee Mass, Deacon Daniel Hernandez (center) assists Fr. Jose Guinta (left) and Bishop Patrick McGrath (right).

times over a few years. The Gospels especially sang to my heart.

"In my search for like-minded people, I started asking questions about religion at work. I happened to work with several people who were Mormons, so I went to a few Mormon meetings and I liked the meetings and the church, so I became a member. I continued to search for a way to respond to the Gospels as they spoke to my heart as a teen, but could not find it. I found a community structure yet not the intimacy or living out of the Word Incarnate, Jesus Christ. After 37 years, I left.

"When I retired from work in 2006, I needed to find something more expressive to do with life. I started looking around for a church and thought: My mother had been a Catholic, why don't I go look at that? I went to Our Lady of Peace and started taking the class for catechumens and really liked it. The Catholic teachings really appealed to me, especially knowing the scriptures as I did. (I read the scriptures for years and have all kinds of translations to read from.) It made a lot of sense to me and I saw some real incredible people in the Church to emulate—a whole collection of them! For example, Mother Teresa: I wanted to serve as she served. Fr. Kolbe and his perseverance in World War II made an impression on me. In their lives, I saw something that perhaps I could try to emulate.

"As I was sitting in the congregation at Our Lady of Peace one Sunday, the president of the Society of St. Vincent de Paul (Denise Lee) made an appeal for money. She said, 'If you want to serve and help those who are needy, come help us out.' So I went in to see what things were like and could see its value right away, what it was doing, and how well it fit my search for service. I read the St. Vincent de Paul manual and gained a sense of how this charity operates.

"Denise was leaving to attend nursing school, and there was a vacancy for the president's role. I was voted in, even though I voted against myself! That was in 2010 and I am still president.

"The president's job is to make sure we follow the overall rules of the Society of St. Vincent de Paul. It is not run like a business; this is a volunteer organization and people are not touching a timeclock. In a volunteer organization, it is a different procedure. People need to do things because they want to do them, not because they're forced to do them. They need to be moved by the Holy Spirit from the inside. It is a ministry and people serve according to how the Spirit moves them to serve, which I really like.

"Ultimately, our job is to deliver the love of the Lord and concern for people. We try to keep that in focus and put ourselves in the position of those who are needy and forsaken by society. We aren't a substance agency; the state has a lot more money than we do. Though substance (money) figures prominently in what we do, our first job is to make sure people feel they are not alone. People come to us and meet with our team of volunteers face to face. The volunteers need to see the people, feel their pain, see the terror in their eyes, hear the desperation in their voice, and know exactly what is going on. When you have multiple heads working on a project, solutions appear like magic! After we changed our system to have clients meet with a team of volunteers (versus just one volunteer), we were much more effective. It dramatically increased our chances of helping in the best possible way. A person needs to progress and develop and sometimes they get stuck in a rut. Our mission is not to make them comfortable in that rut, but to get them involved in their own well-being and go forward.

"I always tell people, 'If you want to see miracles, come to St. Vincent de Paul.' Little miracles of life happen like clockwork. It is unbelievable. We witness them every day. For example, many homeless people come to us. We quickly found we couldn't afford to put people up in motels; it becomes tremendously expensive. We got together as a conference (team of volunteers) and developed a '$10/day' program. If clients can find someone to let them sleep on their floor and use their bathroom, we'll give that host ten dollars a day to keep them there while they are in transition to a better situation. It's amazing how many people participate. One man came in and said he didn't have anyone to ask, but he said he'd look around because it was so difficult to sleep under freeways. The next person who walked through our door had an RV with three bedrooms. We put those two together, and suddenly one guy was off the street and they become friends! To me, that's a miracle! I saw the hand of the Lord in that, bringing those two together and making their lives better. We see those kinds of miracles all the time at St. Vincent de Paul.

"A number of people have come back to say they appreciate the help we gave them (assisting with rent, fixing a car, buying clothes for their children, and so on). Yet they continued to say what was really meaningful to them was to know they weren't alone and we were on the journey with them. We were *interested in their lives*, and that made all the difference in the world. I believe that proves the mission of St. Vincent de Paul: we're here to deliver the Lord's love to people. We're not just a give-away agency. We support people in a lot of ways beyond just sustenance: we advocate for people and interface with landlords or utility companies; we have car mechanic to help people fix their cars; we deliver food, give people rides here and there, and work closely with Catholic Charities because they have a legal arm—if people need legal assistance we can send them there.

"Our role isn't to bring people into the Catholic Church. So many people come to us from other churches because they are told the Catholics will help them. If they ask about the faith, we tell them. Our primary role is to love them. They're human beings and that's all that counts. If people have needs, then they are our needs and we try to help them in any way we can. The Lord looks far beyond countries and borders and races, and ultimately people are pretty much the same.

"Over time, word spread of the effectiveness of our ministry. People must have seen what we were doing, and donations today are four times what we had in 2010. We are now able to put almost $80,000 a year into the community and meet with over 1,200 individuals each year. The impact we have is not only on these individuals, but on their families as well. We are very, very careful with how we distribute funds and very grateful for the generosity and faith people have in our ministry. Because of their support, Monsignor Sweeny's legacy of seeing Christ in others, and the IVE pastors supporting our presence here at Our Lady of Peace, we can bring hope and encouragement to those in need. Love of neighbor is second to loving God. As Jesus said, 'You shall love your neighbor as yourself.'" (Matthew 22:39)

Each of us is unique. Every individual is an individual, there is only one of us. We're all individuals who make our final choice, so [the Church can] give opportunities to give our 'Yes' to God. And so if I can multiply that number!

Monsignor John Sweeny

CHAPTER 8
2010s

Missionaries for the New Millennium

Jesus and Mary; Mary and Jesus.
And through Christ, to the Father, in the Holy Spirit.

Institute of the Incarnate Word
Directory of Spirituality, 325

The year 2010 opened another time of transition for Our Lady of Peace. Fr. Walter Mallo had guided the parish for seven years through the transition from Fr. Sweeny's pastoral care to the priests of the Institute of the Incarnate Word. A leader noted for his love for religious life, prayerfulness, and good sense of humor, Fr. Mallo was asked to transfer to a large parish in Dallas in 2010. Fr. José Giunta came to Santa Clara to assume leadership at the Shrine.

Fr. Giunta continued to share the charism of the IVE with the parish and supported the same long-time spiritual values of Our Lady of Peace. Shortly after his arrival, he established a Pastoral Council to help guide the parish. The Pastoral Council helped parishioners document an understanding of their identity and build a stronger sense of community through improved facilitation and communication. Together with Fr. Giunta, the Council also created a mission statement and encouraged all parishioners to share in the parish mission. The mission statement reads:

Our Lady of Peace is a church and shrine dedicated to the greater glory of God and the salvation of souls. It is a place of prayer and pilgrimage with:

- *Perpetual adoration of Jesus in the Blessed Sacrament;*

- *Devotion to the Blessed Virgin Mary;*

- *Frequent celebration of the Sacraments, particularly the Eucharist and Reconciliation;*

- *Integrated formation of the person (spiritual, moral, intellectual, and emotional).*

This mission statement guides and reinforces many of the recommendations and decisions made by the priests and Pastoral Council.

Additionally, noting that many parishioners continued to grieve Monsignor Sweeny's absence from the Shrine and communicated—what some explained as—a "loss to their core" in the years following his death, Fr. Giunta and his fellow priests collaborated with parish leaders to seek ways to bring groups together and provide the spiritual nourishment they could offer.

Fr. Giunta's three years as Pastor were notably challenging because he was usually one of two full-time priests serving in a parish that needed more. Yet despite the many demands for his time, he was appreciated for his presence at as many parish group meetings and activities as possible and his great love for children—who always made him smile.

In 2013, Fr. Gustavo Nieto, the IVE Provincial Superior who originally assigned Fr. Mallo and Fr. Giunta to Our Lady of Peace, ended his term in IVE leadership and came to Santa Clara to replace Fr. Giunta as pastor. Again building upon the foundation set by the priests who came before him, Fr. Nieto welcomed more large events into the Family Learning Center, such as the RISE conference for teens, community gatherings, and Theology on Tap for young adults (which quickly grew into one of the nation's largest Theology on Tap programs). With the Pastoral Council, Fr. Nieto recognized the overcrowding in church and surveyed parishioners regarding possible solutions for expanding the Shrine. In addition to social and visionary leadership, he emphasized a strong spiritual foundation and opportunities for prayer and evangelization in a parish also serving as a Shrine. Upon the occasion of their canonizations, he installed the statues of Fatima visionaries St. Francisco and St. Jacinta at the Family Learning Center entrance, and St. John Paul II across the lawn from Our Lady of the Immaculate Heart. Fr. Nieto was elected Superior General by the IVE in 2016, necessitating his presence in Rome. Fr. Brian Dinkel arrived in September of that year to assume the massive responsibilities of parish leadership, transitioning in with notable grace.

SERVIDORAS IN SERVICE

The IVE's goal, as a religious order, is following Jesus Christ, and Him crucified, through the profession of the vows of poverty, chastity, and obedience, taking the Blessed Virgin Mary as protectress and guide. Their specific goal, following the call of His Holiness John Paul II, is the evangelization of the culture. The clergy and religious sisters live the same founding charism and evangelical mission. Thus, the presence of the Sisters at Our Lady of Peace is in full support of these goals and, in many ways, the hearts and hands that make possible the incredible amount of activities and opportunities for prayer and formation.

On the Solemnity of the Body and Blood of Christ in 2011, Fr. José Giunta, IVE, leads parishioners on a procession to four outdoor altars.

The religious Sisters are essential to the day-to-day functioning of parish life, a joyful presence, and offer much needed support for youth and families. They provide the backbone for all formal catechesis (which occurs daily and is heavily attended at Our Lady of Peace) and education, as well as friendship, good counsel, and prayer.

TO JESUS THROUGH MARY

Pastor to pastor has led efforts to study and implement Monsignor Sweeny's vision for the Shrine. Today, ten Sunday Masses and 22 weekly Masses are filled with worshippers. Priests are available to hear confessions over thirty hours per week, hearing nearly 8,000 confessions during Lent alone. The rosary is prayed in the church every hour, on the hour (unless Mass is in progress). Long-time devotions continue. In 2015, when parish leadership revived Monsignor Sweeny's favorite devotion of the total consecration of True Devotion to Mary, 4,200 people responded. The Divine Mercy Sunday celebration draws thousands to Mass and confession. Every September, in honor of Our Lady's birthday, prayer intentions are gathered from parishioners and formally placed in Our Lady's Immaculate Heart. Nearly 900 children arrive to the church weekly for catechism classes. Thousands of faithful attend events such as family and youth conferences, the Walk for Life rally, spiritual warfare conferences, Fatima Pilgrimages, Divine Mercy Sunday, and Friday Family Nights. The Society of St. Vincent de Paul assists more people in need than any other chapter in the Diocese of San Jose. City buses, flanked with banners inviting all to Christmas or Easter Mass at the Shrine, carry Christ's welcome through metro Santa Clara. And in 2016, Our Lady of Peace celebrated forty years of 24-hour Eucharistic Adoration: church doors remain unlocked and open day and night as people pray round the clock in the presence of Christ in the Eucharist. More than sixty young people from the

Sister Maria Ain Karem Sosa, SSVM, and Mother María Ana de Jesús Carrió, SSVM, lead a Fatima Pilgrimage procession in 2015.

Shrine have discerned full-time vocations to religious life: a dramatic testimony to the fruits of a parish tirelessly dedicated to offering souls the opportunity to know, love, and serve God.

In the late 1960s, a young Fr. Sweeny held a vision of Our Lady of Peace as a beacon of hope in the Silicon Valley. A notable few understood or shared his vision, yet his bishops allowed him to pursue the "impossible." Joined by a handful of faithful, eyes set on Christ and the heart of his Mother, Monsignor Sweeny's Our Lady of Peace Church grew into a Shrine and reaches more people weekly than most churches in the United States. An estimated 190,000 vehicles exit Highway 101 onto Great America Parkway daily and receive a warm invitation in Our Lady of the Immaculate Heart's outstretched arms. Daily life at the Church and Shrine witnesses lives changed, hope restored, and thousands motivated to spread the Gospel message. Hers is the story of remarkable, faith-filled priests, past and present, who work prayerfully and tirelessly to serve souls in an atmosphere of joy, prayer, and learning. It is the story of religious sisters who labor, love, pray, and counsel. It is the story of everyday people who seek hope, find hope, and return to give hope. Our Lady of Peace Church and Shrine, and all it encompasses, offers a powerful testimony to Christ in our midst, and the love of His Mother.

Fr. Gustavo Nieto, IVE, celebrates the Easter Sunday sunrise Mass in 2014.

Banners on Santa Clara city buses invite the public to Holy Week, Easter, and Divine Mercy Sunday Masses and prayer services.

Sister Maria Ng Krus Totanes, SSVM, and Sister María del Los Angeles Garcías, SSVM, celebrate Palm Sunday in 2015.

Fr. Thomas Steinke, IVE, leads the outdoor Stations of the Cross on Good Friday of 2015.

The Knights of Columbus at a Divine Mercy Sunday Mass celebration.
Since the earliest days of Our Lady of Peace Church and Shrine, the
Knights have generously supported parish events and celebrations,
large and small.

Marco Jarero carries the Crucifix for the Good Friday Stations of the Cross, 2015.

Fr. Brian Dinkel, IVE, is welcomed by a young parishioner upon his arrival as Pastor of Our Lady of Peace in September of 2016.

Fr. William Stout, S.J., offers Mass in 2016. Fr. Stout volunteered at Our Lady of Peace Church and Shrine from 1967 until his death on March 14, 2018.

IVE priests, nuns, and young people welcomed over 850 teens to the 2016 RISE Youth Conference.

Over 4,000 pilgrims attended the Fatima Centennial Celebration on May 13, 2017. High-tech office buildings serve as the backdrop for Our Lady of the Immaculate Heart, a dramatically different landscape than when Fr. Sweeny first envisioned the Shrine in the 1960s.

Children prepare to process in to the Fatima Centennial Mass on May 13, 2017.

The statue of Our Lady of Fatima, adorned for procession. Bishop Patrick McGrath presides at Mass on May 13, 2017.

Diocesan priest Fr. Michael Hendrickson offers benediction at Our Lady of Peace.

Fr. José Giunta, IVE
Pastor of Our Lady of Peace Church & Shrine 2010 - 2013

"When I came to Our Lady of Peace, the devotion of the people amazed me. It was something outside of my experience. In my previous parishes, I would offer devotion of the Blessed Sacrament during the day, but few people went to spend time with Jesus in the Blessed Sacrament. I found *individuals* who were very devoted, but at Our Lady of Peace I was very surprised at the *amount of individuals* who were very devoted. So many people went to visit the Blessed Sacrament, so many people went to pray the rosary, and so many people went to pray at the outdoor statue of Our Mother. They came from different places, many driving half an hour or forty-five minutes, just to pray before the Blessed Sacrament. I was very happy to see this.

"One experience I especially remember is the first time I went to offer the 5 a.m. Mass that concludes the First Friday all night adoration. I rose at 4:30 a.m. and went over to the church, thinking two or three people would be there for Mass, because I was accustomed to other parishes. More than 120 people were there! My goodness! And many of them had stayed to pray the whole night!

"To see the devotion at Our Lady of Peace never ceased to amaze me. This devotion came from the work of the priests who came before me: Monsignor Sweeny, Fr. Mallo, and many others. They worked very hard for that, especially Monsignor Sweeny, who established everything there: adoration of the Blessed Sacrament, devotion to Mary, and so on. When the IVE arrived, everything was already set; we just had to continue what Monsignor Sweeny did before. Seeing the level of prayer at Our Lady of Peace, I knew they had years and years of praying at this church and the people understood devotion

355

to the Blessed Sacrament and the role of the Blessed Mother. The amount of people this brought to every Mass and then to adoration during the day and even at night, it was something! At 1 a.m., there were people praying there, and at 5 a.m., there were more!

"Another memorable experience was during Holy Week. It is a very, very busy time for priests. One week we were hearing confessions Holy Thursday, Good Friday, and Holy Saturday. At 3 p.m. on Holy Saturday, I sent a priest to hear confessions for people waiting there. At 4 p.m., I went to the church to see how many people were there, thinking we might finish in one hour. Well, there were forty or fifty people waiting in line for confession. I stayed to hear confessions, brought in a third priest to hear confessions, and we ended at 7 p.m. The Mass was at 8:30 p.m., and you know there is much preparation for the vigil Mass! I asked the people why they came to Our Lady of Peace for confession, and most were from other parishes and confession hours were less available; they knew at Our Lady of Peace there was confession at every Mass. On Holy Saturday, just when we were supposed to be preparing for the Masses, three priests were hearing confessions for the many people waiting. Those were among the good things I experienced at Our Lady of Peace—so many people desiring confession—and these stories show what it was like to be a priest at this parish.

"Another surprise to me was my ability to focus more on priestly ministry. In my previous roles as pastor, the pastor was in charge of everything at the church, including overseeing the building, maintenance, repairs, and so on. At Our Lady of Peace, the pastor only took care of the people because we had good staff members working on the areas of property management. I didn't have to do too much beyond give permissions. For a priest, that was the best! To be concerned with people, helping them, talking to them, advising them, and celebrating Mass, hearing confessions, and doing the work of the priest. Because of the staff, I could do the priestly work.

"Even with our staff, it was a very, very demanding time. When I was pastor, there were sometimes three priests at Our Lady of Peace but, at one point, only two. The work was too much for only two priests. Priests need to have time to pray and rest. At midday on weekdays, we needed two priests in the confessionals and one saying Mass, so three priests were required. Saturday and Sunday was the same, but all day long for every Mass. Sometimes people complained that no one was hearing confessions, because at times we were short priests. Often we had to call for other priests and it could become difficult to find an available priest because they were also busy.

"We sustained ourselves with prayer. The prayers of the people also sustained us. I think prayer is very, very important. You pray and trust in God to persevere and give you the strength to do the work He wants you to do. So my idea was: of course I need another priest, but I only have one. So we have to do what we can with sacrifice, but we were very happy in our work and at the end of the day we were very tired. It was a lot of work but in prayer I'd say, 'Okay God, if you want me here I'll stay here. Just send me another priest if you want, and if you don't want to I will continue to work until I cannot do it anymore.' We trusted in God. God gives us the grace to do what he wants us to do. If he's going to give us a burden, he will give us the grace to carry the burden. I just prayed and spoke a couple of times to the provincial superior, and when the third priest came it was good! We had a better distribution of work. Through this time, the most important response was to pray and trust in God.

"Another difficulty was that sometimes as pastor one has to make decisions that people don't like and some people complain or don't understand. That is the most difficult thing for the pastor. He thinks about what is the best for the parish, and sometimes what is considered the best for the parish is not best for one particular person. But you consider the parish and ask, 'What is the best thing to do?' And you know at Our Lady of Peace, where five thousand people come to Mass every Sunday, you cannot please everyone. People don't always understand your decisions, and it is difficult for them to understand because they have a different point of view or different interests. Usually I understood their point but I had to do what was best for all.

"For support in making decisions, I created the Pastoral Council. The Finance Committee was typically relied on to consider different pastoral plans, so I decided to establish the Pastoral Council to separate the finances from pastoral issues. The function of the Pastoral Council is to advise the pastor on pastoral matters. We met monthly and different representatives of groups were there in the meetings, so I could come to them and ask for advice, such as developing the pastoral programs in the parish, organizing events, catechesis, conferences, perpetual adoration, and so on. The pastor has the final decision, but it is very helpful to have this group of people to help [the pastor] run the parish in pastoral matters.

"Soon after establishing the Pastoral Council, we worked together to establish a parish mission statement. We looked at the most important values of the parish, what we wanted for the parish, and different elements of what a parish is to be. We combined these elements and the mission statement was the final outcome. It was very good, and actually just reflected what we already had in place. We just expressed it in writing to use as a guide for future decisions and confirm it as a parish identity. The mission statement is like the I.D. for the parish, so when someone asks, 'What do you think of the parish? What is the parish like?' the mission statement expresses what the parish should be. We wanted to be recognized as a parish that exhibits the mission statement and encourage people to be a part of this. When the people at Our Lady of Peace identify with the mission statement, it becomes their identity, too. It is important for the people to identify with the mission statement as their own, because the parish is a communion of people. The parish is not the pastor, the parish is not the office staff; the parish is the people and they can identify with that statement and say, 'This is what the parish is to be and this is who I want to be as part of this parish.' "

Michael Luvara
Parishioner 2008 - Present

"For over fifteen years after my Confirmation at Our Lady of Peace, I didn't go to church. As a boy, I wanted to go but for some reason was afraid to ask. Over time, setting foot in a church became something I wasn't comfortable doing alone. Add comments from others and society's labels to that, and it was almost taboo. When I would drive by a Catholic church, my conscience always nagged at me, but I would tend to find some excuse. Though always knowing that I would return one day, my answer was, 'later,' 'sometime,' or 'not yet.'

"Yet through the grace of God I prayed every day since my catechism as a youth. The Lord was always subtly knocking at the door, but it wasn't until I asked in prayer that He revealed himself in powerful ways. Essentially, I asked the Lord to show me He was real through the help of other individuals as instruments, and in return I would glorify Him in everything I do. And He did! Then it was my turn to do my part, as I had promised, so I attended Christmas Eve midnight Mass in 2007.

"At that Mass, I knew I could not receive the Eucharist because I needed to go to confession first. After looking around at different parishes I found it available on limited schedules. However, a week after Christmas, something happened at work that triggered me to call Our Lady of Peace and inquire about confession times. I was shaking when I made the call and an elderly lady answered the phone,

A joyful celebration of Our Lady of Peace Church's 50th anniversary in 2012. Left to right: Archbishop Patrick McGrath, Fr. José Giunta, IVE, Fr. Gustavo Nieto, IVE, and Fr. Lawrence Goode. With his back to the camera is Fr. John Coleman.

welcoming me to the parish. She told me it was available before every Mass. That was it. I got in my car, drove over to the parish, and parked. After sitting in the car for a minute, I took a deep breath and went in, finding the line for the confessionals. It was like a time capsule. The parish had not changed much in fifteen years.

"The Lord did guide me that day. The priest who heard my confession, Fr. Pintacura, was perfect for my situation. When I mentioned it had been fifteen years since my last confession and that I wanted to again receive the Eucharist, he replied excitedly, 'God bless you! Wonderful, I will remember you in all my Masses. Welcome home!' After naming my sins and receiving some counsel, I heard those wonderful words: 'I absolve you in the name of the Father, Son and Holy Spirit. Amen. Go in peace. God bless you, I will keep you in prayer.' At that moment, I know the angels were rejoicing as Luke 15:10 says: 'In just the same way, I tell you, there will be rejoicing among the angels of God over one sinner who repents.' I received the Eucharist for the first time in some fifteen-plus years that day. It was an amazing moment to kneel at the altar rail and receive the Eucharist.

"Needless to say, I walked out of Mass that day with a new look on life and felt like the cloudy stain over my eyes was washed away— sort of like cleaning a really foggy pair of glasses or even the windshield on a car. This day started a wonderful journey. However, little did I know what lie ahead. It was just the beginning of the Lord placing people and events in my life, not to mention the cleansing process of fifteen years of worldly influences.

"Part of my return to the Church were Christians who brought me to Protestant or non-denominational churches several times, which truly showed me what the Catholic faith has. While many of these churches promoted some of the Truth in their teachings, I felt an emptiness there and came to realize what they lacked was the Real

Presence of Christ in the Eucharist. Had I not experienced events at these churches, I would not have researched the Catholic faith as much as I did and come home so powerfully. In fact, it lit a fire beneath me because it became apparent that the majority of Catholics don't really know their faith, nor can they defend it. I sought to know, live, and defend the faith. I wasn't going to be lumped in with the Catholics who said 'I don't know, Fr. Whatever told me.' We're all called to be informed about our faith.

"Because my Protestant friends had a lot of fellowship, I went parish shopping to find the young adult groups. I went around and around with so many parishes, but kept returning to Our Lady of Peace. There was something different about it. Slowly I realized it was because they focused on the sacraments. Also, this time preceded the 2008 election and I realized the priests were talking about the faith and real topics I didn't hear about anywhere else, which caused me to pause and look at the relationship of our faith and secular world in a different way. Our Lady of Peace was a place where I could go listen to what the Church teaches and receive it truth unadultered: this is what it is, don't do this or that, and this is why. For a while I thought they were a bit brash, or hardcore on damnation, but I soon saw a balance between what not to do, that God loves us, and here is the way out and the right way to live life. So I made Our Lady of Peace my home, and they had just opened up a young adult group in 2008, which was great. It was everything I needed and my faith and involvement slowly grew from there.

"At that time, Fr. Walter Mallo was at the end of his stay at Our Lady of Peace so I really didn't get to know him well. However, he did help me to re-learn the rosary quickly, because I vividly remember his voice at the end of a confession, 'Your penance is *one holy rosary...*'!

"After I was back at church for about two years, Fr. José Giunta became Pastor and formed the Pastoral Council, which I was invited to join and eventually become the chair of. The Pastoral Council is a group of parishioners who are stewards of the parish mission statement, help form the direction of the parish, serve as the eyes and ears of the parish, and report to the Pastor on practical matters of parish life.

"The mission statement was our first task as a Pastoral Council because we had to ask: Who are we? What are we supposed to do? As we tried to offer guidance, it came up that we didn't have a mission statement. So we went out, looked at other parishes and read many mission statements, then came back and began to work on ours. I thought it would be quick, but we spent about six months defining and discerning the parish mission statement. In the end, it was brilliant. As a pilot, sometimes I compare flying to the spiritual life. When I was training to learn how to fly and we arrived to the runway, I asked the instructor, 'Now what do I do?' He replied, 'Tell the tower who you are, where you are, and where you're going.' The mission statement says that: This is who we are, where we are, and how we get to Heaven. The mission statement has helped the parish to have that direction.

"Fr. José had a lot on his plate and at one point it was just him and one other priest. I admired the fact that, despite his high demand, he tried to attend every young adult meeting. That presence was important to many, and at Our Lady of Peace we are fortunate to be accustomed to seeing our pastors at events. All the priests at Our Lady of Peace have impressed me because of their dedication to their daily duties and faithfulness to the Magisterium and sacraments. I think they often give of themselves too much, where it wears them down, but they are a shining example (especially in the confessional). Their focus is clearly aligned with the parish mission statement.

"When Fr. Mallo departed and Fr José arrived, I was relatively new and there was concern from parishioners if things would change, which turned out to be more of a worry than reality. Fast forward to Fr. Nieto arriving and I was in the same place. The council had just gotten settled and here's a new pastor, so I was a bit thrown off course because of the change. I soon realized that was a lack of faith and trust in God on my part. Now having worked with Fr. José, Fr. Nieto, and most recently, Fr. Brian, I can say that each one is rooted in fulfilling the mission statement, however, in their own unique way. I believe God placed each one for a purpose: Fr. Mallo to stabilize the parish after Monsignor Sweeny's departure, Fr. José to build a core mission, Fr. Nieto to thrust the mission into action, and Fr. Brian to be a boots-on-the-ground pastor with discipleship as his core. All of these gifted priests have and will continue to add immeasurable blessings to both the parish and the parishioners.

"Today, I attend Mass close to daily, help teach catechism classes, give talks to youth at retreats, and lector. I told the Lord I would glorify Him, and indeed he has provided the opportunities for me to say, 'Yes.' "

Jenny O'Driscoll
Parishioner 2004 - 2013

"Joel and I, with six of our children (two more were born later) came into the church on the Feast of All Saints in 2004. We were welcomed with open arms. As we grew in our Catholic faith, we especially remember Fr. José Giunta's influence.

"Fr. José was an encourager. He preached, perhaps in every homily, about actively pursuing and desiring to obtain and grow in the virtues. He spoke positively and decisively about this. Once, he told me that things had changed so much for young people living in these times. It used to be that temptations against purity were able to

Left, Michael Luvara stands with Fortunata Luvara, his aunt and Confirmation sponsor, after his 1992 Confirmation. Right, Michael today.

be avoided by simply choosing another way home or not walking into a particular shop; now a young person will walk out of the confessional and have a text message right before their eyes, enticing them to sin. On every level, we have to persevere in virtue. Fr. José encouraged us.

"His positive emphasis on virtue was also evident in the way he interacted with parishioners. My son, Stephen, was an altar server and remembers Fr. José's smile and friendliness toward him. He always stopped for a moment to touch my young childrens' heads and I assumed he was blessing them. He met my eyes and took that little bit of time to exchange a genuine hello. Fr. José had thousands of children and yet made time for each one."

Fr. Gustavo Nieto, IVE
Pastor of Our Lady of Peace Church & Shrine 2013 - 2016

"In 2010, we received a call asking the IVE to staff St. Bernard Church in Dallas. It was decided that Fr. Mallo should go there. Fr. José Giunta was asked to go to Our Lady of Peace. He was a priest with experience and said he would go where the Church needed him, yet he always wanted to be a monk and live in the monastery. It seemed he kept getting parish assignments! Then, in 2013, my term was over as Provincial Superior. I was happy as Provincial but my job there was to solve problems. When I received the news that I was going to Our Lady of Peace I was very happy to be returning to pastoral ministry and that Fr. José could finally go to the monastery.

"My greatest joy as a priest is seeing the souls of the people. There are many, many things priests see in the people. And there are many joys, many holy people here, and so many people on Sundays for the sacraments. I remember when I was ordained a priest and was told I would see many beautiful things in souls. And I do. All the labor for Mass and confessions is also very tiring, but it is not a problem. We have many consolations in this work.

"My greatest concern as pastor is the challenge that there are so many possibilities and I don't want to miss the opportunity to do something for the parish. People are so responsive! That is a unique characteristic of the people here. When we propose something serious, there is a hunger. For example, I asked the people if they wanted to install a statue of St. John Paul II for his canonization, and told them the price, and they immediately responded. We started Theology on Tap for young adults and were expecting only 40 people at the first event. We made a program and posters, and the first event drew 240. The next gathering had more than 300, and the next thing I knew Our Lady of Peace was hosting the largest Theology on Tap program in the country. Even devotions that are spiritually a lot of work grow here. These are just a few of many things we've started at Our Lady of Peace and they all worked. It is a very unique parish with a thirst for Christ. Every priest has his own way of doing things, but the Spirit was here before the IVE.

"I always say we need to keep in mind the mission of Monsignor Sweeny. We need to work on his plans. His master plan is always a big part of how we do things here. We have many projects, but the whole idea is to work for the greater glory of God and the salvation of souls. St. John Bosco used to say, 'Have more people in grace and more grace in each person.' We can make many plans or host many events, but the most important work is in the people here: to bring them closer to the Lord and our Blessed Mother. We have many dreams about the Shrine and how we can work here, but our first dream is to bring people closer to God."

Fr. Gustavo Nieto, IVE, offers Mass for the students of the Children's Oratory in 2013.

Youth recruit Fr. Nieto to join them in the RISE conference photo booth in 2015.

Fr. Jonathan Dumlao, IVE
Religious Vocation from Our Lady of Peace
Associate Pastor 2015 - Present

"The oldest of three children, I was born in Santa Clara, raised in San Jose, and studied at San Jose State University. Though I was baptized as an infant at St. John the Baptist Church in Milpitas, I was never initiated into the sacramental life of the Church which, to my knowledge, led to growing up with no faith life. My Mom is Catholic and my Dad is not. We were not churchgoers. In my late teens and early twenties, I had a 'reversion' to Christianity. I didn't come back to the Catholic Church immediately because a friend—and former Catholic—was swaying me toward the Protestant side. But the Lord brought me back.

"On my college campus, there were friendly Protestants inviting people to church. That was welcoming to me. Then I met a staunch Protestant girl and we started somewhat dating and she'd take me to her Protestant mega church. She told me I needed to get baptized and accept Jesus as my Lord and Savior. (I had no idea that I didn't need to be baptized, I was already baptized as a Catholic.) I went to one of their services where they baptized me in a huge pool of water and dipped me under.

"Soon after, she invited me to a Christian pop concert at her mega church. It was followed by a guest speaker. When the speaker, a pastor, was introduced as a 'former Catholic,' everyone started chuckling. But the statement that this man was a former Catholic stuck with me all night. The guest pastor's entire sermon was about purgatory, which was unusual because purgatory is a Catholic doctrine. He continued to critique the Catholic understanding of purgatory and how the Catholics 'got it wrong.' That stuck with me: Why does he keep talking about the Catholic faith when he is a Protestant pastor? There was a Catholic ring in my mind all night such that, after the event, I was reflecting and realized God was calling me to be a Catholic. That upset my Protestant friend, so I let it go but kept searching through the Bible and the Catechism of the Catholic Church. In one last conversation, I told the girl God was calling me to be a Catholic and join the true Church. She became very angry, called me a religious Pharisee, and we never spoke again. The devil may have been trying to sidetrack me, but in the midst of that, God was in total control of everything and it was how I discovered my vocation to the priesthood. God ended this relationship so that I could begin to develop a *real* relationship with Him alone. I began quenching my thirst for the Truth by further study and prayer.

"I had to be fully initiated into the sacramental life of the Church, so I joined RCIA at Our Lady of Peace. Keith Robinson, my RCIA teacher, taught me so much. I really enjoyed RCIA, and it was through RCIA that I eventually became more fully involved at Our Lady of Peace. I also became involved as a member of the 'core team' in the Young Adult Group.

"As all this was happening, I graduated with a Bachelor's degree in Business Administration and started working for Kaiser Permanente in Information Technology. In my job, I had to travel to the various different Kaiser facilities throughout the Bay Area. They would pay for my gas and hotel for weeks at a time. I had a lot of time alone in my commutes by car and train, and in my hotel, which gave me time to pray the rosary and chaplet of Divine Mercy, and to listen to Catholic radio, CDs, and so on. See how powerful the rosary is! It's a faith builder.

"The first priest who inspired me to want to become a priest was Fr. Paul Coleman at Our Lady of Peace. Attending Mass when Fr.

Paul was celebrating and hearing him preach put these strange thoughts into my mind to the effect of: 'I could do that.' I was impressed with his style of preaching. The priesthood slowly started coming into my mind and I met with Fr. Paul to discuss it.

"Even though I was involved with the Young Adult Group, and I never really had a close association with the IVE priests. Entering their religious order was not even on my radar as a possibility! Nonetheless, the IVE's intellectual formation, style of ministry, and the way they said Mass engaged me. In discerning my vocation, I met with a priest from another religious order and though he encouraged me, he never called me back. See how God works: He opens and closes doors as He wills in order to guide us. I continued to speak with Fr. Paul, spoke with Fr. Mark Catalana, the vocations director for the Diocese of San Jose, and started researching online and signing up for newsletters from different religious orders.

"In the Young Adult Group, we had a core team of about four or five young adults. One of the girls left to become a nun. Then another girl left with the same calling. The first one who left is now Sr. Peace, a professed religious Sister of the SSVM (our Institute's female branch). In the midst of both leaving, I was already scheduled that week to attend a Spiritual Exercises retreat led by Fr. Mallo at the Vallombrosa Center in Menlo Park.

"The final sendoff for Sr. Peace was at Saint John the Baptist Church in Milpitas (interestingly, the church where I was baptized). One morning, before her flight departing from the San Jose airport, I went to Mass with her family and friends and after Mass I walked over to a statue of Saint Thérèse at the back of the church. Praying and asking her to pray for me, I said something to this effect: 'Look, I'm going to this retreat. You need to give me some sign—roses, or something—if I'm called to be a priest.'

"That next Friday, I went to the retreat. Although the retreat was only three days, the silence was deafening to me. It terrified me but I persevered through it with God's grace. Nevertheless, God's timing is perfect! He knew that I would have the proper disposition of soul to hear His will only after my two friends left to become religious sisters. This is a lesson on detachment: He had to break me a little bit prior to the retreat so that come retreat time I would be ready to hear His voice. As I began the retreat, God's will was still unclear to me and I was not at peace.

"Walking around praying the chaplet of Divine Mercy, I saw a white marble statue ahead of me and was surprised it was a statue of St. Thérèse...with one white rose set next to her. I thought something along the lines of: 'Maybe it's a sign?' But I was still a bit incredulous and started questioning the veracity of this sign. I had been expecting a red rose. Looking down, I saw a red rose at my feet. There were no other roses around. Ecstatic, at that point my vocation was clear to me and I was at peace.

"I was on a high after that retreat, and when I returned to the workplace I felt I didn't belong there. There were many details that began pointing me toward the IVE and which helped me to recognize this calling. However, I continued to seek good counsel from various priests in varying religious orders, applied the principles I learned from the St. Ignatius Spiritual Exercises, and benefitted from a talk on vocations given by Fr. Michael Pintacura at Our Lady of Peace. Everything just lined up and I entered the seminary in 2006 and was ordained on May 31, 2014, the Feast of the Visitation of the Blessed Virgin Mary. By the sheer grace of God, here I am today, the second Filipino (and first Filipino-American) priest in the IVE and the first to be assigned to Our Lady of Peace.

"I think every priest can agree the greatest joy of our vocation is administering two sacraments in particular: offering up the Holy Mass and hearing confession. It's even more of a special treat here at

Our Lady of Peace because we experience so many conversions. I believe the visible fruits here are something that you don't usually see in other parishes; this is a very special place. The two devotions, to the Eucharist and Mary, which Monsignor Sweeny cultivated, explain why Our Lady of Peace is the way it is today. Here, I truly see this is what a priest is meant to do: offer up Mass, preach, hear confessions, and give spiritual direction. The greatest joy is to be an instrument for souls.

"Before my return to the faith, I was very introverted and had few friends. Only when I became active in my faith life did I start developing solid, Christ-like friendships. After my reversion I was totally transformed. Now I'm not afraid of people. I still get shy, in the normal sense, but not like before. It was totally the grace of God that transformed me, and now I like talking to people and helping them to solve their problems. My nickname in the seminary was, 'Radar.' My priestly radar now hones in on souls!

"St. Paul says, 'Jesus Christ is the same yesterday, today, and forever.' (Hebrews 13:8) Jesus was the same merciful Lord prior to, during, and after my reversion, and will always be so. May He, 'who began the good work' in me 'continue to complete it until the day of Christ Jesus.' (Philippians 1:6)"

Mariano & Maria Quinata
Parishioners 1969 - Present

"It is important to read the Bible. Additionally, the rosary is the history and the passage of Jesus, from the Annunciation to His crucifixion, and now we even have the Mysteries of Light (Luminous mysteries). When you read the Bible, you find it in the rosary because every Mystery (Joyful, Sorrowful, Glorious, and Luminous) tells you

Fr. Jonathan Dumlao, IVE, hears confessions at the Fatima centennial celebration on May 13, 2017.

about it.

"One night, we were praying the rosary for our children as we do every evening. Later, our son called to say that he was in the hospital. He was in a motorcycle accident on his drive home from San Francisco. His motorcycle slid into the shoulder and he was dragged beneath it for a distance. Then, he got up, drove all the way back to San Jose, and checked in to the Valley Medical Center! It was a miracle he was alive. We realized the accident had occurred precisely at the time we were praying the rosary for our children.

"An extra blessing is that Fr. Stout was the Catholic chaplain for Valley Medical. We phoned him. He had just returned to his office, but went right back up to visit our son."

Barbara Wilkinson
Parish Staff Member 1986 - 2015

"Monsignor Sweeny gets the credit for all the solid marriage preparation at Our Lady of Peace over the years. It's not just preparation for the Sacrament of Matrimony! It's also making sure the couple is ready for marriage itself.

"We have a wonderful team of priests and married couples who share the faith and work with the engaged couples for two days. In March of 2015, we had 67 couples here for marriage preparation. We have weddings at Our Lady of Peace nearly every weekend.

"After the marriage preparation course, some have actually canceled their weddings. After all the preparation, they realize they are not compatible. In another case, one groom was atheist and set against marrying in the Catholic Church except that his bride held it important. He was actually angry about having to attend the preparation sessions and learn about the Catholic Church's teaching on marriage. After the marriage preparation was all over, he hugged me and said, 'Thank you. I've never really known what the Catholic Church was about and...I want to become a Catholic.' His bride heard him and was so happy she screamed! Even some Catholics come in without much preparation or understanding of their faith. We do our best to offer them more.

"I wanted to work for Our Lady of Peace because in Monsignor Sweeny I saw a priest who was a spiritual leader for his people. That doesn't always happen in all churches. Because of Monsignor Sweeny, I'm very strong in my belief system. I know I get that from him because I walked the walk with him for so many years. There is no peace without the Lord."

Br. Kevin Stolt, IVE
Religious Vocation from Our Lady of Peace

"I was born in Phoenix, Arizona and raised both there and later in North Dakota. My family was always faithfully Catholic. Most of my religious experience growing up was going to Mass every Sunday. Confession was not a big part of my parish experience, it was less accessible. But growing up in North Dakota I had a great community and my formation both in that community and in the love I experienced in my own family led me to want to have children and a family of my own. That's what I thought my vocation was for many years. I always knew the priesthood was a possibility, but as something maybe, *maybe*, in the future to consider.

"After high school, I didn't have a deep sense of wondering what God wanted for me, so I did what most people do and went to college. I attended the Massachusetts Institute of Technology (MIT) and earned an undergraduate degree in Computer Science and Engineering. Then I stayed on for a Master's degree in the same field.

"There were two important occurrences in my faith life at MIT. First, I had to start making the faith my own. It was no longer my parents who drove the family to Mass on Sunday. When you're away at college, you're there alone. If you don't go to Mass, no one is going to take you there. It has to be your faith. Second, I was introduced to ways of living my faith not just on Sundays, such as daily Mass and adoration of the Blessed Sacrament. Before college, I don't think I understood adoration.

"The chapel at MIT was shared between many faith groups. They had daily Mass twice a week and adoration once a week for an hour. Toward the end of my time at MIT, I started attending both. I also found a small group of men who gathered in the evenings to pray the rosary together. When I started to pray the rosary, I noticed a change in my countenance. On the days I prayed the rosary, I had a greater sense of peace. Progressively, over time, I noticed a difference.

"There at MIT, I started making the faith more a part of my daily life. And I can't neglect the moral teachings of the faith that my parents were instrumental in teaching me. I felt very strong in that throughout my life before college and during college, and it helped me to make the faith my own. There are a lot of pressures for immorality when young people go off to college. Having a solid background in what is right and wrong helped me to reject those pressures from others. All my parents taught me was rooted in love.

"After earning two degrees, I looked for a job. Software engineering was the next step, but at the same time I knew something was missing. It was conscious. I could use my talents as a software engineer and all I had learned, yet now I look back and see what I was feeling was that it wasn't God's ultimate goal for me. I knew there was something missing, but didn't know what it was. I would later discover God's ultimate goal for me through the help of Our Lady of Peace Church.

"Google was recruiting at MIT and was seen as one of the best software engineering companies. I moved to California to work at their headquarters in Mountain View, California. At the beginning, I struggled to find the right place for practicing my faith. After attending Mass in various places, one priest suggested I go to Our Lady of Peace. So I started coming to Our Lady of Peace more and recognized there was a difference here compared to a lot of other parishes. Not that other parishes are bad, there was just something that seemed really special about the sacraments here. As a result, I started trying to make the sacraments more a part of my daily life. It turned out that Our Lady of Peace was half-way between my work and home, so I started stopping in occasionally in the morning before work for Mass or in the evenings after work for adoration. At first it was pretty infrequent, maybe a couple of times during the week. Then maybe three times a week, then five or six days, and then every day. And then I started spending more and more time in adoration. I'd work late to avoid the traffic and on the way home stop at Our Lady of Peace and spend an hour or two in adoration.

"The reason I needed to go to Mass and to receive the sacraments more was because I found myself focusing inward. The first couple of years at Google, I was becoming more self-centered and was not really giving of myself. Sometimes that can be a part of the culture: 'I've got to make a difference, I've got to stand out.' I didn't like to see this in me and felt focusing on myself so much was not being the person I should be, so I began frequenting the sacraments more and coming to Our Lady of Peace more often. To have them so available really was instrumental in helping me to achieve that goal of giving more of myself. As a result, my desires began to change and the sacraments were changing me. I didn't care about things concerning money or honor—personal recognition, prestige—and felt myself wanting to give my time more. That continued for about a year.

"In 2010, I went to a half-day retreat in San Francisco hosted by another young adult group. I still never considered the priesthood. Up to that point I had always thought the priesthood was something God might be calling me to in the future, but never at the present moment. At that retreat, I realized, 'God isn't calling me to consider this in the future, God is calling *me* to consider it *right now.*'

"It didn't take long after that for me to fully realize my vocation. Once I actively started to consider the vocation and continued to increase my reception of the sacraments by attending regular confession at Our Lady of Peace, going to adoration, and attending Mass, within the course of nine months I quit my job and entered the religious life.

"After realizing my call to religious life, the desire grew stronger and stronger for the priesthood. Seeing the work of the priests at Our Lady of Peace, their dedication to the sacraments, spending all the hours in the confessional, all the hours they spend in spiritual direction, the many Masses that are celebrated, and the devotion to the Eucharist—you can come here any time for adoration—seeing that impressed upon me the importance of the priesthood in a way that I realized more definitively it was the vocation God was calling me to. I didn't feel that God was calling me to the diocesan priesthood and I wasn't sure where He wanted me to go. After visiting different religious communities, one day during adoration at Our Lady of Peace I realized He was calling me to the Institute of the Incarnate Word (IVE).

"When I entered the IVE, I knew the work of some of the apostolates the priests do. Some priests work in the houses of charity that we have for the disabled or for orphans. Others are parish priests in big cities, others in small towns. We are all over the world. Some are doing first contact missions, while others are in mature, busy parishes. I liked the idea that God might call me to anything, that it wasn't determined beforehand—some are teachers, some are professors—that what God might call me to do is entirely up to Him. The other aspect I liked was the aspect of poverty. It wasn't easy because I had become attached to things, but I wasn't giving up anything! Rather, it was God's grace that gave me everything.

"In particular, the IVE represented a different kind of choice for me. When I was deciding on colleges, I chose MIT because it was considered the best for the career path I was pursuing. I didn't consider God's will for me and didn't even know to. It wasn't until I was 26 years that I started asking that question: What is God's will for me? And God's will is absolutely the best thing for me. God doesn't want anything that is not the best for me, and yet I never asked Him. If I was in high school and asked God His will instead of, 'What career do I want? What do I want to do when I grow up?' it may have changed my path. In his Providence, there are these things that are now part of my history: I went to MIT and worked for Google. In his Providence, God allowed that for me, but at the same time I didn't ask Him if that's what He wanted for me. How I feel about my life now versus how I felt about my life then is that I have an incredible peace, a certainty of knowing that I'm doing what God wants. That makes everything right. That's the beauty I find now in the religious life and in the day-to-day activities. It fills me with great joy, great peace, that I know I'm doing what God wants me to do and He gives me the grace to enjoy it. That's what I was missing. After college and graduate school, I was uncertain. I know now, with certainty, what God wants."

Our Lady of Peace Church in 2014.

Peter Hoonhout
Parishioner 2013 - Present

"I attended Our Lady of Peace during a college internship. After graduation, I returned to the Bay area to work and started getting involved at the parish in the Young Adult Group and as a volunteer teacher at St. Joseph Academy.

"The Young Adult Group offers a community where young adults can have Catholic friends and a community. The big event that drew me into it was the Theology on Tap program. At the first event, over 200 people showed up even though advertising was limited! I believe the whole diocese was ready for it and the turnout was several times more people than the Fr. Nieto, Sr. Nikopoia, and the other organizers anticipated. People wanted something like that and finally a parish got around to offering it. Fr. Nieto realized they could turn Theology on Tap into a monthly activity and was very generous in moving forward and helping the young adult community. After the impressive response to Theology on Tap, other parishes in the diocese realized there's an interest in young adults for gathering and becoming active. A few parishes have started up their own young adult groups, a young professional organization has kicked up, and the diocese is getting more organized about advertising young adult activities diocesan-wide so opportunities reach more people.

"Additionally, the Young Adult Group at Our Lady of Peace has snow trip weekends, a camping trip, and Wednesday night gatherings for game nights, adoration, Bible study, sports, community service, and so on. Theology on Tap caters to all the young adults in the diocese, and the weekly activities are parish-based. Everything we do is to build community and faith in individuals.

"I go to Our Lady of Peace because I'm a fan of orthodoxy and taking our faith seriously. Behind the orthodoxy are the IVE priests and the Sisters' efforts to make Catholicism real. There is less 'feel-good' Catholicism and more of an authentic faith. I think that's what young adults are looking for: they don't want a story that makes everyone feel good, they want the truth that's behind our faith. My generation has started critiquing the culture that corporate America is pushing. We're really antsy, questioning, whining, and we want to figure it out. Our Lady of Peace gives that to me: I know the priests are really trying to help everyone in their faith and make everyone a better Christian, not only to attend Mass every Sunday but to be active in their faith and community. They offer a straightforward message and live an authentic faith. They aren't just trying to attract people, they're really behind it. For example, the Sisters run a school for low-income families who can't afford parochial school but want their children to have a Catholic education. They provide a classical education through St. Joseph's Academy homeschool co-op that would cost an excessive amount of annual tuition anywhere else in the Bay area. The Sisters are there every morning from Tuesday through Friday at 7 a.m., teaching and administrating. They put their souls into it. I see the same in the priests. At the all-night vigil for the closing of the Holy Doors [to conclude the Year of Mercy], they were there all night hearing confessions. People at Our Lady of Peace know about confession because the priests speak so highly of it. So many confessions are heard at Our Lady of Peace and there's always a line there of people trying to do better."

Parishioner Healed from Addiction

"My life has been filled with not only great sorrow and pain, but also intense joy. I have been suffering from an eating disorder for almost ten years. It all started in high school at age sixteen, a time when a teenage girl's bodily image is of the utmost importance. As the years went by, the disorder grew worse. I went from almost totally abstaining from food to a toxic obsession with food. I would binge and purge over twenty times a day. It seemed like my addiction was growing stronger by the hour. I was bulimic and there seemed to be no turning back.

"The purging was terribly detrimental to my physical and mental health and had a terrifying effect on my heart and lungs. I couldn't stand for any length of time because my electrolyte-depleted body had no energy. I always felt faint and tired. There would be times when my heart would be pounding so hard that I prepared myself for death. I would pray and ask God every night to have mercy on me because I never knew if I would wake up the next day. I was in and out of the emergency room as the disorder continually threatened my life. I knew I was going to die if I didn't change my life, a fact I just accepted.

"I also suffered from a deep depression and constantly prayed, 'God, I cannot take another day. Deliver me from this misery. Take me home to you.' Indeed, I contemplated suicide every night, but never acted on it. At this point in my life, I had not only given up on myself, but on God as well.

"As if I didn't have enough problems, I also gradually became addicted to prescription pills and marijuana. I was numbing the pain by getting high each day. I was trying to forget about life. In 2011, I overdosed on smoking, drinking, and pills and was rushed to the emergency room. My body started to shut down. A man named Bob came into my room and asked if he could pray with me. Bob asked Our Lord to heal and protect me. I lay there choking back tears, knowing at that moment God had answered my prayers. I quit smoking, taking pills, and drinking alcohol from that day forward.

Fr. Brian Dinkel, IVE, formally closes the Holy Doors to conclude the Year of Mercy on November 20, 2016. Mother María de la Caridad Asensio, SSVM, and many parishioners witness the ceremony.

Yet my biggest fear and weakness was not being able to get over my bulimia. I continued to binge and purge every day.

"It wasn't until December 14, 2014 when I went to Mass at Our Lady of Peace and heard a homily by Fr. Thomas Steinke that things started to change. He mentioned how people suffering from addictions get a physiological impulse, which overpowers them, and how God alone could bring joy into their lives.

"Two days later, I got very ill again from excessive binging and purging. I was so scared I immediately searched for Fr. Thomas's email address on the internet. I felt that he understood people like me, people suffering with eating disorders and addictions. I met with Fr. Thomas the very next day and went to confession. That was the first day I won the victory over bulimia in a long time.

"Fr. Thomas said the best therapy is to go to daily Mass and receive Holy Communion. I was so desperate at this point that I never once questioned his advice. It made even more sense when I heard of others who were healed from addictions to drugs and pornography from receiving the Holy Eucharist each day. I walked into church that day feeling incredible. I felt like the weight of the world had been lifted off my shoulders. I knew that God had answered my prayers.

"I went to Mass each day asking God only to help me to abstain from binging and purging that day. It was an absolute miracle that I made it through the first three days without binging and purging. Those three days turned into a week and that week into two weeks. I was so overwhelmed with joy. I couldn't imagine anything more important than going to daily Mass and allowing our Eucharistic Lord to transform me. My complexion gradually changed from a dark yellow to a glowing warm olive tone. My hair, formerly brittle and dry, became soft again. I was so full of joy that nothing or no one could bring me down.

"I felt delivered from certain death. Each day I felt more alive after receiving Holy Communion. Nevertheless, each day was a battle. The temptations were very intense, but the Body and Blood of our Lord was my shield of protection. The first two weeks were the hardest... but Our Eucharistic Lord protected me. I trusted in *Him*.

"It is important to understand all this spiritual and physical healing couldn't have been possible without trusting in Him. The Holy Eucharist is *not* a magical pill that takes away all our troubles. The Holy Eucharist is *God Himself* and He communicates His heart to ours. I was healed because I received supernatural strength from Jesus Christ, truly present in the Most Blessed Sacrament. Every day as I gave my thanksgiving I prayed, 'Jesus help me get through this day. I know I cannot do it without your help. It is through your Body and Blood that I have become strong.'

"I continue to practice my faith with great dependence on God. I know I will have to battle for the rest of my life, but my journey and even my addiction have, in some sense, helped me. It is because of this addiction that my relationship with God has become stronger than ever. I live my life for Him and nothing and nobody can ever take Him away from me.

"I was tormented physically and psychologically for years and now Jesus Christ has set me free. Life is beautiful and I treasure each day."

Daniel Alva
Parishioner 2014 - Present

"In November of 2017, Fr. Brian walked into our Confirmation class and asked if any of the kids would be interested in an Advent challenge to go to Mass every day during Advent. He suggested he would offer a 6:30 a.m. Mass for kids who had to get to school and couldn't attend the later Masses. I thought it would be cool to get up early at serve Mass at 6:30 a.m., so I volunteered when he asked for a show of hands. The next week, he returned to our classroom and passed out sign-off sheets for the priests to sign every day we went to Mass, to keep us accountable.

"At first it was hard to wake up early, but then we got used to it. The food and socializing afterwards was a bonus: people started to bring food and one day there were two boxes of Stan's Donuts waiting for us after Mass. When the challenge was over, Fr. Brian hosted a Kansas City-style barbecue, cooked by Chef Fr. Brian, for the thirty kids who completed the challenge. We also played basketball and frisbee.

"I was glad I did the Advent challenge because it was a good way to start the day. So many people attended the early Mass, Fr. Brian made the 6:30 a.m. Mass permanent."

Glenda Dubsky
Parishioner 2010 - Present

"I was at Mass on October 22 in 2013, and it was the Feast of St. John Paul II. Fr. Nieto gave a very powerful homily on Totus Tuus, John Paul II, and then the Total Consecration to Jesus through Mary as given to us by St. Louis de Montfort. I was very much inspired by it, such that I prayed, 'Mother Mary, do you want me to ask Fr. Nieto to bring the Total Consecration to Jesus through Mary to this parish?' After Mass, I told Mother Mary I would know if I saw Fr. Nieto waiting outside. Mass concluded, I took my time to leave, and headed to my car. Fr. Nieto was right outside near the parking lot.

"We spoke, and I told Fr. Nieto he really excited me about his homily and asked, 'Can we bring the Total Consecration to Jesus

A group of 2017-2018 Confirmation students gather at the Rally for Life on January 26, 2018.

Fr. William Stout, S.J. (left) and Fr. Michael Pintacura (right) distribute Holy Communion in 2016.

through Mary to Our Lady of Peace?' He said, 'I think that's a great idea. What group are you with?' I didn't have any group at that time, in fact, I didn't really know anyone at the parish! But I told him, 'Father, there will be people who will help us.' I knew Mother Mary would help us. He gave me his business card and told me to contact him. I contacted him in early December and asked to meet with him. I was surprised he responded! He asked me to call the office to schedule the appointment.

"I researched the Total Consecration to Jesus through Mary, gathered the materials and examples, and created a plan outline and presentation for Fr. Nieto. The day I was scheduled to meet with him, I went to Mass and afterward saw Regina Rivera and Gloria Natividad and asked them to come with me. One other person joined us and I presented the plan to Fr. Nieto.

"Fr. Nieto was very excited. He brought in Fr. Joseph LoJacono. We met monthly for about seven months, created a plan, and set up a website. I created the basic website but Fr. Nieto made it functional and attractive. He established topics for the talks that were patterned after the True Devotion to Mary. He wrote welcome letters to all the people who signed up. He gave everything a personal touch and made it so much better with his ideas and artwork. Finally, it was time to roll out the program and I needed people to help. I asked the Blessed Mother to help me find people, started talking to people, and all kinds of people said 'Yes' and joined our group.

"Fr. Nieto told us, 'If we have 50 people sign up, I'll be very happy.' I said, 'Let's sign up a thousand!' He replied, 'Glenda, if this goes well, Mother Mary will use you in a big way.' We signed up people after all the Masses. It was a lot of work. When we were so tired, Fr. Nieto would say, 'Your vacation is in heaven!' When we complained, 'Father, we need to go home,' he'd say, 'This is your home.' We were working until 2 or 3 a.m. to enter all the data—

addresses, names, and so on—in the database, because so many people were signing up. There is a lot of work behind the Total Consecration program, yet I recall when we were working into the early hours of the morning, we were given a special grace in that we were not tired. The reason it was more work than we anticipated was because 4,200 people signed up the first year! Then we had to send them letters and receive RSVPs for people attending the talks, and plan accordingly. The church was packed for the talks. The people we signed up were from all over! Many were local, but others were from Monterey, Sacramento, Modesto, Daly City, Fremont... people drive from all over to Our Lady of Peace. It is like a melting pot. We even had people from distant places sign up, such as Korea and the Philippines, and people from out of state who were visiting and wanted to consecrate themselves. They brought the materials home and consecrated themselves on the same day and at the same time as our group at Our Lady of Peace, because the prayer is so powerful when everyone says the prayer on the same day.

"From this experience, our group of Total Consecration promoters became known as the Consecration Group. Our mission is, first, that people consecrate themselves to Jesus through the Blessed Mother. Then, to help them deepen their relationship with the Lord by understanding the Consecration, Jesus, the spiritual battle, and carrying our crosses.

"After the Total Consecration, we felt there needed to be a follow-up so people would learn to live their Consecration, not to just do it once and be done. It is really a spiritual battle in this world and we need to understand by knowing what happens in the spiritual battle, how to recognize it, and how to respond. The four parts of the Total Consecration are knowledge of the world, of self, of Mary, and of Jesus. By understanding what is causing us to sin in the world, we are able to fight it. This is why we hosted a spiritual warfare conference in 2016. Fr. Joseph in particular understood our need to

Fr. Brian Dinkel, IVE, speaks to the Consecration Group's 2018 book club, where nearly 300 parishioners met to study St. Louis de Montfort's "Letter to the Friends of the Cross."

organize this and was very supportive and helpful. From there, we organized a book club and read St. Louis de Montfort. In 2016, 40 people attended and we read *True Devotion to Mary*. In 2017, we read *The Love for Eternal Wisdom* with 70 participants. And in 2018, studying *Letter to the Friends of the Cross*, almost 300 people attended and we had to move into the gym. Even within the large group, we broke into small groups of six people for discussion.

"Fr. Thomas Steinke had the idea to produce a program on the Eternal Word Television Network (EWTN) about the Total Consecration. We spoke with some people we knew, including Fr. Melvin Castro who has hosted programs for EWTN, and somehow everything came together. A team of people met by phone, planned thirteen episodes, and the EWTN crew came to Our Lady of Peace in 2017 to film them. In California, some local parishes have asked the Consecration Group to help them begin the Total Consecration program in their parishes. We have given them the materials and they established their own. Now, EWTN brings the Total Consecration to a worldwide audience."

Chris Schaper
Parishioner 1972 - 2003

"The beginning of the story of Our Lady of Peace is Monsignor Sweeny's mother and father and who they were. Through it all, the grace continues. That's what Monsignor always said: 'We don't know where this is going to go. Why do I have a parish with no people?' He came to a parish as if he was unwanted and there was nobody here.

"Look at what it is today! Our Lady, here in the United States, built through rosary checks, is turning hearts to Christ. It almost makes one laugh! No one expected us to become anything! That didn't bother Monsignor Sweeny. He just said, 'We need to pray.' He entrusted it to Our Lady. The IVE priests and nuns continue to lead with the same faith.

"Today, the parish continues to thrive and visitors are always at the Shrine. Through the IVE, the church's mission and ministry continue and have grown significantly. There's never, ever been a calculated plan for growth at this parish, just a tireless effort to reach out to others, bringing hope and joy to this life and leading souls to heaven."

. . .

Eucharistic adoration at Our Lady of Peace, 2017.

On the eve of the third millennium the whole Church is invited to live
more intensely the mystery of Christ by gratefully cooperating in the
work of salvation. The Church does this together with Mary and
following the example of Mary, the Church's mother and model:
Mary is the model of that maternal love which should inspire all who
cooperate in the Church's apostolic mission for the rebirth of humanity.

St. John Paul the Great, Redemptoris Missio

Historical Timeline

1777
First Mass is offered by Franciscan Missionaries seeking to establish Mission Santa Clara de Asís (January 12). The territory is part of the Diocese of Sonora, Mexico.

1848
Mexican Cession occurs.

1850
Santa Clara becomes part of the Diocese of Monterrey.

1922
Santa Clara is transferred to the Archdiocese of San Francisco under Archbishop Edward Hanna.

1935
Pope Piux XI names John Joseph Mitty as new Archbishop of San Francisco.

1952
The people of Alviso create their own Catholic chapel and dedicate it to Our Lady Star of the Sea.

1960

Archbishop Mitty purchases 13 acres of farmland for $130,000 as the future site for Our Lady of Peace Church.

1961

Archbishop Mitty appoints Fr. Joseph Sullivan as founding pastor. He is to assimilate Star of the Sea parishioners into the new parish.

1962

Construction begins on Our Lady of Peace Church in the spring.

Flooding in Alviso forces Fr. Sullivan to offer Masses in the unfinished Our Lady of Peace Church.

Pope John XXIII opens the Second Vatican Council opens in Rome.

Joseph Thomas McGucken is named new Archbishop of San Francisco by Pope John XXIII.

1963

Construction is completed for Our Lady of Peace Church and hall. Archbishop McGucken dedicates the new church to the worship of God and confers the Sacrament of Confirmation on the first confirmation class.

The City of Santa Clara re-zones land surrounding Our Lady of Peace for business and industry, threatening the parish closure.

1964

The "New Mass" (as per the Second Vatican Council) is introduced in all United States Catholic churches.

Our Lady of Peace Gift Shop (later expanded to Gift Shop and Bookstore) is established.

1965

Pope Paul VI closes the Second Vatican Council.

1969

Latin Masses are fully phased out in the United States.

Fr. John Joseph Sweeny replaces Fr. Sullivan as pastor of Our Lady of Peace.

Fr. Sweeny establishes the Legion of Mary at Our Lady of Peace.

First Friday All-Night Vigils begin.

1971

Fr. Sweeny formalizes praying the rosary in the church before every weekday and Sunday Mass.

1972

Fr. Sweeny visits Fatima, Portugal and returns with the statues of Our Lady of Fatima and the Sacred Heart of Jesus.

Fatima Pilgrimages begin at Our Lady of Peace (July 13).

First of the pear trees are cleared to make room for 4 mobile classrooms.

1973

Fr. Sweeny initiates first year of pear harvest to help pay parish debt. The parish harvested approximately 55 tons of pears for 4 years.

1975

Sr. Mary Jean Kula arrives to assist at the parish.

The Sacred Heart of Jesus is officially enthroned in Our Lady of Peace church (April 26).

True Devotion to Mary (as taught by St. Louis de Montfort) study group is formed and led by Fr. Sweeny.

1976

Fr. Sweeny meets sculptor Charles Parks and commissions him to create a 90-foot statue of Our Lady of the Immaculate Heart.

Perpetual Adoration begins.

The Archdiocese of San Francisco sells some of the parish acreage to alleviate debt. Other acreage is leased.

1977

Archbishop McGucken retires and Pope Paul VI names John Raphael Quinn as Archbishop of San Francisco.

The ten-foot model of Our Lady of the Immaculate Heart is installed in the parish courtyard.

1980

Fr. Sweeny commissions a 32-foot statue (to precede the 90-foot statue).

1981

The Diocese of San Jose is created and Pope John Paul II names Pierre DuMaine as bishop.

Bishop DuMaine halts Fr. Sweeny's plans to pay for the statue.

1982

Charles Parks completes the 32-foot statue of Our Lady of the Immaculate Heart.

A temporarily "homeless" Our Lady of the Immaculate Heart travels across the United States on a flatbed truck, stopping at various sites for viewers to enjoy, pray, and honor the Mother of God.

1983

Donations sent to Fr. Sweeny pay for the statue in full.

Our Lady of the Immaculate Heart arrives to Santa Clara and is installed by Bishop DuMaine on October 7, the Feast of Our Lady of the Rosary.

1984

Our Lady Star of the Sea in Alviso is formally recognized as an independent parish.

1986

Our Lady of Peace Church celebrates her 25th anniversary.

1988

New rectory and parish offices are constructed.

1996

The Family Learning Center and Pilgrimage Hall is constructed.

1998

Pope John Paul II names Patrick McGrath as coadjutor bishop of San Jose.

1999

Bishop DuMaine retires and Patrick McGrath is installed as Bishop of San Jose.

Our Lady of Peace library opens (May 31).

2000

Pope John Paul II extends the title of "Monsignor" to Fr. Sweeny in grateful recognition for his exemplary priestly service to the Church.

2002

Pope John Paul II recognizes Fr. Sweeny as a Prelate of Honor. He is now addressed as Monsignor Sweeny.

Bishop McGrath asks Monsignor Sweeny to retire and invites the priests of the Institute of the Incarnate Word (IVE) to assume pastoral leadership at Our Lady of Peace. Fr. Walter Mallo, IVE, arrives as the new pastor.

Fr. Mallo renames the Family Learning Center the "Monsignor John Sweeny Family Learning Center."

2004

The Servants of the Lord and the Virgin of Matará (SSVM), female branch of the Religious Family of the Incarnate Word, founded their apostolic community at Our Lady of Peace (August 28) under the guidance of Mother María Ana de Jesús Carrió, SSVM ("Mother Ana").

2006

Monsignor John Sweeny dies (March 6).

2007

The outdoor Stations of the Cross are completed and installed for Good Friday services (April 6).

Sr. Mary Jean Kula dies (July 22).

2010

Fr. José Giunta, IVE, is assigned as new pastor of Our Lady of Peace Church.

2013

Fr. Gustavo Nieto, IVE, assumes pastoral leadership at Our Lady of Peace.

Mother María Regina Pacis Cáceres, SSVM ("Mother Pacis") assumes leadership of the apostolic community of sisters at Our Lady of Peace.

2014

The statue of Saint John Paul the Great is installed and dedicated.

2015

4,200 people make the annual total consecration of True Devotion to Mary.

2016

Fr. Junipero Serra, founder of Mission Santa Clara de Asís, is canonized by Pope Francis.

Our Lady of Peace Church celebrates 40 years of Eucharistic Adoration.

Statues of Blessed Jacinta and Francisco are installed at the entrance to the Monsignor John Sweeny Family Learning Center.

Fr. Gustavo Nieto is elected General Superior for the IVE and transfers to Rome. Fr. Brian Dinkel, IVE, becomes pastor of Our Lady of Peace Church.

Mother María de la Caridad Asensio, SSVM ("Mother Caridad"), assumes leadership of the apostolic community of sisters at Our Lady of Peace.

2017

Fr. Brian Dinkel, IVE, places a relic of St. Junipero Serra in the altar stone (April 14).

Our Lady of Peace Church & Shrine celebrates the 100th anniversary of the Fatima apparitions in an outdoor Mass celebrated by Bishop Patrick McGrath and many concelebrating priests. Over 4,000 people attended.

2018

Mother Marie Notre Dame de Bon Secours Casadaban, SSVM ("Mother Bon Secours") assumes leadership of the apostolic community of sisters at Our Lady of Peace.

Acknowledgments

A few months into researching for this book, I discovered Our Lady of Peace's story is more profound, far-reaching, multi-generational, tireless, generous, miracle-rich, and teeming with authenticity than I could have anticipated. Yet coupled with her depth and draw is simplicity: a tireless dedication to inviting souls to the fullness of life in Christ, a mission remarkably on-focus since 1963. This is the dedication that built this Shrine and fills these pages. I am the messenger, but this is your story. It is a story now shared because of the many people who generously shared their own memories or supported my research.

To the generous contributors who humbly shared their time, stories, information, and archives: you are the co-authors of this book. Through interviews, emails, and surprise archive drop-offs at the rectory, you hosted a parish history celebration year-round. In every encounter was a gift to unwrap, large and small, now penned on these pages. Thank you.

My sincere thanks to Fr. Gustavo Nieto who initiated and encouraged this project and Fr. Brian Dinkel who arrived to Our Lady of Peace mid-project with a love for her story and her people, seeing this book to completion. To Fr. Jonathan Dumlao, Fr. Joseph

LoJacono, and Fr. Thomas Steinke, thank you for many thoughtful contributions and responses to my countless inquiries. Your insights and prayers add strength to the reader's journey from chapter to chapter.

To Grace Laxamana, I extend my gratitude for connecting me to the deep, complex web of Our Lady of Peace past and present, yielding indescribable assistance, and propelling me forward toward people and resources otherwise unknown. You navigated, removed obstacles and, of course, laughed often!

To Br. Blaine Halley, always reliable for genuine feedback, thoughtful opinions, and an honest edit, I am tremendously grateful for your caring heart and writer's professionalism. Karen Ruiz, Genevieve Van Tuyl, and Gloria Relloma, volunteer content editors with priceless feedback, thank you for the hours you spent reviewing early drafts and yielding a more complete story.

Above all, I thank Joe Mastroeini, the unknown hero of Our Lady of Peace's parish story. Over many years, Joe safeguarded archives, names, dates, and "all things Our Lady of Peace." He rescued archives when others saw in them no value, priceless resources we would have never known today. As I worked, Joe questioned, challenged, and researched. It is most fitting that Joe, our unofficial parish historian, titled this book.

The above mentioned individuals were moved by love for the story of our church and shrine to volunteer more time and attention than they anticipated. Your selflessness has many times moved my own heart to seek the cause of your joy.

On the home front, my family's day-to-day faithfulness and steady support made this book possible. Rafael Sr., Rafael III, Elizabeth, Emma Rose, Daniel, Catherine, and Mary Carmen, thank you for listening to my dinner table anecdotes, taking an interest as chapters unfolded, accompanying me, giving me quiet time to write, and loving the Shrine and her people. Our hearts, and four years of our lives, are wrapped in these pages.

Finally, I close in thanksgiving for the intercession of Our Lady of the Immaculate Heart and the Sacred Heart of Jesus. May our stories continue in union with their love.

Ad majorem Dei gloriam,

Rosemary Alva